To W.

From
[signature]
5/7/15

Passing in Review

by

Hal Sacks

Passing in Review

30 Years of Literary Criticism and Articles from
Jewish News of Southeastern Virginia

by Hal Sacks

Edited by Terri Denison

PARKE | PRESS
Norfolk

Passing in Review • Copyright © 2015 by Harold H. Sacks
All rights reserved.

All rights reserved, including the right to reproduce this work
in any form whatsoever without permission in writing from the publisher,
except for brief passages in connection with a review.

PUBLISHED BY
PARKE PRESS
Norfolk, Virginia

www.parkepress.com

Designed by Marshall McClure

ISBN 978-0-9883969-6-8

Library of Congress Control Number is available upon request

Printed in the United States of America

Contents

7   Preface

9   Introduction

11 BIOGRAPHIES

25 ESSAYS *and* ARTICLES

43 FICTION

69 FOR COOKS

99 HISTORY MATTERS

141 HOLOCAUST

151 MEMOIRS

175 POLITICS

205 THIS *and* THAT

242 Afterword

243 Appendix: Index of Titles

PREFACE

IN 1976, at age 46, I went on my first study mission to Israel. It was a highly subsidized "Professor's" Mission, put together by Joyce Strelitz. My wife, Annabel, was the professor; I schlepped along. It was kind of a Birthright trip for the rapidly middle-aging, and with it, my life was forever changed.

Soon after I returned from the trip, I attended a breakfast in Room 400 of Norfolk's Jewish Community Center. The late "Col." Henry Zetlin took charge of me and I learned how to "call cards" for the United Jewish Federation of Tidewater. Seven years later I had been "Campaign Worker of the Year," Division Chairman, Allocation Chairman, UJA Regional Cash Chairman, Vice Chairman of the UJF Campaign, and Federation Treasurer. I was on a search committee to hire a Campaign Director, so I quit my job as General Manager of Checkered Flag Motor Car Company and hired myself. In January of 1983, ensconced in my office in the absolute rear of the Federation suite (where I could smoke my cigars in peace), I fell under the spell of that wicked witch, Reba Karp, editor of the *UJF News*.

Hal Sacks

We were quite a bawdy crew back there, the third member of which was the octogenarian, Sydney Gates. Reba yelled and screamed a lot, especially when facing a deadline (she published 44 newspapers a year single-handedly, and ultimately up to six issues of *Renewal* magazine a year). Sydney regaled me with stories of the philandering of bygone members of the community. Each morning Reba or I would jot down on the board a "new" word, like "segue" or "eponymous." We were all poorly paid, but had so much fun we probably would have worked for nothing (thankfully my kids were already out of college).

One day Reba asked if I would try my hand at a book review. The rest is history.

Marc Jacobson, then-president of the United Jewish Federation of Tidewater (UJFT), asked me where I found the time to read all those books. "Oh," I told him, "I read them while I'm at work since I have so little to do." Marc was shocked until he realized I was pulling his leg. After all,

HAL SACKS PHOTOGRAPH BY STEVE BUDMAN

I was Assistant Executive Director of the Federation, charged with being Campaign Director; Women's Division Director; Director of Planning, Budgeting and Organization; and Mission Planning Director. In retrospect, I wonder what it was my boss was doing, if anything.

Now, three decades later, I am shocked to learn, upon retrieving my old reviews in preparation for the *Jewish News* Archival Project, that I had more than 475 reviews and dozens of articles printed in several iterations of the *News*.

So, with a respectful nod to Reba Karp, great appreciation to a fantastic editor, Terri Denison, and thanks to our publisher and book designer, Marshall McClure, I humbly express my gratitude to all who had a hand in making this collection possible.

Hal Sacks
Norfolk, Virginia

INTRODUCTION

BOOK REVIEWS are generally meant for two types of people: bibliophiles who seek recommendations, and readers who don't have time to read but appreciate a good synopsis and analysis. Both types prefer to get their information from a reliable reviewer who often becomes like a trusted friend.

For readers of *Jewish News*, for more than 30 years Hal Sacks has been that friend, that source of good advice on what books to invest precious reading time, and conversely, as he might note, which tomes are best for wrapping fish.

I've had the daunting task of choosing which reviews to include within these pages. What a pleasure to read, some for the first time, Hal's literary criticisms, his summaries, his opinions. Through the process, I've learned so much—akin to taking exhilarating crash courses on a variety of subjects.

A student of history, Hal has written reviews on books with themes of politics, history, Israel and the Holocaust that are enlightening, comprehensive and, best of all, understandable. Hal's reviews of memoirs and biographies manage to vividly portray the subjects' lives. Since Hal serves as his family's primary chef, he knows his way around the kitchen, making his takes on cookbooks (from a cook's perspective!) an important ingredient when sizing up recipes and cooking methods. When it comes to his fiction reviews, Hal deftly offers just enough details to entice readers, and yet not enough to spoil the fun of the read. Not one to shy away from opinion, Hal has written essays and articles on topics dear to his heart, several of which we have also included.

Because these reviews were initially written for a Jewish audience, most have some sort of a Jewish connection, i.e., the author or topic, but not all. This really is a book for everyone. Along with Hal's Jewish approach and perspective, his viewpoint stems from his roles and experiences as a retired U.S. Navy Commander, New York native, avid traveller, arts aficionado, professional fundraiser and husband, father, grandfather and great-grandfather.

Each review is clearly written with respect for his audience's intelligence. It is as if Hal is having a personal conversation with his reader.

Intelligent, articulate and, when appropriate, sprinkled with a touch of humor, this collection of reviews may be read cover to cover or by topic, or just by skipping around. With each review, the title's pertinent information is included so the reader may locate the book if so inclined.

Imagine the hours spent reading and evaluating these many books, which are but a mere fraction of what we chose from! How gracious of Hal to make the commitment, so that his readers may reap the benefit.

Terri Denison

BIOGRAPHIES

Reading *Chutzpah* proves to be 'learning experience'

"THE MAN WHO DOES his own public relations has more than *chutzpah*; he has a *schlemiel* for a client." So concludes the *Time* magazine review (June 24, 1991) of Alan Dershowitz's latest book, *Chutzpah*. Either the reviewer was looking for an opportunity to use that clever line or he didn't quite understand the purpose and title of the book.

Dershowitz clearly states in his introduction, "This book reflects my concern that despite the unmistakable contributions of Jews to the American success story, we seem to be willing to accept less than first class status." From that premise he proceeds "to generalize from [his] personal experiences" in an autobiographical, *chutzpalulik* journey from Borough Park boy to one of American's greatest trial lawyers.

Chutzpah
Alan M. Dershowitz
Little, Brown and Co., 1991   378 pages

En route, Dershowitz repeatedly demonstrates the necessity for "boldness, assertiveness, a willingness to demand what is due, to defy tradition, to challenge authority, to raise eyebrows"—in a word, chutzpah. He deplores the behavior described by "the offensive concept of *shanda fur de goyim*— an embarrassment in front of the gentiles," too often a Jewish rationale for lack of action. "*Sh'a shtill* (keeping quiet) has never served us well," Dershowitz writes.

Reading *Chutzpah* was also a learning experience for me; I was not aware of how deeply involved Alan Dershowitz is in Jewish "causes:" Natan Sharansky's lawyer; Jonathan Pollard's lawyer in his sentence appeal; Rabbi Avraham Weiss's lawyer in the slander suit against Cardinal Glemp of Poland (related to the Carmelite convent at Auschwitz), to list a few.

Dershowitz provides personal incidents as well as excerpts of his anti-Semitic hate mail as evidence that although we believe "the old anti-Semitism is waning [per Charles Silberman]... the new Judeopathy is alive and well." Refusing to recognize it or pretending that it doesn't exist won't cut it. "Notwithstanding the stereotype, we are not pushy or assertive enough for our own good and for the good of our more vulnerable brothers and sisters in other parts of the world," Dershowitz asserts.

Chutzpah is Dershowitz on Dershowitz, the Jewish civil libertarian attorney taking on the extreme right, the extreme left, the Holocaust, anti-Semitism, Israel, Jewish leadership and an assortment of well-known personalities including Pat Buchanan, Noam Chomsky, Norman Podhoretz and Leonard Fein, to name several. Dershowitz minces no words (word-mincing is not *chutzpahdik*). He is direct, sure, strong and merciless in his criticism and arguments—and, if you agree with him, you'll love it. *Chutzpah* is, as the *Time* reviewer comments, "In a word, gall. In two words, Alan Dershowitz." May he live to 120 and keep giving us lessons!

July 1991

'Tabloid biography' of Madeleine Albright is an easy read

MICHAEL DOBBS, the *Washington Post* reporter who in 1997 broke the story of Madeleine Albright's Jewish roots, has written what can best be described as a tabloid biography of the first female Secretary of State—biography from the vantage point of newsworthiness. Whether it fits into the category of "authorized" or "unauthorized" biography is questionable; the author received what is described as "limited cooperation," a total of three hours with Madeleine Albright devoted exclusively to the purposes of the book.

Madeleine Albright
A Twentieth Century Odyssey
Michael Dobbs
Henry Holt & Co., 1999   466 pages

Dobbs, writing in an easy-to-read journalistic style, devotes the first quarter of the book to a history of Albright's family, the Korbels, "a typical Central European Jewish family." He follows the family from its roots in southern Poland, into what is now the Czech Republic, through the 19th century, into the 20th century with its two world wars and the horrors of the Holocaust, and finally to the promised land of Denver, Colorado in 1949, when Madeleine was 12 years old. His details of Jewish life in Central Europe, the ambitions of Madeleine's father, and her parents' conversion to Catholicism in the context of Hitler's rise to power, provide the medium for understanding this unique individual.

To say that Michael Dobbs wrote this book with an "attitude" is probably an understatement. Throughout, Dobbs tends to accentuate the negative, up to and including Albright's tenure as Secretary of State. Clearly, she is a product of her personal history—intelligent, ambitious and determined to succeed as a powerful citizen in her adopted country. From Wellesley to the State Department, Albright created a persona that finally landed her the top job available to a non-native born American. It was neither a meteoric rise nor a slow climb up a long ladder, but many years of diligent accomplishments in the cauldron of Washington politics.

To the question of when she knew of her Jewish origins, it would seem to require an extraordinary suspension of disbelief to acknowledge that such an intelligent and creative woman could live almost 60 years without knowing that three of her grandparents had perished in concentration camps, to say nothing of the more than 25 other family members who were victims of the Holocaust.

Like everyone else, Madeleine Albright is the product of her life. Dobbs begins and ends the book with the same quotation from *The Great Gatsby*, which he considers "the greatest American novel of the 20th century" (as a literary maven, he's a pretty good journalist): "So we beat on, boats against the current, borne back ceaselessly into the past."

July 1999

A focus on Sharon's political life

PUBLISHED IN 2002, this first biography in English of the Israeli prime minister has finally been read by your reviewer, just on the eve of what appeared to be an unnecessary general election, one destined to be merely a waste of about $100 million. That view, of course, prevailed when it seemed that Ariel Sharon was sailing serenely toward reelection, having trounced Benyamin Netanyahu in the struggle for leadership in the Likud party. This was before the revelation that Likud leaders were corruptly deciding who would serve in the Knesset after the election and the leaked story (immediately denied) that Sharon's sons had engaged in some hanky-panky with excessive campaign donations. Thus, at this writing it is not clear that Sharon, the perennial "hawk" and current "dove" will successfully defend his position as prime minister, but by the time this brief review is published, the results will be in.

Sharon
Israel's Warrior-Politician
Anita Miller, Jordan Miller,
Sigalit Zetouni
Academy Chicago Publishers, 2002   630 pages

Outside of Israel, not much is known about the personal life of Ariel Sharon. Early biographies by Uzi Benziman and Matti Shavitt, translated from the Hebrew, were reported on in the *Southeastern Virginia Jewish News*, but they were for the most part not complimentary, colored by the emotional reaction to the massacres at the Sabra-Shatilla refuge camps. And this contemporary biography by academicians Anita Miller, Jordan Miller and Sigalit Zetouni, while dutifully detailing Sharon's early life on a crude farm near Tel Aviv and his brilliant military career, both as fighter and tactician, devotes the major part of their readable work to his political career after the Lebanon incursion of 1982.

Forced to step down as Defense Minister, but permitted to remain in the cabinet without portfolio, Sharon spent the next 15 years opposing peace without guarantees, and when the opportunity arose, promoting and actively ordering the creation of new settlements.

The defeat of Likud in the elections of 1992 saw Sharon out of the Cabinet, forced to content himself campaigning against the peace accords throughout 1994, and fundraising in the U.S. and Canada on behalf of the settlers (where, despite the overwhelming approval of the peace process, he was enthusiastically received). But following the assassination of Prime Minister Rabin and Netanyahu's smashing victory over Peres in 1996, Sharon was snubbed, offered a minor Cabinet position, but finally became head of a new Ministry of National Infrastructure which gave Sharon control over land management, rural development, water, roads and energy. Sharon's struggle for power in the Netanyahu government continued through 1999, and the authors cover his role in the Wye negotiations and other important missions undertaken in the U.S. and France. Sharon's political fortunes continued to wane until Ehud Barak's landslide victory over Netanyahu, following which Sharon took on the leadership of Likud.

The authors take us over the events of the next few years in a respectable feat of contemporary historical reporting. Sharon's ascendance to the Prime Minister's role, the Al-Aqsa Intifada, the Passover massacre, Operation Defensive Shield are very well covered, but fall in the category of "too soon to judge." Whether one considers Sharon too far to the right or relatively in the middle, contrasted with those further to the right, his persistent presence for over half a century in the midst of the military and political scene brings the reader into the thick of events and into the company of many world leaders. The verdict is still out on Ariel Sharon. His legacy may yet be in the making, however *Sharon* is a reasonably balanced portrait of his life and activities to date.

January 2003

Fascinating reading

THIS IS THE FOURTH BOOK on Ariel Sharon reviewed in this column since 1982. The first was a derogatory biography that belittled his military achievements and went along with the general effort to blame him for the Lebanese Phalangist slaughter at the Sabra and Chatila refugee camps. (Current opinion is that his defamation was simply part of a political effort to topple the Begin government.) The second appeared in the mid 1980s at about the time Sharon successfully sued *Time* for defamation, and the third was his autobiography, *Warrior*, published in 1988.

Ariel Sharon
An Intimate Portrait
Uri Dan
Palgrave Macmillan, 2006   292 pages

Now, just published, comes Uri Dan's panegyric to a 50-year personal and professional friendship. Dan, as a young reporter, undertook combat training in order to accompany Colonel (and then General) Sharon into battle, a classic case of what we now term "embedding." This close relationship, based on trust, respect and real affection that matured over the decades, is what makes this insider's biography of such great interest and is also the source of its principal weakness.

Uri Dan, acolyte and disciple, is no Boswell. Not content to allow his clearly intimate access to Sharon and his family reveal itself through the content of his interviews and discussions, Dan feels it necessary to insert himself into the text as though demonstrating over and over just how close he has been. Thus, we must be told that on arrival at Sharon's farm, Dan is served his "usual black coffee and soda water."

Nonetheless, the mere fact that Ariel Sharon's life and career spans the entire life of the State of Israel; that even in disgrace he had pivotal roles to play; that beyond all of his military success this was the man who created the Likud Party and who built the settlements and who finally, as prime minister, engineered the disengagement from Gaza and created the Kadima Party; makes this portrait an important and fascinating one.

During the Lebanese incursion of 1982, I was part of a 1,000-person solidarity mission to Israel and was bused to a settlement town for a meeting with Sharon, then Minister of Defense, sworn to oust Arafat from Lebanon. (Sharon never would shake the hand of Arafat.) He arrived by helicopter, a bit overweight, but hugely charismatic, and it was clear that had the government of Lebanon taken advantage of the Israeli presence at that time, a different history might have been written.

Despite the fact that Dan is so unabashedly sympathetic to Sharon (with a few minor exceptions) and that his encomium never fails to portray Sharon in the best light possible, his extensive one-on-one interviews make fascinating reading and reveal a warmer, much more sympathetic warrior than we have imagined him to be.

In Ariel Sharon's own words, Uri Dan was "above all, a true friend who has always been there, in moments of laughter and celebration, in difficult times of pain and personal tragedy, in the luminous joy of victory, as well as during the dark nights of heavy fire in the court of death..." How could Dan's biography, therefore, be less than required reading?

November 2006

A monumental work for a monumental person

WHEN, IN 1948, a group of American Jews desired to create a non-sectarian community of scholars and students united by their commitment to the pursuit of knowledge, the founders sought to name the university after an individual of impeccable moral fiber, leadership, intellectual ability, integrity and social conscience. The name that shined the brightest was that of the late U.S. Supreme Court Justice, Louis D. Brandeis. Brandeis University has since grown to become a national model of ethnic diversity and pluralism.

It is unlikely that today's reader will remember that Justice Brandeis survived a six-month confirmation fight in Congress following his 1916 nomination by Woodrow Wilson. That fight was fomented as much by his alienation of industrial and financial powers who despised his social reform contribution to sweeping regulatory legislation as by deep-seated and overt anti-Semitism (although there was more than enough of that). For most, Brandeis is simply installed somewhere among the icons of our legal history along with his contemporaries, Justices Oliver Wendell Holmes, Jr. and Felix Frankfurter.

Louis D. Brandeis
Melvin I. Urofsky
Pantheon Books, 2009   955 pages

Louis Dembitz Brandeis, born just a few years before the Civil War, died just a few weeks before Pearl Harbor. His life as a ground-breaking attorney and his 23 years as a Supreme Court Justice encompassed an era of unbridled industrial and financial consolidation, followed by groundbreaking governmental activism.

Melvin Urofsky, Professor of Law and Public Policy and Professor Emeritus of History at Virginia Commonwealth University, has given us a huge (almost 1,000 pages) and, to date, definitive biography of one of the most influential jurists in American History.

Born in the United States into a largely non-observant, middle-class, German-Jewish immigrant family in Louisville, Kentucky, Brandeis graduated from Harvard Law School with high honors despite the fact that he had not met the minimum age of 21. After a brief period in St. Louis, he returned to Boston to practice law, becoming very successful as a pioneer in the creation of large practices which include attorneys specializing in the various fields of law. Brandeis revolutionized how lawyers presented appellate briefs in cases of reform legislation by citing relevant factual information in addition to legal theory. For decades, such briefs would be referred to as "Brandeis briefs."

Many believed Brandeis, a strong campaigner for Woodrow Wilson, would be awarded a cabinet position, but White House insiders considered him too much of a lightning rod for conservative opponents of the administration. He remained, however, a highly trusted advisor to the President on economic matters, as well as legal issues. During Wilson's administration, Brandeis opposed the huge consolidations that created U.S. Steel, Standard Oil, and the railroad combines. In *The Curse of Bigness* he warned of the harmful effects of large scale industrialization on society, labor, the environment and the political process.

His remarkable prescience a century ago remains applicable today. Called upon by President Wilson, Brandeis was in the forefront of national reform politics from 1912 until he was named to the Supreme Court in 1916. He helped draft the Federal Reserve Act, the Clayton Antitrust Act and the law establishing the Federal Trade Commission. His exposé of the banking industry led to the creation of the Glass-Steagall Act in 1933. The Glass-Steagall Act mandated federal regulation for banking. As a result of its repeal in 1999, we are all suffering the worst financial crisis in 80 years.

In 1914, Brandeis joined the Zionist movement, a monumental step for one who harbored strong feelings on the matter of dual loyalty. Powerfully pro-American, he had always opposed labels like "Italian-American" or "Jewish-American," holding that we were all equally "Americans." But Brandeis came to understand the importance of the cultural contributions of diverse ethnic groups and appreciated the richness they added to American society, provided they all subscribed to a common set of ethical and social principles. When he joined the Zionist movement he was asked what brought him to that decision. This formerly unaffiliated peripheral Jew said that he had come back to his people through his Americanism, citing the democracy he had seen at work while a mediator during the garment industry strike of 1910. (During those negotiations it became apparent that most of the labor representatives were Jewish, as were most of the owners).

Admitting his lack of a Jewish background, he declared nonetheless that "Jews were by reasons of their traditions and their character peculiarly fitted for the attainment of American ideals." Thus he was able to form the link bridging Zionism and Americanism: "To be good Americans, we must be better Jews, and to be better Jews, we must become Zionists."

Brandeis anticipated that there would be a fight over his confirmation following his nomination by President Wilson to the Supreme Court, and he was not disappointed. Wall Street firms deluged the Senate with condemning letters. Anti-Semitic Boston Brahmins were outspoken opponents, and seven of the 16 living former presidents of the American Bar Association signed a letter proclaiming his unfitness for the office. Months later, on strict party lines, Louis Brandeis was confirmed and received a one-word message from Oliver Wendell Holmes— "Welcome."

Author Urofsky provides, sometimes in mind-numbing detail, the intricacies of Brandeis' incomparable contribution to the effort of American Jews in support of the struggling *yishuv* in Palestine and their preparation for eventual statehood. What remains, of course is the meat of the Brandeis story. Louis Brandeis is credited with the development of the modern jurisprudence of free speech and the constitutional protection of the right to privacy. We continue to observe the ripple effect of those decisions. Perhaps most important of all is Brandeis' development of what is termed the "doctrine of incorporation," by which the Due Process Clause of the 14th Amendment to the Constitution was used to apply the Bill of Rights to the states as well as to the federal government.

Urofsky also reminds us that as a commercial lawyer, Brandeis' work on *Other People's Money and How the Bankers Use It* and "similar indictments of immoral banking behavior will likely find a new audience." "For Brandeis, regulation was not supposed to be a restraint on innovation or the entrepreneurial spirit, but rather a check on unbridled greed."

Brandeis is a monumental work, but then, nothing less could do justice to such a monumental human being.

November 2009

On Potok

CHAIM POTOK, who died in 2002, shared two things with your reviewer. We both graduated with BA degrees in Literature in 1950 and we both had our minds opened to literature by Evelyn Waugh (among others). He was smitten by *Brideshead Revisited*; I by *A Handful of Dust*. We both studied James Joyce, particularly *A Portrait of the Artist as a Young Man*. Potok went on to join the pantheon of great American writers, and more particularly of great American Jewish writers.

Chaim Potok
Confronting Modernity Through the Lens of Tradition
Edited by Daniel Walden
Pennsylvania State University Press, 2013
184 pages

Daniel Walden, Professor Emeritus of American Studies, English, and Comparative Literature at Pennsylvania State University, was the founder and longtime editor of the journal, *Studies in American Jewish Literature*. We both received our Masters degrees in literature at Columbia University, but our paths never crossed until recently. Readers of this column know that this reviewer is generally untroubled by bouts of humility, but Professor Walden has assembled essays from such a distinguished group of scholars that any reader should be a bit intimidated.

Nonetheless, for any fan of Chaim Potok, especially one who has read most of his novels decades ago, this collection is as much a joy as it is a challenge. Walden and his contributors made me recall that, whereas Saul Bellow, Bernard Malamud and Philip Roth captured and ruminated on the conflicts engendered by Jews fitting and not fitting into the fabric of American culture, Potok's early works such as *The Chosen* and *The Promise* did the same—but within the context of Judaism alone. This is one of the reasons Potok seems to be considered a kind of "outlier" among Jewish American authors.

The structure of the book is twofold. The first half is a significant body of criticism of Potok's novels, including some of his later and less well-known works, providing a review for those who may be a bit rusty on Potok—as well as the basis for scholarly and critical discussion. The second half consists of more personal considerations, notably a wonderful essay by Potok's widow, Adena Potok, who in addition to her own career as a psychiatric social worker, was his "first reader" until his death in 2002.

Herman Harold (*Chaim Tzvi* in Hebrew) Potok was born in 1929 in The Bronx, New York. (We were chronological, geographic and name contemporaries, and I have wondered my entire life what it was in the name

Harold, a Middle English name derived from the Scandinavian, that fascinated Jewish mothers in the Bronx at that time.) His father was a Belzer Hasid and his mother descended from the Hasidic Ryzner line. A *yeshiva borcher* from childhood through rabbinic ordination, Potok was enamored of painting until Orthodox concerns with idolatry forced him to seek other intellectual pursuits. Brought up in the tight Jewish world of the Bronx, he emerged blinking in the powerful light of what he termed "Western secular humanism." One could argue that this was a western extension of the European *Haskalah,* the Jewish Enlightenment movement in Europe of the late 18th to late 19th centuries inspired by Moses Mendelssohn. It could be further argued that there was a line of connection going back to writers like Sholom Asch, who emigrated to America and whose novels, such as *East River,* foreshadowed the work of E.L. Doctorow and Herman Wouk, as well as Saul Bellow, Philip Roth and Bernard Malamud.

Chaim Potok concludes with the reprint of an address by Potok himself in 1982. In it he acknowledges that "the Eastern side of our planet has some overlap with our side, but at the heart of things, I think the two sides of the planet really think the world structures reality in ways quite different, one from the other." The new world, only about three hundred years old, begins with the Enlightenment, thus our "civilization makes no appeal to the supernatural." No wonder Potok has been described as a *"Zwischenmensch,"* a "between person," and not only Jews but Christians, Muslims, Hindus and Buddhists have taken to his works as they also struggle to live in constant tension with tradition and everyday reality.

Re-reading one's favorite books has become more and more difficult as we are bombarded with a surfeit of new publications on our Kindles, Nooks, Kobos or good old paper. However, re-reading the perennially relevant Chaim Potok is what your reviewer has in his bucket, and Daniel Weldon's *Chaim Potok* will certainly be an invaluable guide to that task.

November 2013

ESSAYS
and
ARTICLES

A dining experience 'worth trying again for first time'

ANNABEL AND I, in the first of what we hope will be a series of visits to local restaurants on behalf of the *UJF Virginia News*, had an exceptional dinner recently at the Ships Cabin. So what's new? Isn't the Ships Cabin a Golden Fork Hall of Famer? Hasn't it been one of the area's best known and favorite restaurants for years? Well, yes, but, like the cornflake commercial, we encourage you to "try it again for the first time."

We approached our invitation from owner Joe Hoggard as an opportunity to dine in a frequently visited restaurant as though we had not been there before. We also concluded that the entire point in writing about a restaurant devoted primarily to serving superior seafood was to explore the items not on the "no no" list.

Ships Cabin Restaurant
Norfolk, Virginia

So what did we find? Well, as you probably know, the restaurant is comprised of a series of handsome rooms—but the room overlooking Chesapeake Bay offers a view of which we never tire. And there we dined.

Wine lists today are frowned upon as lacking in class if they don't include a fair number of pricier wines, and Joe's list is no exception. However, more important than the high end choices are the number of good wines at moderate prices. We chose and enjoyed a Sinskey Aries Merlot '91, Carneros ($5 by the glass; $22 per bottle) and a Laboure-Roi Pouilly Fuissé '90, France ($5 by the glass; $22.50 per bottle). For those dining as a couple who prefer a white wine with starters and salads and a red with entrées, and for whom the thought of downing two full bottles is daunting, Ships Cabin offers an above-average list of half bottles and splits.

The appetizers were wonderful—but for the purposes of this article we are going to move along smartly to the salads: a generous House Salad at $3.25, a classic Caesar Salad at $3.75, and a Goat Cheese Salad, tossed with California field greens, the creamiest chevre we have ever tasted, and a not-too-tart, not-too-sweet white wine vinaigrette, a $4.75 delight!

Chef Bobby Huber, relatively new at Ships Cabin having arrived from Fire and Ice in Hampton about a year ago, has changed about 25 percent of the menu items and generally enriched already first-rate selections. Of special note, among the fish entrées are Salmon Maurice, grilled and served over black beans with a pungent tomato relish at $13.75, Horseradish Encrusted Tuna, oven roasted and garnished with a citrus soy sauce at $15.50, and Herb Crusted Salmon rolled in fresh aromatic herbs and topped with sundried tomato butter at $14.50.

Meat entrées include a braised, melt-in-your-mouth Lamb Shank (*Bubbe* never made one like this!) draped in exquisitely caramelized onions over a pile (no other way to describe it!) of mashed potatoes (like *Bubbe* used to make—but the heart-stopping schmaltz!) at $14. If you're starving, for $16.50 you can have the Lamb Shank plus a generous portion of fresh Herb-Crusted Salmon. The accompanying veggie was a substantial portion of perfectly cooked fresh carrot sticks tossed with tarragon (no precisely placed, countable miniature veggies here!).

Scrumptious desserts vary in price from $3.25 to $4.50. The Pecan Lace (giant) Cookie with fresh strawberries and white chocolate mousse is a delectation not to be found elsewhere in the area; save room to at least share this one.

Having read recently of the peripatetic nature of chefs, we can better appreciate the difficulties in maintaining a standard of excellence over the years. It is more difficult still to continually freshen and improve one's menu while maintaining the old favorites. At Ships Cabin, Joe Hoggard and his enthusiastic young chef have accomplished just that, which, aided by the ministrations of what has always been a well-trained staff, results in continued fine dining—and great eating too!

May 1994

Secrets of the 400 Club revealed

THIRTY YEARS AGO, as the newly hired Campaign Director for the United Jewish Federation of Tidewater (so named due to the merger of the Portsmouth Federation with the United Jewish Federation of Norfolk and Virginia Beach), I had tried to create an affinity group of past leadership—a group that would meet quarterly to receive briefings on what was going in the community. Sydney Gates had another idea. Since then, losses, gains, and time have brought the two concepts closer together, as will be revealed below.

Jewish Community Club Comes of Age

Hal Sacks

Strictly speaking, the 400 Club is a misnomer. The ages of the original five members added up to only 398. They were Sydney Gates, Lester Sherrick, Morton Kushner, Archie Harris and one kid still in his fifties, Marvin Simon. I used to tell Sydney Gates that as a bunch of merchants they should call it "The 398 Club, Marked Down from Four Dollars." The whole number thing quickly became moot as they immediately allowed Buddy Kantor, a youth not yet 70, into the club as a "full member."

Sydney was the Treasurer, Secretary, and unpaid and unappreciated general factotum. His task was to send out the meeting notice each month along with the venue, which varied from such places as Burroughs (Military Highway) to The Circle (Portsmouth) to AJR Doubleday's (Ghent) and Johnny Lockhart's (Tidewater Drive). Several times a year they were in for a real treat—having lunch at the Sandler warehouse.

Sydney would read the minutes:

"No minutes."
"Treasurer's report: No money in the treasury."
"Agenda: No agenda."
"Let's eat."

So what did they do at these exclusive meetings? Well, they told dirty jokes, talked over old times (like who was arrested when their floating poker game was raided by the police), and recalled the peccadilloes of various contemporaries in the Jewish Community of the 1920s, '30s and '40s. Membership was initially restricted to Federation presidents, JCC presidents, or Chairmen of the "drive" (as the Federation's Annual Campaign was dubbed). Their motto was: "No fancy stuff for the 400 Club; just fellowship for old friends."

Membership restrictions were relaxed to include anyone over 60 who had worked hard for the Jewish community and was still active one way or another. Somehow Leonard Strelitz and Sam Sandler made it in, followed shortly by Bernard Jaffe, Mickey Kramer, Sam Weisberg and Sam Swersky. And in time Arthur Kaplan, Sonny Lefcoe, Julian Rashkind, Malcolm Rosenberg and Henry Zetlin were inducted. Of course, there was no "induction" ceremony, just a phone call inviting the new member to lunch.

They are all of blessed memory now, but they have left an indelible mark on our community. Survivors of the "old" 400 Club include Tavia Gordon, Arnold Leon, Marc Jacobson, Kurt Rosenbach, Morty Goldmeier, Bob Rubin, Dave Furman,* Walter Segaloff,* and the undersigned.

Every day we continue to be thankful for what the 400 Club did to create this [Simon Family Jewish Community Center] campus. When, in 2003, Steve and Art Sandler (inducted despite their youth) asked the Club to assure them that it would back the Simcha Campaign if they took the lead, the members responded with over $8,000,000 in pledges. Within two weeks of breaking ground the example set by the Sandler and the Simon families and the 400 Club resulted in pledges in excess of $20,000,000.

But what of the 400 Club now? Some old friends remain; some new friendships are being made; not many dirty jokes or racy stories. In many respects the Club is as different as the Tidewater Jewish community has become in three decades. When the original group kicked things off thirty years ago our agencies were small and almost fifty percent of our Campaign dollars were allocated to the United Jewish Appeal. However, in many ways the Club is very much the same. Still relevant, its members have all been involved in some aspect of the Jewish Community—Federation, Foundation, Agencies and Synagogues. Meetings are once a month for lunch and fellowship and, from time to time, to receive briefings from the Federation, the Tidewater Jewish Foundation, and their recipients, constituents, and affiliates. Mostly it's schmoozing, talking about the Jewish world, and expressing our gratitude that we can continue to gather in harmony.

As Sydney Gates used to say, "Don't call us, we'll call you."

Hal Sacks

* of blessed memory since originally printed

What a privilege to have gone!

Guantanamera,
Guajira Guantanamera!
Guantanamera!

Yo soy un hombre sincero, De donde crecen las palmas
Cultiva la rosa blanco... Para el amigo sincero...Que me da su mano franca.
Guantanamera!

I am a truthful man, from the land of the palm...
I cultivate a white rose... for the sincere friend who gives me his hand.
Guantanamera!
> – José Marti, National Hero of Cuba

WHAT A COUNTRY! Liberated at last from the colonial grasp of Spain, Cuba then suffered a century of dictators. Some were murderous and corrupt thieves, and finally during the last 40 years in Cuba, a generation of inept ideologues, clinging irrationally to a failed system.

As for the Jews of Cuba, their second Diaspora in one generation left a bare remnant of Jewry in Cuba, a country whose constitution declared it to be an atheist state. Thus we heard little of the remaining Jews, who couldn't make a living under the Communist regime while practicing their religion.

A Cuban Journey
1991

The constitutional change in 1991, which declared the state secular rather than atheist, and the subsequent visit of Pope John Paul II, signaled an opportunity for Cuban Jews to renew their practices. As the U.S. State Department says, "Cuba's small Jewish community continues to hold services in Havana and has pockets of faithful in Santiago, Camaguey and other parts of the island. Assistance from Jewish communities abroad, including arranging for visiting rabbis and rabbinical students, helps to keep the Hebrew faith alive in Cuba."

Thus we journeyed to Cuba, that beautiful beggar nation, on a humanitarian mission to share fellowship with the Jews of Cuba: to pray together, to gain strength from their strength, their commitment to hope, to *hatikvah*.

The Jews of Cuba are not starving; they are poor, but not ragged. They need help, but remain proud and are determined to keep the faith alive. Despite a 90% rate of intermarriage, a large percentage of the intermarried convert to Judaism, thus helping the small community grow. They are relearning Hebrew and teaching their children. They depend on volunteers and two

Joint Distribution Committee representatives, virtually the total JDC aid.

Early in the mission I joked that my purpose in going to Cuba was to look for the 1953 Dodge Coronet, which I left there in 1959 when leaving for the U.S. after the revolution. Certainly the streets were filled with cars of the '50s and '60s, as well as horse-drawn buggies and man-powered cyclos. I also looked with great sadness on the beautiful colonial buildings which had been allowed to decay and crumble. But mostly I loved the conversations, some brief and some quite in depth, depending upon the available mix of English and Spanish.

Robert Acree is 58 years old, an engineer, in charge of the waterworks for the city of Santiago de Cuba. He earns 250 pesos a month, which at 22 pesos to the dollar comes to just under $12. His ration card permits him to buy six pounds of rice each month for the highly subsidized price of 25 centavos per pound. He lives with his married daughters and their families, and by pooling their resources they manage not to starve. But to maintain a modest, yet decent, standard of living, he depends on the stipend which he is allowed to receive from his son in Tampa, Florida. The $100 he receives monthly doubles the earnings of Robert, his daughters and sons-in-law—all put together.

Robert's father worked in the Public Works Department on the Naval Base in Guantanamo Bay. Robert remembers that when he was 11 years old his father took him to see the first of the new supercarriers (U.S.S. *Forrestal* CVA 59). What an irony—there was Robert, on shore, looking at the beautiful new ship. There was the undersigned, at that very time, an instructor on the ship—looking at the *verde claro*, the light green hills of Cuba. And there we were, in the plain but magical synagogue of Santiago. I will write to Robert—but have no confidence that he will receive my letters.

Two weeks later, I wonder, "Was I really in Cuba?" It flashed by so quickly: the little Orthodox synagogue with its unusual *mechitza*; the *Museo de Art de Cubana,* with its ominous revolutionary tones; a few days; we did so much. Too soon it was over.

Y para el cruel que me arranca
El corozon con que vivo
Cardo ni ortiga cultivo
Cultivo la rosa blanca

And for the cruel one who would tear out
This heart with which I live.
I cultivate neither thistles nor nettles
I cultivate a white rose.

What a privilege to have gone!

March 2006

Trip to Israel

AGE PROMPTS ME to pose the same question each time I contemplate a trip to Israel. Will this be the last? It's such a long and tiring trip! How important is it for me to make the effort, and will it be worthwhile?

My daughter, Judy Anderson, and I traveled to Israel on July 17 with the express purpose of visiting Tidewater Jewish community project sites and renewing friendships made during 25 years of partnership activities. I think Judy was motivated at first by concern for the "old man" traveling alone, but grew increasingly motivated by the opportunity to revisit places and people encountered in several previous visits.

Visiting UJFT Project Sites in 2009

Hal Sacks and Judy Anderson

On July 19 we traveled to Pardes Hana to visit Neve Michael (pronounced *nevay meechal*), the crisis center and youth village that has received financial support from the United Jewish Federation of Tidewater and private individuals in our community for about 15 years. Greeted by the redoubtable Hava Levene, the "face" of Neve Michael, we joined a Partnership 2000 group from Knoxville, Tennessee, for a tour of the facility. Although we had taken the standard tour many times, we were delighted to have the opportunity to take it again since we had brought a trio of Israeli friends with us who were interested in volunteer activities. It also provided an easy way to become familiar with the updates at Neve Michael:

Crisis Center: This is one of just a few crisis centers and they are funded by the State of Israel for the purpose of taking in children who are wards of the courts for one reason or another, but usually as witnesses and/or victims of sexual, physical, and psychological abuse. Children remain for up to six months until deemed "ready" to join one of the family group homes on campus, or to be returned to their family if such is determined to be safe. The Crisis Center depends upon donations for operational and capital support over the minimal support provided by the State.

Group Homes: Funds have been made available to upgrade some of the children's rooms but additional dormitory space is still needed.

As usual, the children are the stars of the tour, but some of the "foster" mothers I have met over the years are soon to retire. Some have been on the job for over 20 years. It was touching to see how reluctant they are to leave Neve Michael.

Hava Levene sends heartfelt love to our community.

July 20 found us in Pardes Katz, formerly a Sephardic neighborhood in the ultra-religious municipality of B'nei Brak. Our relationship with this underprivileged enclave is a quarter of a century old, stemming from former Prime Minister Menachem Begin's creation of Project Renewal. Diaspora communities have helped revitalize 69 down-at-the-heels neighborhoods that had been bypassed by the miracle of Israeli growth and had succumbed to the urban ills of drug abuse and crime. Tidewater's contribution over the years has been construction of an education wing to the *Matnas* (their JCC), development of a daycare center, furnishing a library, creating a dental clinic, and funding the operation of a summer camp in English.

In previous reports I furnished the community with updated demographic information about Pardes Katz as the *olim* from the Former Soviet Union displaced some of the Sephardic families who successfully moved to better neighborhoods. It became immediately apparent during our visit that additional important changes to these demographics have occurred. (I have initiated an effort to update this information which I will present when it's available.)

The most obvious change has been the assignment of over 60 Ethiopian families to Pardes Katz with no special State assistance for dealing with their unique problems. The Municipality of B'nei Brak has, however, opened a second *moadonit* (a daycare center in a home-environment model for at-risk children). The original *moadonit* is still in operation. Formerly, Tidewater funded "extras" for these children, like field trips to museums or the circus, or purchase of audio/video equipment, for about $2,500 per year. It is this observer's opinion that some funds, even if a lesser amount, be once again considered for the *moadonitim*.

Some readers will recall the youth director of the *Matnas*, Ayelet. She has left the position for further study in India. Several years ago Tidewater had the pleasure of hosting two Pardes Katz volunteers and *Matnas* Director Michal Zehavi. Sadly, one of the volunteers, Yossi Dror, passed away this past November. A new daycare classroom has been named in memory of Yossi. The other, Yoni, has transitioned from volunteer to director of Cultural Activities at the *Matnas*.

The number of children requiring daycare has doubled. There are now four daycare classrooms. Special one-on-one work with Ethiopian children of school age is a major project. These children speak conversational Hebrew well enough, as do their parents, but their parents basically can't read Hebrew and are no help to the children in their school work. The children tend to fall behind and become disciplinary problems. Thus, the Association of Matnasim (our national Jewish Community Center Association) is funding the staff to work with these children.

The Calvin Belkov Dental Clinic is very busy, furnishing quality dental care at about 40% of the going rate, and the small profit it generates is going directly into the programming of the *Matnas*. A new dental chair funded by Tidewater has been installed and one of the older chairs has been recovered. Matching some of the funds sent by Tidewater, the clinic has been renovated and one wall removed (formerly separating the clinic from the waiting room) thus enlarging the clinic. While I was visiting, workmen were installing a newly purchased (used) X-ray machine as the one that we sent to them 15 years ago has failed. I have separately recommended that funds for this machine ($1,600 U.S.) be forwarded to the *Matnas*.

One of my personal reasons for visiting Israel at this time was to visit Dr. Harold Burstein, age 96. "Doc," a retired veterinarian, is the founding president of the Hebrew Academy of Tidewater (HAT) and among other accomplishments, my son Skip's godfather. What a joy it was to sit with Doc and talk over old times! This remarkable man still reads three daily newspapers in English and several periodicals spanning the political spectrum from left to right. Despite his frailty he has a good appetite, an excellent memory, and returned the regards I brought for him from the children of his now-departed friends.

We stayed with his son Joel, a consulting engineer who made *aliyah* about 40 years ago. Joel's daughter Lior took Judy and me to *Yad LaKashish* (Lifeline for the Old). *Yad LaKashish* was begun over 40 years ago with assistance from the American Jewish Joint Distribution Committee (JDC). Five mornings a week about 300 elderly and disabled men and women find stimulating and creative work opportunities in an array of artistic workshops. They produce beautiful handmade Judaica and craft items, earn a stipend and benefits which include transportations costs, a daily hot lunch, and dental and eyeglass allowances. What is most noteworthy is that *Yad LaKashish* is a totally independent non-profit, receiving no government support.

Everyone said that I must revisit *Yad Vashem*, newly designed and organized. I resisted slightly, having been there over a dozen times. But Judy and I went and were overwhelmed by the architectural statement and the excellence of the new displays. The additional testimony of survivors living in Israel was so powerful. We strongly advise visitors to Israel to revisit Yad Vashem and see it for the first time all over again.

One result of the impact of our current financial crisis is the need to reexamine the nature of our Israel & Overseas commitment. My discussions with lay leaders and professionals in Israel revealed a tendency to focus efforts, at least within Israel, on one project with which the greatest impact may be achieved, leaving the regular allocation to the Jewish Agency for Israel (JAFI) and JDC through UJC to "cover the waterfront." I met with Judy Yoda, director of Partnerships, Israel Department of JAFI. She confirmed this trend and I defended Tidewater's different strategy in recent years. Our relationships with a variety of programs in Israel, in Eastern Europe, Argentina and elsewhere developed as small groups traveled to different places and were attracted to the idea of fulfilling needs in a variety of locations. Yet, on reflection, should we become greatly restricted in funding, perhaps it would be wise to question this and think about focusing on a smaller number of projects.

But how does one measure the impact? There are no scientific tools readily available for this purpose. Anecdotally, we *can* observe impact. Perhaps the following is illustrative:

One of my daughter Judy's objectives was to seek out and thank a young woman who had befriended and helped my granddaughter Miche during her eight-month stay in Israel more than a year ago. Miche, currently employed at our Jewish Family Service, was working as an intern with the newspaper *Ha'aretz*. Her housing in Ra'ananah was over an hour's bus ride from downtown Tel Aviv where she worked. On many late evenings Liron Berger, a new friend, invited her to stay at her apartment in Tel Aviv. Liron, a recruiting officer for a technical college in Tel Aviv, met us for lunch at the Carmel *shouk*. A stunning young woman in her mid-20s, Liron asked me what I was doing in Israel. I replied that I wanted to visit friends and project sites, such as the Matnas in Pardes Katz. Without pausing for breath, I began to tell her of some of projects there, including the *kefiada* (an English language day camp for which we provided American college students as counselors. We stopped sending our kids during the second *intifada* but continued the funding by paying for Israeli counselors.) Liron stopped me there and said that she knew about the *kefiada* because she grew up in B'nei Brak and went to the *kefiada* in Pardes Katz for two years. "That's where I learned my English," she said, "and without that I wouldn't have the job I now have." Now that's what I call impact!

During most of this trip to Israel, Judy and I stayed with the Shaked family in Shoham, a peaceful and charming new city near Ben Gurion Airport. Shuli Shaked, now Einhorn, formerly of Pardes Katz, but now living in the Fairfield neighborhood of Virginia Beach, teaches at the Bina High School and at the Hebrew Academy of Tidewater. When I ask myself, "Was this my last trip to Israel?" I think about the hospitality of the Shakeds and the rest of my second family and how amazingly changed Israel is each time I visit.

Why wouldn't I go back? I can hardly wait.

July 2009

A thumbnail history of the Jews of Tidewater

WHILE THE ARRIVAL in 1787 of Moses Myers, a New York native of Dutch descent, whose Georgian home in downtown Norfolk is an integral part of the Norfolk Tour, is commonly accepted to signify the arrival of the first permanent Jewish settler, records exist of the family of Jacob Abrahams, who lived and worked in Portsmouth well before that date.

A Thumbnail History of the Jews of Tidewater

Adapted by Hal Sacks from the histories published by Irwin Barent and (Mrs. Alvin) Elise Levy Margolius

Shortly after Moses Myers arrived in Norfolk, in the Berkley section of Norfolk County, a close-knit Orthodox Russian-Jewish community began and established the first cemetery in the area. For a time it was believed that George Washington favored this area as the site for the nation's capital, and for half a century the Berkley section was known as Washington Point.

It is thought that by 1840 there were, in Tidewater, a sufficient number of Jews to make a *minyan*. The wave of German Jewish migration in the following decade led to the establishment of the first congregation in the area, Chevra B'nai Jacob, Friends of the House of Jacob. The first synagogue was constructed a year or so before the outbreak of the Civil War. Hand in hand with the creation of a congregation went the establishment of cemeteries, such as the Hebrew Cemetery on Princess Anne Road, which remains in use today.

The 19th century was a time of very slow growth for the Jewish community and it was not until the turn of the next century that the Jewish population of Norfolk, increased by the arrival of immigrants from Russia, Lithuania and Poland, reached about 500. Thus, 1900 found the Ohef Sholom congregation (about 120 members*) ensconced in the former Methodist Protestant Church on Church Street; Beth El Congregation (about 75 members*) in the former Ohef Sholom Temple on Cumberland Street (just opposite the former Norfolk Academy, then the Chamber of Commerce and now the Hurrah Players' building).

The Orthodox synagogue, B'nai Israel (about 50 members*) was likewise

---

*The numbers probably refer to family units because wives and children were not likely to be counted as members.

first housed on Cumberland Street. As the new century began, one could perceive the beginnings of Jewish communal life outside the synagogues, with the creation of two Zionist organizations, the B'nai Zion Alliance, and the Ladies Zion Alliance, as well as the proliferation of charitable organizations including the Ladies Hebrew Benevolent Society, the Jewish Board of Guardians, and the Hebrew Board of Charities. Educational, social and fraternal orders followed apace.

From the founding of the Hadassah chapter in 1912 and the organization of fundraising activities for the Jewish National Fund to the regional meetings in Norfolk of the Zionist Organization of America in 1923, local Jewry continued to expand its horizons, on behalf of the overseas needs of the Jewish people, while voicing concern about the needs of Jewish youth at home. As early as 1912 leaders were demanding the establishment of a YMHA. The community's present-day efforts to provide expanded JCCT facilities and/or programming is reflective of an editorial by Dr. Lazarus Karp in 1914:

> It is true the Kehillah of Norfolk maintains a very modern Hebrew school for the children, and can also boast of several very attractive synagogues and temples, but what precautions has the Jewish community of Norfolk taken to prevent the backslidings of the youth and what have they done to abort the sorrowful consequences of an unguided generation? ... The Jewish community of Norfolk owes it to their growing sons and daughters to provide the proper surroundings and institute the proper refining influences within its midst.

The Jewish community continued to grow and prosper following the first World War, devoting energy to the relief of those suffering as a result of the war, raising funds for a hospital, and conducting the first of many campaigns for the newly organized United Palestine Appeal, precursor of the United Jewish Appeal. By 1926 a goal of $20,000 was established. Then as now, it wasn't easy, but the few persevered for the good of so many.

The Jewish community weathered the Great Depression alongside the general community, while casting a worried eye as news of anti-Jewish atrocities in Germany began to trickle home. Irving Kline was selling two-year-old Chevrolets for $295 and a five-year-old sedan cost less than a kosher brisket today ($35). L. Snyder offered men's winter union suits for 49 cents.

By 1935, the B'nai B'rith Lodge in Norfolk was formally reorganized. From its leadership evolved the Jewish Community Council of Norfolk, forerunner of the present day United Jewish Federation of Tidewater.

Between those early days and the present, two generations of leadership built a community with two principal objectives: significant support to our Jewish brothers and sisters overseas; and fulfilling our obligations nationally, regionally and locally. By the early 1970s, the community boasted a nationally applauded campaign, a fledgling Hebrew day school, and successful Jewish

Family Service and Jewish Community Center operations.

The Jewish population passed 5,000 in the 1960s, and by 1974 the influx of Jews to Virginia Beach swelled the population to over 12,000. By 1982, according to the first professionally directed demographic study, the United Jewish Federation of Tidewater served over 15,000 Jews in Norfolk, Portsmouth, Virginia Beach, Chesapeake and Suffolk.

A 1988 update estimated our population at 18,000, with about 8,000 in Norfolk and 8,000 in Virginia Beach. As we approach the turn of the century, the Jewish population of Tidewater is probably closer to 20,000 with about 60 percent in Virginia Beach.

November 1998

Thriving community gone

OUR JOURNEY to Egypt, which began on Christmas Day 1987, juxtaposed the legend of the three wise men and the reality of the last three Jewish children in Alexandria. But more of them later.

In 1947, there were about 65,000 Jews in Egypt, almost half of which were in Alexandria, an ancient Jewish community enriched over 400 years earlier by an influx of Spanish Jews fleeing the Inquisition. The establishment of the State of Israel and King Farouk's declaration of war signaled the beginning of the second exodus from Egypt. Half the Jews of Egypt had departed by 1950.

By 1957, following the Sinai campaign, there were fewer than 3,000 Jews in Alexandria. By

The Last Three Jewish Children in Alexandria, Egypt

Hal Sacks

1970, it was down to 1,000 and at mid-day on Dec. 25, 1987, there were 18 men, 80 women and three Jewish children in Alexandria. But more of them later.

It was still dark in Cairo when my wife, Annabel, and I rendezvoused with our driver for the journey through the desert to Alexandria. Recent rains had flooded the old and more charming Nile Delta road, but the drive through the desert brought its own flood of memories as signs pointed the way to Merse Matruh and El Alamein of World War ll fame, and in our mind's eye, we could see the ghostly legions of Rommel, Montgomery and Patton pursuing each other across the trackless dunes.

Rain was falling when we arrived in Alexandria. Clement Sellon, 82 years old, nattily dressed in handsome blue blazer, rose to greet us. I thought of George Burns. There was a twinkle in his eye, which could not be subdued by the grimness of his responsibilities.

It is difficult to say with certainty why we had arranged with the Joint Distribution Committee (JDC) for this visit. Perhaps we felt a little guilty over a visit to Egypt strictly on holiday without some "meaningful" Jewish component. Perhaps reports from others who had been to Egypt and visited the synagogue in Cairo were just too negative. Whatever the reason, we knew of the work of the JDC in helping to maintain the remnants of Alexandria's once flourishing Jewish community and thought it would be interesting to see it for ourselves. We were prepared, yet unprepared.

The official Jewish community lies just off a major shopping street lined with fine shops. Many of these formerly were owned by Jews, but had been sequestered by Nasser in 1956. Surrounded by the protecting walls common to both Jewish and Christian religious centers, we were surprised to find the entrance guarded by two Egyptian soldiers bearing the automatic weapons common to the region. As in Vienna, Paris and Holland, their presence, to guard against the daily terrorism, was chilling in itself.

Our amiable host talked about his hopes and fears, with the earnestness of a man with a mission, but with the resignation of one who has told his story before—each time praying for results that might never be achieved in his lifetime. He told of the necessity in the past of selling off the other synagogues in the city, to raise the funds to support the one remaining, exceptionally beautiful Eliahu HaNavi Synagogue.

"The community here is disappearing," said Setton. We used to have 30,000 Jews in Alexandria. Then we were a community. But now we are a family, that's all."

Setton took us into what had been the study of the Chief Rabbi of Alexandria and then into the archives, where he maintains the files of *ketubbim* and marriage licenses. Even as we spoke, a gentleman who had emigrated to Brazil 38 years ago arrived with his wife to seek a copy of their wedding certificate.

Then it was off to the great synagogue itself: imposing, 100 years old, well maintained by a caring and loyal group of Arab workers whose affection for the old man was obvious and touching. As we entered, the lights were turned on, the electrified candles glowed and we approached the Holy Ark. I was by now a little shaky in the knees.

"Open it," he commanded. I complied, feeling the honor of this *aliyah*, to see inside over 50 Torah scrolls, some of unusual age and beauty. I realized there were more scrolls than worshipers because as each synagogue closed, the scrolls were collected and placed in Eliahu NaHavi.

"What will happen when I die?" Setton asked. "They'll turn this place into a museum. The scrolls will lie here, unopened, unstudied... like children whose lives will go to waste. My dream is to get them out of here, to send them, not to museums, but to synagogues around the world where they will be opened and used and will live their own lives after we are gone."

Leaving the synagogue, we looked at the deserted school building where the voices of 1,200 Jewish students studying Torah and secular subjects once echoed. Imagine a Hebrew day school in a community of 30,000 with 1,200 students. I could not help but think of our own community and its struggle to operate a school with 180 students. Setton then told of another dream—a dream of a group of Hebrew students who would come to Alexandria, live in the many rooms that are within the compound and who would study, using the school and its library.

"We could house them and, if we had to, I suppose we could feed them. But they could stay here for a few months and learn from ancient works."

A hopeless dream? Perhaps, but perhaps not. Who were we to discount the dreams of this brave man?

Setton took us next to the "Le Foyer," the small nursing home maintained by the community with major support from the JDC—with funds from us, through our annual campaign commitment. Again, the passage between the ever-present and watchful armed guards.

How to describe this building of fading splendor? Exceptional, by Egyptian standards, yet on this chilly day, it was cold and not very bright. The paint was fading, but funds for this job were not yet available. Victor Ballasiano, director of "Le Foyer" showed us around. A young man appearing to be in his 40s, he had taught French for almost 15 years at the community school and when it closed, he stayed on to do what he could for the home. Although there were only eight residents, others were expected, as the 18 men and 80 women, all seniors, were each alone with no spouses or family to help them in their declining years. The home was there for them when it would be needed, and Victor was committed to seeing them through their last years with some measure of dignity. Some of the residents approached Setton, kissing his hand as he offered a word of care here, of encouragement there. Zelda Hollander, articulate and mentally alert, begged us to visit her room. She showed it with pride, apologizing that she hadn't expected guests and had not yet made her bed. The room was spacious, though shared with two others, and I guessed we would consider it spartan. But Zelda had a home and a community and people who cared for her.

We visited the kitchen and the dining room, where the principal decorations were drawings from children in the States, which had been placed on the walls.

It was then that we met Victor's wife, Denise, and the last three Jewish children in Alexandria—the couple's three beautiful children: Rachel, 7; Esther, 6; and Jacque, 4; who greeted us. It was then that the impact of Victor's commitment reached Annabel and me. We realized that they lived in a home surrounded by age, with young children for whom there are not, nor can there ever be, any Jewish playmates. What were their hopes, their dreams, their future?

Reluctantly we said farewell to this singular and exceptional family and drove Setton back to his office, where he had a full schedule of appointments. Then we said our goodbyes to him. He begged us to return, to make a *minyan*, to pray with them and for them.

"I don't know what will happen when there are not Jews left in Alexandria," Setton said. And the twinkle in his eye dimmed, as we embraced in the rain in the courtyard. His final words broke our hearts: "I am alone here. It is my destiny."

April 1988

AUTHOR'S NOTE: Since this article was written, Clement Setton, president of the Jewish community in Alexandria, Egypt, died. May the lifelong struggle of this gallant *tzadek* be an inspiration and blessing to us all.

FICTION

A slightly surrealistic I.B. Singer-like tone

AHRON APPELFELD, author of a dozen internationally acclaimed novels, lives and writes in Jerusalem having made his way to Palestine in 1946. Born in Czernovitz, Bukovina, Ukraine, in 1932, he was imprisoned by the Nazis at the age of nine, was separated from his family, escaped, and hid in the forests until he joined the Soviet army as a kitchen boy.

The Conversion, a tale of reparation and retaliation, taking on a slightly surrealistic I.B. Singer-like tone (possibly due to translation) is set two generations before the Holocaust, at a time when many Jews, in order to abet their advancement, abandoned their Judaism and converted to Christianity.

The Conversion
Ahron Appelfeld
Schocken Books, 1998 228 pages

The protagonist, Karl Hubner, a highly regarded municipal bureaucrat, having watched his parents work themselves into early graves in an unsuccessful shop, converts in order to be promoted to a top echelon position. At first he suffers no regrets. The reader is introduced to three converts: Martin, an attorney; Freddy, a physician; and Hochhut, a corrupt city official and real estate developer.

The only observant Jews left in the city are the elderly owners of rundown stores in a shabby section of town. Their businesses are practically worthless, but they haven't the means to leave. In the name of development and progress, Hochhut has designated the dilapidated area for razing. Karl, despite his desire to put Jewish life behind him, cannot avoid his compassion for his dead parents' contemporaries.

Martin is haunted by guilt, Freddy throws himself into a life of sacrifice, and Hochhut is driven insane by the exposure of his crimes and the collapse of his financial empire. Karl, against his will and better judgement, is reunited with his past in a Kafkaesque series of dramatic events.

As the principal instrument of the redemptive spirit, Gloria, a Polish maid who was taken into the Hubner family as a young girl, reappears in Karl's life. Out of love and respect for Karl's deceased parents and relatives who gave her a home, Gloria has become an observant Jew in practice. Her return to the family home, now occupied only by Karl, their becoming lovers despite the difference in their ages, leads them to leave the city for a peaceful existence in the countryside. Implicit in Appelfeld's tale is the understanding that the conversions of convenience of that era did not absolve the apostate from the contempt and suspicion of both Jews and Gentiles. Nor, in Kurt Hubner's case, did his belated acts of *teshuva* prevent the tragic events which conclude Appelfeld's study in sepia.

February 1999

Revitalizing short-story genre with Jewish tales

YOUR FAITHFUL REVIEWER meant to write about this collection months ago when it received rave reviews in *The New Yorker* magazine and in the *New York Times Book Review*. Meeting the author at the UJC General Assembly in November was a rare treat. Upon hearing him read (beautifully) a thoughtful, yet immensely entertaining tale of a down-at-the-heels rebbe who augments his pitiful living by serving as Santa Claus in a department store (Reb Kringle), I silently promised to bring Englander to the attention of those who might not be aware of this new literary star.

For the Relief of Unbearable Urges
Nathan Englander
Alfred Knopf, 1999   205 pages

The pre-publication in magazines of two of the stories only reinforced the growing recognition that there has rather suddenly appeared on the literary scene a brilliant Jewish author, revitalizing the short story genre with Jewish tales, stories reflecting tremendous imagination and penetrating insight, served up with humor and angst.

While the eponymous story, "For the Relief of Unbearable Urges," and others such as "The Last One Way," find their humor and their poignancy in the depth of Jewish experience, Jewish history and particularly in the customs of Orthodox life, the story that perhaps best signals the emergence of an immense talent is the first one, "The Twenty Seventh Man." Selected in error, along with 26 famous Soviet-Yiddish writers, for arrest and swift execution, is Pinchas Pelovits, reclusive reader and writer whose work has been seen by no one, and who composes a tale in his head during the brief period of imprisonment and torture prior to being shot.

The Jewish writers are all tortured to force confessions of anti-revolutionary crimes, but on the eve of their deaths they question the presence of Pelovits, the writer with no readership. Convinced that he is not there as the result of a clerical error, but in satisfaction of some cosmic scheme, Pelovits reads the brief tale which he composed without pen or paper to three of the great writers in his cell.

> Bretsky stood. 'Bravo,' he said, clapping his hands." And later, "'Did you like it?' Pinchas asked. 'Very much,' Zunser said. 'You're a talented boy'.

Pinchas goes to his death having increased his reading public three-fold.

Not a bit ashamed to confess Englander's book was read by yours truly at poolside, and possibly somewhat dazed by the Arizona sunshine, I had a slight vision of young (30) Nathan Englander, not in a cell but in a room, reading one of his short stories to Sholom Aleichem, Isaac Bashevis Singer, and Bernard Malamud.

Malamud stands up. "Bravo," he says, clapping his hands ...

Unquestionably, Englander is a talented writer, with a special voice. As he explained to us in Atlanta, he grew up a proper *yeshiva borcher*, but now has removed himself from his youthful milieu. His stories reflect these tensions, and while we have been given to expect his next work to be very differently cast, somehow we know that the rich interweaving of Jewish life will not long be abandoned. It may be possible for Nathan to take Englander slightly out of Judaism, but from what I have read and from what I intuit, having met this extraordinary young man, is that it will be impossible to take the Judaism out of Nathan Englander.

May 1999

Bellow does not accept dullness

CHARGED WITH WRITING the biography of his longtime friend Abe Ravelstein, a brilliant professor of political philosophy at a Chicago university, the narrator Chick, an elderly writer (read: the author Bellow himself, now at 84 giving us his first novel in a decade) produces no less than the distillation of a life. And what a life! Bellow has been criticized for "outing" his friend, Allan Bloom, whose bestseller, *The Closing of the American Mind*, so closely parallels Ravelstein's late-in-life success which brought him millions and the ability to enjoy a prodigal lifestyle.

Close to death from AIDS, Ravelstein shares his thoughts with Chick who, although declaring his place to be merely a tolerated "presence on the margins," likewise shares his thoughts with Ravelstein and the reader alike. Ravelstein stares down infirmity and death and Bellow/Chick reprises his well-known themes, meditating on truth, compassion, love, mortality, and nihilism.

Ravelstein

Saul Bellow

Viking, 2000   233 pages

Biographical without being a biography, autobiographical as well, the exchange of wit between old friends is tempered with criticism and self-criticism. Ravelstein pooh-poohs the countrified lifestyle adopted by Chick (along with Roth, Updike and others). "In the country he never set off on his own across a field. He looked the woods and meadows over but had no other business with them… Plants were not Ravelstein's dish. He'd eat a salad but he couldn't see the point of meditating on it."

Chick suffers a writer's block and is unable to undertake his promised life story, until he himself narrowly escapes a life-threatening illness, which forces him to reflect on the intricacies of his friendship and his rivalry with Abe. It has been said by other reviewers that Chick here plays Boswell to Ravelstein's Johnson, and so he does in a superficial way. But Boswell, while portraying Johnson's idiosyncrasies with sufficient candor, never fails to convey the simple fact of Samuel Johnson's greatness and his powerful and unique influence on the thought and manners of the late 18th century. Chick/Bellow, on the other hand, doesn't quite come across with respect to placing Ravelstein/Bloom in the pantheon of late 20th century intellectual shakers and movers.

Near the end, Ravelstein, the Jewish atheist, totally peripheral to his people during his adult life (except for his relationships with Jewish intellectuals), begins to follow a trail of Jewish ideas and Jewish essences in his last conversations with Chick. No longer quoting Plato or Thucydides, "he was full of Scripture now," concluding that "…it is impossible to get rid of one's origins, it is impossible not to remain a Jew. The Jews... were historically witnesses to the absence of redemption." Thus Ravelstein, as he was dying, was thinking of such matters, and concluding "that a Jew should take a deep interest in the history of the Jews." Even at the end, Chick admiringly observes that "his clarity was like a fast-freezing liquid."

Asked by Abe how he envisions death, Chick replies, "the pictures stop ... but no one believes in his mind of minds or heart of hearts that the pictures do stop."

What a spring and summer it has been, with new works by Roth, Wouk, Updike and Bellow. Bellow, Nobel laureate and the only novelist to receive three National Book Awards, surprises still, and delivers an exquisite portrait. Like Ravelstein, Bellow does not accept dullness and boredom, rather working "to make certain if he could that the greatness of humankind would not evaporate in bourgeois well-being."

August 2000

An 'over-the-top fantasy' about a rabbi who becomes a quarterback

NOT A PARTICULARLY AVID FAN of farce, your reviewer had serious doubts about reading, much less reviewing, this modern-day fable, the premise of which involves a young rabbi who becomes the starting quarterback for the New York Giants, leading to the apparent conversion of most of the world to Judaism.

In this over-the-top fantasy, Ezekial "Ziggy" Cantor, through an improbable sequence of events, becomes a superstar quarterback, drilling passes with unparalleled accuracy, kicking 60-yard field goals with aplomb, inspiring his hulklike teammates toward invincibility.

The Pigskin Rabbi
Willard Manus
Breakaway Books, 2000   300 pages

Against the background of rigid disapproval from his father, a widowed congregational rabbi, and the loving and protective lavishing of kosher food from his grandmother, Ziggy continues to play principally for the love of the game. Ziggy's Judaism, formerly viewed as a burden in a gentile society, now becomes the source of good for him, his team, the coaches and owners (an absentee European conglomerate), for the fans and sportswriters. Before long the cheerleaders are chanting:

Give 'em a zetz; Give 'em a whisk. Give 'em a frosk in pisk!
Giants, Giants, Giants!

And 73,500 fans, wearing Gucci-designed *yarmelkehs* (most of whom wouldn't know a *yarmelkeh* from a *yentzer*), are soon singing:

Zum Galee, Galee, Galee,
Zum Galee, Galee!

By this time, it is not surprising that the redneck linesman, just prior to Ziggy's attempting a 61-yard field goal, offers "a *glick ahf dir*," and the rest of the team, in the huddle, chants "Yeah, *zol zein mit glick*."

Yes, there is the inevitable backlash from a band of Christian fundamentalists, a jealous benched quarterback, an affair with a gorgeous *shiksa*, and a pervasive tension between Ziggy's faith and his newfound eminence in the sport he loves. Mostly irreverent, this sports novel, nevertheless, has some modest theological underpinning. Lightweight stuff, a little raunchy, a little touching, more than a few laughs.

March 2001

Good listening

I.B. SINGER, characterized by one biographer as "The Magician of West 86th Street," was born in 1904, the second son of a Hasidic rabbi, in a tiny village of eastern Poland and grew up in a poor crowded Jewish quarter of Warsaw. From his mother he inherited an intellectual curiosity, which complemented his spiritual background. His language was Yiddish and he really was a character from one of his own Nobel Prize-winning tales of Polish Jews, and the demons and passions which possessed them. He emigrated to the United States in 1935, following his brother, Joshua. The murder of his mother and another brother by the Nazis in 1939, followed by Joshua's death of a heart attack, led, paradoxically, to an unprecedented burst of creativity on Singer's part.

The Magician of Lublin

Isaac Bashevis Singer

Jewish Contemporary Classics
Audiobook 9 hours

Yascha, the eponymous magician, player to small town crowds while dreaming of making it big in Warsaw, led a kind of "Captain's Paradise" existence, with a loving and devoted wife, Esther, at home and two serious lovers away. Magda, his magician's assistant and caretaker of the animals and props used in his performance, entertained dreams of a life with Yascha, and Amelia, a young widow with a daughter to care for, had hopes of marriage to him, including his conversion to Christianity. Yascha, on more than one occasion, had the opportunity to repent of his duplicitous life and return to the pious religious life of his youth, but managed to reject such a path. His friend and confidant exclaimed, "to you, Yascha, women are like flowers to a bee. Always a new one. A sniff here, a lick there, and 'whist'—you buzz away." Not without its tragicomic and picaresque elements, which include a foiled robbery, a suicide, and a retreat from the world, *The Magician of Lublin* concludes with Yascha's act of *tshuva*, which finally brings him forgiveness and peace.

In another work (*The Spinoza of Market Street*) we read, "heaven and earth conspire that everything which has been, be rooted out and reduced to dust. Only the dreamers, who dream while awake, call back the shadows of the past and braid from unspun threads, unspun nets." For those who enjoy a good "listen," this rare taped translation from the Yiddish celebrates the narrative art of the master dreamer and magician, I. B. Singer.

May 2002

Two works juxtaposed

UNDER THE RUBRIC of *Judaic Traditions in Literature, Music, and Art,* two works are juxtaposed; one the magnum opus of a seminal figure in modern Yiddish and Hebrew literature, first published in Yiddish in 1865; the other a slender, subtly surrealistic novel published first in Hebrew in 1998.

Abramovitsh wrote under the *nom de plume,* Mendele Moykher Sforim, (Mendele the book peddler), and Mendele managed to produce literary landmarks in both Hebrew and Yiddish. For *The Wishing Ring,* the mythical shtetl of *Kaptsansk* (Poorsville) was created, from whence we have seen the later writer, Sholom Aleichem, create the more well-known *Anatevka,* and for that matter, William Faulkner's Yoknapatawpha County, and Grover's Corners, New Hampshire in Thornton Wilder's classic play, *Our Town.* The truly impoverished Jews of *Kaptsansk* are driven by lack of opportunity and sheer starvation to seek employment in the nearest town, *Glupsk* (a city of fools), where the Gentiles have left the Jews no one to prey upon but themselves. Thus we are introduced to various forms of "white slavery," unsuccessfully disguised as marriage brokering, apprenticeship, and home service.

This reviewer is not qualified to comment on Michael Wex's translation, however Wex appears to have captured Mendele's descriptions and shifting narrative voice most skillfully.

The Wishing Ring

S. Y. Abramovitsh
Translated by Michael Wex

Syracuse University Press, 2003 280 pages

F AST FORWARD a century and a half, and Israeli poet and novelist Miron Izakson's novel about Nathan, essentially a powerful, shameless Israeli control freak, is told through the eyes of Meir, his personal secretary. Just as Mendele's tales explore the complicated personalities of his characters and the manner in which they exploit one another's human weaknesses in the context of mid-19th century Pale of Settlement Jewish society, *Nathan and His Wives* speaks to the intricacies of human relationships in contemporary society.

Nathan and His Wives
Miron C. Izakson
Syracuse University Press, 2003   280 pages

Nathan's obsessive collection of art and antiques leads to his quest for a rare manuscript, one in which the faithful Meir's assistance produces ironic results. Izakson utilizes elements of Jewish belief and culture in his exploration of the issues which confront his characters.

Betsy Rosenberg, who has also translated the works of Ahron Appelfeld, among others, translated *Nathan and His Wives* from the Hebrew.

January 2004

A great ear for *shtick*

YOUR REVIEWER has had this first novel by Eliezer Sobel on the desk for a couple of months and when the author emailed *Jewish News* recently with a gentle nudge, like, "Nu? When are you going to read it already?" we duly noted that it had taken him 20 years to write it, so what was the rush?

So here's the deal. The eponymous *minyan* is immediately reduced to nine adult males in their mid- to late-30s having just buried one of their number.

Minyan:
Ten Jewish Men in a World That is Heartbroken

Eliezer Sobel

University of Tennessee Press, 2004 244 pages

Freddy Lipschitz is dead of an overdose, but this gathering is no "Big Chill," rather a hilarious introduction to the narrator, Norbert Wilner, and his band of misfits. From Goldberg, the impecunious composer with a *shiksa* girlfriend who craves clothes; to Bernstein, the *Shiva-borcher* turned drug dealer who returned from wandering around India in a loin-cloth spreading *namaste* instead of *sholom;* to Goldberg, Greenblatt, Finkelstein and the rest, all losers to some degree, Sobel has created a picaresque work which will frequently force the reader to laugh out loud, causing family members to wonder if at last you have lost it. If this were a movie, Sobel could be a kind of Yiddish Almodovar, directing a male version of *Women on the Verge of a Nervous Breakdown.*

Norbert Wilner, irreverent, brainy, and going nowhere fast, is full of doubt and self-loathing, still finding himself, unable to commit to a permanent relationship, and able to shed the harsh light of self-criticism on himself and his immature friends.

Jewish News readers may recall the recent review of *Shanda: The Making and Breaking of a Self-Loathing Jew,* by Neil Karlen, in which Rabbi Manis Friedman, a Hasidic Rabbi kabbalah scholar serves as the motive force through which the author works his way back to Judaism and what can only be described as a happy ending. Norbert, too strikes up a friendship and accepts a kind of mentorship from the eccentric Reb Miltie, whose *simcha* may be suspect but whose bagel-and-cream-cheese-inspired sessions with Norbert serve as the device by which Sobel's more spiritual message is introduced.

Sadly, there is no traditionally happy ending for Norbert, who manages to fall in love but chooses "friendship" over marriage in the end. He does find a kind of salvation through humor and the teachings of the Baal Shem Tov. If Neil Karlen starts out as an "insufferable jerk," Norbert and his friends are at best "sufferable" jerks, baffled by the prerequisites for success in an adult world. Wilner at least is able in the end to make a couple of adult decisions, although the reader, by the end of *Minyan*, knows him well enough to doubt that he will follow through on anything.

Sobel has a great ear for *shtick* and never fails to find the comedic grain in life's situations, however grim they may be, but there are times when the reader may be forgiven for shouting, "enough already." That said, one could only hope that another 20 years will not elapse before this very talented writer produces his second novel.

March 2004

Preserving a literary milieu

DESPITE THE EFFORTS of a few Yiddish enthusiasts, it is unlikely that the generation coming of age in the early part of the 21st century will demonstrate any significant mastery of the language. If we are to preserve some appreciation of the immense contribution of Eastern European culture to American Jewish life, we are dependent upon high quality translations of the master works of late 19th and early 20th century artists such as Abramovitsh, Rabinovitsh (Sholom Aleichem), and Peretz.

Classic Yiddish Stories of S.Y. Abramovitsh, Sholom Aleichem and I.L. Peretz
Edited by Ken Frieden
Translated by Ken Frieden, Ted Gorelick, and Michael Wex
Syracuse University Press, 2004 286 pages

Sholem Yankev Abramovitsh (1836–1917) played a seminal role in the emergence of modern Yiddish fiction and is generally recognized as the first writer to produce Yiddish novels on a par with 19th century fiction being published in other European languages.

We have recently reported on Abramovitsh's novel, *The Wishing Ring,* and Editor Frieden, the B.G. Rudolf professor and director of the Judaic Studies Program at Syracuse University, includes here two powerful novellas, *The Little Man* and *Fishke the Lame.* Abramovitsh turned to Yiddish in the 1860s along with many leaders of Jewish Enlightenment *(haskalah)* because only a small, elite group could read secular Hebrew. He created the fictional "Mendele the Book Peddler," through whose voice his powerful tales are heard. These are among the most vivid descriptions of shtetl life.

In *Fishke the Lame,* there are three narrators: Mendele, Alter, and Fishke. Their distinctive voices represent three strata of Jewish life in Eastern Europe: Mendele, the traditional, yeshiva-educated man; Alter, the average guy, struggling to make a living as a tradesman; and Fishke, a cripple, hobbling along at the bottom of the social hierarchy.

Sholem Aleichem (1859–1916), dubbed by many as the "father" of modern Yiddish literature, considered Abramovitsh the "grandfather," and continued his satiric bent, softened, however, by humor. Thus his marvelous Tevye stories, two of which are included here, demonstrate our tendency for "laughing *mit yashicas* (with tears)." Much of the translated Sholom Aleichem work fails to convey his great comedic talent, even though the retranslations in this collection are by Michael Wex, a humorist in his own right.

Freiden's volume moves from Abramovitsh's Enlightenment beginnings through Sholem Aleichem's humoristic monologues, to Peretz's neo-hasidic tales. Peretz, not a religious man, draws from the Jewish religion the material from which he creates secular art and culture. Two selections, *The Kabbalists* and *The Shtrayml*, translated by the editor, typify Peretz's technique and round out the collection.

Included are biographical essays which the reader will find "must" reading if the authors are to be understood in the context of their times and their literary milieu.

June 2004

A fast read

RIGHT FROM ITS OPENING 15 line-long sentence, the reader knows a treat is in store; this is vintage E.L. Doctorow, the novelist at his best, painting one of his huge murals. Author of *Ragtime, City of God, The Book of Daniel,* and *Billy Bathgate,* Doctorow assembles a huge cast of characters—which is one of the reasons several of the movies made of his novels failed to succeed financially. For *The March* to reach our movie theatres (and there is little doubt but that therein lies the making of a great movie) prospective producers would need to pony up about $200 million.

The March

E. L. Doctorow

Random House, 2005   363 pages

Such is the scope of William Tecumseh Sherman's march through the South with 60,000 troops, foraging as he went, destroying what could give comfort to the Confederate enemy (all that wasn't put to the torch by the retreating *secesh* forces), and joining to his advance thousands of freed slaves and now-destitute former slaveowners.

Doctorow, past winner of the National Book Award, the Pen Faulkner Award and numerous other literary accolades, lets us in on the chess-like maneuvering of the retreating Confederate forces and the advancing Union Army. He brings to life the generals on both sides, and the reader is given a deeper glimpse into the paradox of close college (military academy) friends sworn to destroy each other, but moved to tears when learning of the death of an opponent's young son in battle. The poignant sacrifice and bloodletting on both sides in the final weeks of the Civil War is grimly highlighted through the professional work of Colonel Wrede Sartorius (a tip of the hat to William Faulkner), regimental surgeon, who vainly tries to introduce more humane and effective methods to the butchery of the surgical tent.

Every drama must have its Rosenkrantz and Guildenstern, and *The March* is no exception as we follow the misadventures of Will and his dominating brother Arly, both fated not to survive the war. Similarly, Emily Thompson, representative of the now-impoverished white aristocracy and Mattie, the hapless widow of a plantation owner, each typify a different response to the situation. Emily moves forward with her life while Mattie, whose husband dies of a head injury and one of whose sons is killed in service, seeks to return home to she-knows-not-what. And if Mattie is rendered a little crazy by the destruction of her bucolic plantation life and her confrontation with the white-skinned slave, Pearl, product of Mattie's husband's liaison with one of his slaves, who could blame her? (For a deeper examination of the tangled and fraught relations between women slaveholders and women slaves, see Elizabeth Fox-Genovese's *Within the Plantation Household.*)

The loyal Doctorow reader will recognize the names of some of the characters whose descendents (we presume) have already appeared in earlier novels such as *Ragtime*; however, the author leaves it up to the reader to speculate as to the connection.

This is a fast read. One gets so swept up in the action and interaction that the book is finished in a couple of sittings. Doctorow ties up most of the loose ends, yet leaves the reader itching for a bit more. Perhaps that's a good thing.

October 2005

From the greatest

RESPONDING TO the recent publication in *The Times Book Review* of a list purporting to be the "single best work of American fiction published in the last 25 years," as chosen by a select sampling of prominent writers, A.O. Scott noted that the top five American novels are the work of a single generation born between 1931 and 1936—Don DeLillo, Toni Morrison, John Updike, Philip Roth and Cormac McCarthy. Surprisingly, the "boomer" generation, long ascendant in popular culture as well as in politics and business, has not produced a "great novel," generally eschewing "great" themes. Toni Morrison's *Beloved* was the winner. If asked who the best writer of that period was, Philip Roth, with seven titles receiving votes, would clearly have been the winner. Roth, whose primary concern has been the past and whose production has been so steady and so various, continues to dominate.

Everyman is unnamed in this too-brief but brilliant novella by Roth, arguably "our most accomplished novelist," recipient of two National Book Awards, two National Book Critic Awards, two PEN/Faulkner Awards, a Pulitzer Prize and most recently, for *The Plot Against America*, the Society

Everyman
Philip Roth
Houghton Mifflin, 2006   182 pages

of American Historians' Award for the outstanding historical novel on an American theme for 2003–2004. *Everyman*, however, takes its title from a 15th century allegorical play whose theme is the summoning of the living to death. Thus Roth's work must inevitably evoke Arthur Miller's unforgettable representation of Everyman in the persona of Willy Loman, protagonist of *Death of a Salesman*. Half a century ago it was remarkable that Miller's tragic hero was tragically flawed, yes, but was merely an ordinary salesman, falling from no great height, and now it is not terribly remarkable that Roth's Everyman is a Jew.

The recently reviewed *Brooklyn Lullaby* dealt with a retired insurance salesman looking for a peaceful place to spend the last part of his life. Everyman, a retired successful commercial artist, serial husband and chronic philanderer, seeks a similar peace returning to the Jersey seashore, scene of his childhood summers. Troubled by his bare survival of a long series of life-threatening diseases and surgeries, musing on the twists and turns of his life, exacerbated by his estrangement from his sons (abandoned emotionally when he divorced his first wife), he attempts with dubious success to reawaken his artistic muse, seeing "the advancing green Atlantic, rolling unstoppably toward him like the obstinate fact of the future."

Everyman, fully aware of his mistakes, nonetheless resists apology. "There's no remaking reality," he says. "Just take it as it comes. Hold your ground and take it as it comes." I kept thinking of that old jazz lyric, "it ain't what you do, it's the way that you do it..." as Everyman rationalizes his failed relationship with his sons. "He had done what he did the way that he did it and they did what they did the way that they did it." At first, reviewing his journey, he concludes that "...what he learned was nothing when measured against the inevitable onslaught that is the end of life."

In the end, however, he perhaps gets the picture. Visiting the cemetery where his parents are buried, he speaks with his mother, the first of a series of women who cared for him despite all. She asks him how old he is and he replies that he is 71. "Good," she says, "You lived," while his father reminds him that it is not too late to atone for his sins.

By the end of his life, he concludes:

Had he been aware of the mortal suffering of every man and woman he happened to have known during all the years of his professional life, of each one's painful story of regret and loss and stoicism, of fear and pain and isolation and dread, had he learned of every last thing they had parted with that once had been really theirs and of how, systematically, they were being destroyed, he would have had to stay on the phone through the day and into the night... old age isn't a battle; old age is a massacre.

Willy Loman, Miller's Everyman, achieves a kind of salvation as his mourners declare he deserves respect. The Christian allegory, *Everyman*, concludes with the mercy of God granting eternal life. There is cold comfort to be gained from Roth. His *Everyman* lives, enjoys, suffers and dies, just like the rest of us.

June 2006

A strongly suggested read

WHAT DO PATRICIA COHEN, Michiko Kakutani and Terence Rafferty have in common with Hal Sacks? We all read Michael Chabon's (pronounced *shay-bone*) new book, *The Yiddish Policemen's Union*, with great relish and not a little amazement at the author's ability to create a fantasy world, his 2001 Pulitzer Prize-winning, *The Amazing Adventures of Kavalier and Clay*, notwithstanding. In that novel he presented a detailed look at New York in the 1940s.

Chabon develops a minor historical footnote in which Secretary of the Interior, Harold Ickes, proposed the creation of a sanctuary in Alaska for European Jews slated for extermination (there have always been such proposals, from Madagascar to West Africa, but "not in my country"), creating a Jewish world on

---

The Yiddish Policemen's Union

Michael Chabon

Harper Collins, 2007   414 pages

Sitka Island, Alaska. Literature is replete with the usage of this literary device, from Samuel Johnson to Voltaire, from Edward Bellamy to H.G. Wells, and more recently the brilliant Roth novel, *The Plot Against America*, as well as the less brilliant, if timely, *Jamestown*, by Matthew Sharpe.

But what Chabon has done is use this complex and multi-layered venue as the setting of a murder mystery, which pays serious homage to the great Raymond Chandler. Replete with Chandleresque skeins of description, our admirable, if somewhat dissolute detective hero, Meyer Landsman, along with his ex-wife, (Detective Inspector) Bina and his sidekick, the half-Tlingit, half-Yiddish giant Berko Shemets, set out to solve what appears to be a simple murder, but instead find themselves embroiled in an immensely complicated plot with major international repercussions. What drives the matter is the impending Reversion, as the refuge that was provided to the million-plus Jews was for 60 years only and is slated to revert back to the original people of Sitka very shortly.

Among the numerous Hasidic sects living on Sitka is that of the Verbover (a made-up group), who have more or less controlled the crime scene and have greatly enriched themselves as a sort of Jewish mafia. When the murder victim turns out to be the estranged son of the Verbover Rebbe himself, Landsman's investigations meet with interference from some unrevealed (until the end) higher authorities. He perseveres, however, taking more than a few knocks, both physical and emotional, along the way.

Just published in May of this year, *The Yiddish Policemen's Union,* was #2 on the best-seller list within its first week. The non-Jewish, and to some extent the younger Jewish, reader will confront a surfeit of Yiddish expressions, particularly in the first half of the book, for Yiddish is the *lingua franca* on Sitka Island, and conversations switch back and forth from Yiddish (translated) to "American." Of course this is part of the charm of the novel. Cell phones are *shoyfers,* and a handgun is a *shammos*; a popular song of the day is *Noch Amol.* Now my recollection of *noch amul* (once again) is that it was generally used as a rhetorical question, something like "Again? Are you still at it?" Or, "Do I have to hear it again?"

Here are a few words you may wish to look up in advance: *Alenu, emes, eruv, freylekhs, gabay, Galitzer, luftmensches, maven, purimshpiel, schlosser, shkotz, shtekeleh, shpilkes, shtarka, shvartsn-yam, smikha, tateh, tzaddik,* and *yekkes.*

And understandably, but somewhat disturbingly, the characters are constantly referring to each other as *yid.* ("Hey, yid," do this, or do that. Or "this yid" did this or that. Or what is "a yid" supposed to do, or think?) But upon reflection, and understanding that these are mostly Central European Jews, where *Zhid* was the common term applied to Jews, and thinking about the common appellation of *nigger* used by African-Americans to each other (also disturbing), one more or less gets used to it.

But the Chandler aficionado will recognize the descriptive gems:

The wind carries a sour tang of pulped lumber, the smell of boat diesel and the slaughter and canning of salmon.

When Landsman steps outside the Ickes building and fits his hat to his voided head, he finds that the world has sailed into a fog bank, the night is cold sticky stuff that beads up on the sleeves of his overcoat. Korczak Platz is a bowlful of bright mist, smeared here and there with the paw prints of sodium lamps.

A badge of grass, a green brooch pinned at the collarbone of a mountain to a fast black cloak of fir trees.

So what does it matter in the end that the humble Review section of the *Jewish News* strongly suggests you read this book? After all, it has been called "a towering achievement," and "a towering swashbuckling thrill of a book" and "gosh-wow, super colossal." This writer doesn't know from towering. But he does know from good writing, and it's Jewish, and it's Raymond Chandler and Michael Chabon all wrapped up together. Enjoy!

Fall 2007

From tradition to chaos

Caspian Rain
Gina B. Nahai
Macadam Cage, 2007 298 pages

DALIA SOFER'S chilling novel, *The Septembers of Shiraz* (reviewed here last year), dealt with Jews struggling to live in an oppressive regime. Farideh Goldin's poetic *Wedding Song* (reviewed here five years ago), opened a window for this reader into a Jewish society and culture closeted from view, always driven to avoid criticism from within and without. The reader will recall Goldin's father burning her books lest she "corrupt herself, giving all of us a bad name."

Gina B. Nahai, professor of creative writing at the University of Southern California, further fills in the landscape of Jewish society in Iran during the permissive reign of Shah Reza Pahlevi. Jewish merchants, bankers and civil servants, although only a few generations removed from the Ghetto, formed a kind of unofficial aristocracy not unlike that of elite Jews in 16th Century Poland, and were socially integrated with the mostly Muslim, upper-class elite. *Caspian Rain* tells its story through the eyes of Yaas, the hearing-impaired daughter destined to become totally deaf. She is the child of a dysfunctional marriage. Omid, scion of one of Tehran's wealthiest Jewish families, against his parents' wishes, impetuously plucked Bahar from the slums of South Tehran, one street away from the former Jewish Ghetto. Sadly, Bahar is no Eliza Doolittle, and Omid is no Professor Higgins.

As the marriage crumbles amid Omid's infatuation and love affair with the beautiful Niyaz, daughter of a noble Muslim family, Yaas' childish and naïve struggle to save her family becomes a metaphor for Iran's descent from tradition to the chaos of the Mullahs' successful revolution against the Shah. Helpless in a male dominated society, ill equipped to extricate herself from her horrible marriage, Bahar, despite having all of her material needs satisfied, is ultimately no better off than the unfortunate women encountered in Khaled Hosseini's excellent novel of survival under a despotic theocratic system, *A Thousand Splendid Suns*.

It has been a number of years since journalist/novelist Geraldine Brooks' *The Nine Parts of Desire* opened our eyes to the degrading treatment of women in Saudi Arabia and, of course, Farideh Goldin's ultimate joy at her liberation from an intolerable destiny is not to be realized by Bahar. Even Bahar's love for Yaas is tempered by her denial of her daughter's growing deafness, driven by her fear of criticism from the close-knit Jewish community. Within Bahar's own family, a past denial ultimately led to the devastating death of her brother. His memory persists in haunting the living as a boy on a bicycle. The guilt surrounding his family's refusal to recognize and deal with his deafness pervades the novel. *Caspian Rain* is graceful and poetic, written with wit and, while hopeful, is not mawkishly so.

October 2008

Relationships drawn with master strokes

WE DON'T USUALLY review books that have been out for over two years, but this one was given to me to read while on a recent trip to Israel and it turned out to be an excellent companion, meriting our readers' attention. Meir Shalev is a prize-winning Israeli author, honored in Italy, France and Israel, whose previous work includes *The Blue Mountain, The Loves of Judith, Esau* and more than a dozen successful children's books.

As pointed out by a *New York Times* reviewer, Shalev attracts a primarily Jewish readership in the United States. However, even though *A Pigeon and a Boy* may be filled with reference to Jewish tradition, the story is told from a distinctly secular point of view.

A Pigeon and a Boy
Meir Shalev
Schocken, 2007 311 pages

Yair Mendelsohn is an Israeli tour guide specializing in nature tours, particularly bird watching. While conducting a tour, Yair is told a story by an old Palmach fighter, speaking as a witness to a battle during the war for independence in 1948. At a time when pigeons were still used as reliable military communication, a gifted young pigeon handler lies bleeding to death in battle. He manages to dispatch one last pigeon, a bird carrying a special gift to the girl he loves. Yair then takes over as narrator and the tale spins itself out, resulting in a beautifully written novel of two love stories connected over half a century by a singular act of devotion.

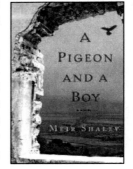

Some may find the first few chapters a bit slow, but once the reader gets into the story, it is compelling. We learn a great deal about raising homing pigeons (perhaps a bit more than we need to know), yet there is a mystical connection to the entire enterprise, one which adds a poetic sheen to this novel. In finely wrought passages the novel explores the ways in which faith and destiny determine our lives.

Shalev, a master storyteller on the order of Gabriel Garcia Marquez, manages without sounding didactic to provide commentary on the early builders of Israel—those who labor with their hands along with the intellectuals whose product makes an equal contribution, the social chasm thus created notwithstanding.

This is a story of love found, lost, found again, and lost again. In some ways it is heartbreaking, but relationships between man and woman, parent and child, friend and friend are drawn by Shalev with master strokes. Shalev rightfully belongs with A.B. Yehoshua, Amos Oz and others in the pantheon of contemporary Israeli authors.

July 2009

FOR COOKS

Southern-style kosher cookbook's recipes somewhat unevenly served in this work

IT SEEMS that when you're on a roll, you keep on rolling. The premise, I take it, for this work, is the success of two previous books (not examined) by two New Orleans balabustas, *Kosher Cajun Cookbook* and *Kosher Creole Cookbook*.

The premise is a good one, but is somewhat unevenly served in this work, which is a lot better than the too-cutesy effort to yiddishise the names of all the recipes would lead us to believe. Organizing the recipes by states of the south, with a brief historical introduction to each state, the authors are oddly

Kosher Southern Style Cookbook

Mildred L. Covert and Sylvia P. Gerson

Pelican Publishing, 1993   245 pages

partial in specifying pareve margarine in meat dishes, Kosher seasoned bread crumbs, and Kosher white wine, but not specifying Kosher condensed mushroom soup (*oi vey*, can you believe a cook from New Orleans would use canned soup for a sauce?), or Kosher picante sauce.

Names like Lunts Mon Lamb Chops (made with shoulder steaks—yuk), and Taka Tacos or Gottenyu Guacamole and Chai There Chowder (made with canned salmon—not exactly yukky... but why not fresh fish?) really detract from some very solid recipes which, if followed with some inventiveness will simplify the problem a traditional cook has in adapting *glattraif* recipes to the Kosher kitchen. An example of this would be the Pinsk Fish Platter which specifies "defrosted flounder fillets," but which would not be spoiled by the presence of other fish—preferably fresh.

Gratuitously, the Klezmer Chicken recipe directs us to use a whole chicken "cleaned and innards removed." In general there is a great dependency upon canned vegetables, such as peas, beans and tomatoes; and on prepared spices such as Worcestershire sauce and ketchup.

Fortunately, however, there are recipes for a good Cajun Gumbo and a Tex-Mex Cholent which provide the necessary regional flair in a kosher context.

It is not always clear whether this book is intended for experienced cooks or relative newcomers to the kitchen. The newcomer may wish to prepare Cajun Jambalaya, which calls for cut-up pieces of cooked duck meat, but might not have the foggiest notion of how to cook a duck.

The authors are to be complimented on making even a perfunctory effort to include microwaving instructions. These, unfortunately, are inconsistent and in some cases (i.e., Breaded Veal Cutlets or what is termed Vulcan Veal: perhaps vulcanized would be better), inadvisable. Truth to tell, there are dozens of recipes in the *Kosher Southern Style Cookbook* which lend themselves perfectly to the microwave for some or all of the process.

On balance, if one takes the position that a cookbook need contain only a few good ideas for a change of direction in meal planning, particularly for parties, then this entry will do fine, even if it's a bit overdone. One can only wonder if their next book will feature Kabbala Kabobs with Minyan Mashed Potatoes and Mitzvah Marshmallow Mandelbrot.

September 1993

Kugel Story 'a pretty funny cookbook'

ACCORDING TO the publisher and author, "kugel could be love at first bite." On the surface *The Kugel Story* is a pretty funny cookbook with more than 175 recipes for the whole gamut of kugelry: meat, dairy, fruit, flat, round, square, long and board. The author has taken the trouble to expound on the great "kugel, keigle, koogle" pronunciation debate, and furnishes important hints about eggs and their substitutes, storing cottage cheese, and chopping onions without tears. She tells us how and when to freeze and when not to, provides a quick but useful discourse on *kashruth* as well as a fairly comprehensive "ingredients" index and glossary of cooking terms.

The Kugel Story
Not Just Noodle Pudding
Nina Yellin
Symlan Reed Books, 1993   204 pages

Having said that, why then, when I showed this to my sous chef, did she give it a quick once-over and put it aside? "Well," she said, "I looked through it and didn't find one recipe that particularly appealed to me."

Not one, I thought to myself? But there are more than 175 recipes, many of which I would like to have served to me. Now I, the chef, may complain, as I do of many new cookbooks, that not enough respect is given to modern applications. For example: Can the blintze or other dough be made in a food processor? If so, how? Or noodles in the pasta machine, or bread in the bread machine? What about the great zapper, the microwave? Where can it be used? Where should it be avoided? Cookbook authors do need to write for those young couples who register before their weddings for Waterford crystal and great china, but who mainly order in pizza.

Finally, it is difficult to determine if the book's small print, crude drawings, and inconsistent typography is part of the cuteness of the book or just plain amateurish. In either case I would advise those who like a little background material with their recipes to overcome all the above objections and buy the book anyway. For the publisher, I would advise purchasing some updated software, and I don't mean kugel. Without a more professional layout, typesetting and printing job, thousands may never know the heavenly heartburns they are missing if they don't tune in to *The Kugel Story*.

September 1993

Chinese Kosher Cooking
not merely a book of recipes

NOT A NEW BOOK, but certainly a favorite, having gone through at least four printings, *Chinese Kosher Cooking* is worth a second look for two reasons; first, it is a cookbook, not merely a collection of recipes; second, it is readily available at the Temple Israel gift shop.

The Jewish-American love affair with Chinese food is legendary and our comedic archives are replete with such humor. Chinese restaurants of the '20s and '30s are probably the single greatest source of defection from Kashrut. And here we are, two generations hence, using this truly great cuisine as the basis for *t'shuva*.

There are, of course, some great enduring myths about Chinese food. First, that it is low in fat because things are cooked in a minimum of oil. False! Just read about Rabbi Belzer's Beef Lo Mein and cringe at the liberal use of oil—albeit vegetable oil. Chinese food is loaded with fat, sugar, salt, and every steamed dish is complemented by half a dozen fried delectations. But it's good!

Chinese Kosher Cooking
Betty S. Goldberg
Jonathan David Publishers, 1993   351 pages

Betty Goldberg's book, first printed ten years ago, is based on over a decade of prior experience with both teaching and cooking "Chinese." Thus the good news is that the teacher has provided an excellent chapter which explains much about basic methods and terms, ingredients and techniques. And of course, this doesn't go out of style. The beginning cook can really cook from this book. And if you don't keep kosher, don't bother—this is very labor intensive and if it's not done right it won't have that Chinese-Yiddishe *tam*. But if you are into cooking and kosher and really want to delight your family and friends, *Chinese Kosher Cooking* is a great basic text.

If I were revising it today, I would wish to get a bit more "cutting edge" in ingredients and veggies and the light cooking techniques of the '90s. After all, there is life after the mung beans and tofu.

What is really needed is not "wok on down," but a few rim shots, that is, Pacific Rim—Kosher, wow. *Ess, ess, mine kind!*

September 1993

Cooking Jewish and *Jewish Cooking*

SO LITTLE TIME and so many books to read. We had hoped to get around to a review of several Jewish cook books in time for Chanukah, but books we had ordered failed to arrive in time. Happily we continue to eat, even after Chanukah, and the Jewish home cook is ever in need of new ideas. Which is not to say that most cook books, of whatever stripe (cook books are second only to the bible in popularity) have much merit. Collections of recipes which fail to inform the mystified amateur

Harriet Roth's Deliciously Healthy Jewish Cooking
Harriet Roth
Dutton, 1996   461 pages

of necessary techniques seem to abound. Every now and then a book is put together which is true to its promise and which is genuinely worth owning.

One such is Harriet Roth's *Deliciously Healthy Jewish Cooking*. A former director of the Pritikin Longevity Center Cooking School, Roth has adapted over 300 dishes from our culinary tradition to meet our current preoccupation with avoidance of fat, sugar and salt.

This is a truly useful basic work which clearly reduces the content of unwanted ingredients while managing to salvage more than a little of that old *yiddishe tam*. For the "30-something" generation just beginning to think beyond ordering in a pizza to eat on their Spode, each recipe is labeled (dairy, pareve, or meat) and each contains an analysis per serving of fat by types, calories, sodium and fiber. Roth's introductory chapter is filled with good information that the neophyte, attempting to create a Kosher meal for the first time, or the experienced Kosher cook, will welcome, for while this book is not strictly speaking a kosher cookbook, it endeavors to find a meeting ground for religious law and healthy eating. The few pages devoted to how the low-fat, low-cholesterol kitchen (refrigerator, pantry, cupboard, and freezer) should be stocked is worth the price of admission. With a little practice you can become "the maven of *matzoh brei*, the baron of *borscht*, the queen of *kugel*, or the king of *knaidlach*."

LORRAINE GERSTL'S EDITION of *Jewish Cooking Secrets,* adapted from the Congregation Beth Israel (Carmel, California) cookbook is a much more modest affair, and makes little pretense to be other than a collection of recipes, albeit a pretty good collection which has attempted to adjust many of the recipes down in calories and

Jewish Cooking Secrets from Here and Far
Lorraine Gerstl
Millennium Publishing, 1996   192 pages

fat. It's one of those recipe books from which an experienced cook will glean half a dozen recipes she may wish to try, but which doesn't have the range and depth necessary to serving as a basic kitchen guide.

THERE'S NOTHING MODEST about *The Great Chefs of America Cook Kosher.* This is a very classy package indeed, one which opens flat and which has had a lot of design effort put into it. The executive editors, Idee Schoenheim and Ruth Madoff, were motivated to create this culinary delight out of concern that hundreds of thousands of kosher consumers in America seldom eat out due to the paucity of kosher restaurants, and severely limited menus are offered by the few that are avail-

The Great Chefs of America Cook Kosher
Edited by Karen MacNeil
Vital Media, 1996   185 pages

able. Thus began a three-year process of contacting America's top restaurant chefs and challenging them to "kosherize" their best-known dishes. Not satisfied with merely collecting the recipes, our plucky editors spent a year testing each and every recipe.

The result is a modishly eclectic collection of dishes varying from "wok-seared duck breasts" to "skirt steak with chimichurri and sweet potato fries." Those lucky enough to get their hands on some of our wonderful local rockfish will wish to try Chef Lidia Bastianich's striped bass salad, and for who have forgotten that tuna ever came other than in those little round cans, there are several mouth-watering tuna recipes, blackened and otherwise.

Oddly enough, these truly elegant dishes are for the most part not difficult to prepare. Some effort will be required to assemble all of ingredients without access to a substantial kosher market. Imagine serving Wolfgang Puck's potato parsnip pancakes, direct from Spago of West Hollywood, or our own Trellis' Marcel Desaulniers' "absolutely deep dark chocolate fudge cookies."

As in the Roth book, every recipe is identified as meat, dairy or pareve. This is a handsome gift book for the serious home cook.

FINALLY, JOAN NATHAN, author of *Jewish Cooking in America*, which won many awards in 1994, has now given us more than a collection of recipes, but rather a family workbook, if you will, which entwines tradition and proven recipes with techniques to teach children how to cook in the context of a Jewish kitchen. Organized around the holidays, there are the playful activities such as baking edible *hanukkiot* and dreidels, chocolate covered *matzahs*, and Golda Meir's chocolate chip cookies.

The Children's Jewish Holiday Kitchen

Joan Nathan
Schocken Books, 1996   157 pages

Author Nathan scripts the kitchen activities carefully, thus while it generally falls to the adult to light the oven, or boil the water, the child, using a plastic knife, is asked to peel the apple, beat the eggs, or smear the chicken with honey.

This is a neat book, filled with activity-oriented pages along with considerable collateral educational material. The thought of a young mother working through some of the recipes with her children is a charming one. Is it ever to come to pass? It is true that Nathan does not say "mother" or "daughter," but "adult" and "child"—yet it is difficult to picture Dad and Richard making the pot roast while Mom finishes making her rounds at the hospital. But if they did—would they wish to use a recipe from this book—or one written on a card that Grandma (or Grandpa) used?

January 1997

What's cooking for the holidays?

WHAT'S COOKING for the Holidays? What Holidays? We never had to ask; Passover was Passover, but the holidays began with Rosh Hashanah, and that meant food and family. So did you ever think of serving a real gefilte fish? Not the pallid patties from the jar, nor even "fixed up" with a few carrots, onions and celery, nor even homemade from scratch balls of fish, but real *Farshirovannaya Riba Zharenym Lukom*?

As the faithful reader of this column can attest, we have

Kosher Kettle
International Adventures in Jewish Cooking
Edited by Sybil Ruth Kaplan
Five Star Publications, 1996   496 pages

generally been unkind in our reviews of collections of recipes as opposed to "cook books," the distinction being centered around the inconsistencies which accompany the usual hodgepodge of recipes from Gertrude, Polly, or even Hal, from Utica, Fresno, or Norfolk, which confuse even the experienced kitchen hand. There are a few such inconsistencies in Sybil Ruth Kaplan's *Kosher Kettle*, but the inexperienced cook, or the young homemaker wishing to have a kosher kitchen with a few snazzy menu ideas, will not be deterred, even if it means ferreting out and discarding such heart-stopping recipes as the baked haddock dish for four to six people which uses a quart of sour cream and a quarter pound of butter.

One can amaze the family with a dazzling array of Thai, Israeli, Greek, Indian, Russian and Italian style meals, *fleishig, milchig,* or *pareve,* dishes which are not inordinately complicated to prepare and cook. Even the stuffed fish looks fairly easy and I plan to try it myself for this holiday. There is a brief guide to *kashrut* and sprinkled throughout the book are personal notes and anecdotes which make this eclectic text a particularly flavorful one.

THAT MARLENE SOROSKY, what a trickster she is, and what a terrific book her *Fast & Festive Meals for the Jewish Holidays* is. Convinced that there must be a happy medium between a self-flagellating round of exhausting preparation of tedious

Fast and Festive Meals for the Jewish Holidays
Marlene Sorosky
William Morrow, 1997   370 pages

and heavy recipes of the past, and simply "ordering in," she has provided us with a first-rate collection of time-saving recipes for 13 Jewish holidays and *simchas*, generally organized into complete menus a la James Beard, which both experienced and neophyte cooks will appreciate. But her trickery lies in understanding and communicating the advantages of advance preparation. Thus, whether putting together a tuna mousse for a *brit milah*, or a *Shana Tova*, luncheon for after services, Sorosky gives a few notes on the rituals, the "game plan," (which includes prep time, cook time, and advance prep) always alert to reducing fats and inserting new ideas for a fresh taste.

The book is printed on heavy paper, attractively presented in a user-friendly format, and no adult child or child-in-law will fail to appreciate such a gift. Conversely, if you have wondered how to impress a mother or mother-in-law, try a carrot *tzimmes* (prep time: 10 minutes; cook time: 15-18 minutes) which may be cooked a day ahead and reheated. Or a "brisket from hell" with burgundy-orange sauce that takes 10 minutes to prepare for the oven. Oy, is she clever! Far from being content to rest on the laurels of her traditional recipes, Sorosky, winner of numerous awards, has the *chutzpah* to offer up a Mexican Matzah Brei Omelet, a Salmon Gefilte Fish, and Mushroom, Goat Cheese, and Pine Nut and Potato *Knish Hamantashen*. Obviously the years spent working with such notables as Julia Child, James Beard, and Jacques Pepin were not wasted. If you are only going to buy one cookbook this year, hers is the one.

M*IRIAM'S KITCHEN* is a 350-page book with only 26 recipes; it is a guide to setting up, operating, and maintaining a kosher kitchen created in the *shtetls* of Poland and Latvia three generations ago; it is a memoir, written by a living author of lives and times of generations gone by; finally, it is a compelling intertwining of the life of the author with family tales.

Lest the reader be put off by the notion that this is a "how to," book, let me assure all that it is not, yet learning "how to" is the path taken by author Ehrlich on which she journeys from life as an ambivalent "ethnic" Jew to one which includes observance and tradition in her home.

Miriam's Kitchen
A Memoir
Elizabeth Ehrlich
Viking Press, 1997   370 pages

If last year's *Memories from a Russian Kitchen* revealed a rich tapestry of experience among women who had lived through two world wars and the transition from Tzar to commissar to democracy, all through the medium of food, and if the heart-stopping *In Memory's Kitchen*, reviewed early this year, showed us the heroic defiance of women in Theresienstadt, who used the memory of food as the medium to dream of a world after the camps, then we more fully understand the author when she writes that "serious cooking is an essentially optimistic act. It reaches into the future, vanishes into memory, and creates the desire for another meal."

Elizabeth Ehrlich, a journalist and editor, "...wondered what to teach my children. I wanted to build a floor under my children, and to live on it, too."

Thus began her pilgrimages to the kitchen of her mother-in-law, Miriam, a Holocaust survivor who carries on the traditions first learned in Poland, and then tempered in Israel during the lean years following the War for Independence. Ehrlich learns much more than how to make *chulent, lukchn mit laybem* (chicken livers with noodles), and *danishkes* (cheese pastries). Not unmindful of the marginalization of women in Jewish life, she nevertheless questions "the fashion in which I am raising my kids. I should be cooking and cleaning, my children beside me, so that they also can learn the ingredients of everyday life."

Miriam is the Mina Pachter of *In Memory's Kitchen*. Just as our own Anne Friedman triumphantly declares, "My name is Anne, too; I am the Ann Frank who lived," so Miriam, through the loving exploration of her daughter-in-law, is the triumphant Mina who lived, to nurture through her food and her living the tradition, the children and grandchildren who take the place of all those who perished.

One Yom Kippur, Ehrlich's father, not a synagogue-goer, took his daughter in a small rowboat out on a lake. "So where is God?" he asked the child. "Inside a synagogue or out here?" The child shivered, and now an adult, continues the search for an answer.

At this time of retrospection and re-consecration, your reviewer trusts that his dwelling on food is taken by the reader not as a tribute to the satisfaction of one's sense of smell or taste, but as part of the shaky rope bridge, swaying over the ravine of time, which we cross and recross in our attempt to hold once more the hand or caress the cheek of past nurturers.

L'shana tovah!

April 1998

Kosher Light — healthy and traditional

LAST YEAR we reported on *Faye Levy's Low Fat Jewish Cookbook* (Clarkson N. Potter, $24.95), wherein none of the recipes have a fat content exceeding 30 percent. More commendable was the fact that many of the recipes themselves were easy to prepare and produced satisfying results. There was a concise yet adequate chapter on dietary laws and recipes were labeled dairy, meat, or pareve.

Now Zillah Bahar has provided another entry into the search for traditional meals cooked healthy. *Kosher Light* attempts to offer help to the diet-conscious eater who refuses to give up taste. The recipes are divided into separate *milchig* and *fleishig* sections for convenient menu planning, and go beyond

Kosher Light

Zillah Bahar

Penguin, 1998   112 pages

the mere reduction of fat, using easy-to-find ingredients yet listing fat, calories, sodium and cholesterol content while preserving the flavor and quality of traditional kosher cooking.

Author Bahar is a food and lifestyle journalist based in the San Francisco Bay area where she is a columnist for the *San Francisco Examiner* and the *Jewish Bulletin of Northern California*.

That stuffed cabbage, beef *cholent* or brisket *tzimmes* or cheesecake, *hamantaschen* or noodle kugel could fall into the category of light and delicious is the result of a deeply felt conviction that salt (which we once needed to preserve our food) and fat (the persistent metaphor for abundance) are now to be regarded as *traif* as a slab of bacon. *Kosher Light*, then, transforms the salty and fatty Jewish favorites into wholesome (safer) dishes.

In some cases the use of low cholesterol substitutes actually improves the flavor of the dish. A case in point is the classic Passover Matzah Brei. Few are adventurous enough to try Marlene Sorosky's marvelous Mexican Matzah Brei Omelet (*Fast and Festive Meals for the Jewish Holidays*, William Morrow & Co.). According to Zillah Bahar, on the other hand, the *Kosher Light* version with onions brings out the taste and versatility of egg whites, which in this case produces a fluffy texture and a crisper Matzah Brei.

Similarly, her pareve and kosher for Passover potato latkes suffer mainly from being feather-light. The taste is O.K. but we re-enactors will miss the heaviness of the deadly latkes of our youth.

Another recipe worth trying is the no-chicken-fat, no-egg-yolk-kosher-for-Passover potato kugel, kicked up in flavor by a little rosemary and sage, and baked in muffin cups so that everyone gets the crispy piece.

The brief but appropriate introduction by Rabbi Joel Landau and the attractive book design with illustrations by Maria Mayr combine to make *Kosher Light* a particularly fine gift book for every Jewish cook, or every cook who cooks Jewish.

ACCORDING TO ITS AUTHOR, "this little cookbook is a collection of secret family recipes ... It is designed for non-kosher as well as kosher cooks ... All recipes are coded pareve, dairy, and meat ... The necessary ingredients are readily available." The author believes that the soul of Jewish cooking lies in the culture of its people, and has therefore included a description of each Jewish holiday.

Little Cookbook Full of Secrets
Mark Stark's Amazing Jewish Cookbook
Text and Illustrations by Mark Stark
Alef Design Group, 1997   320 pages

This is a cookbook for the entire family which allows beginning cooks and seasoned chefs alike access to the world of Jewish cooking. The charming but functional drawings which accompany each recipe detail how many people the recipe will serve; what ingredients and tools (*sic*) are needed; and the steps involved in preparation. More than a collection of recipes, the *Amazing Jewish Cookbook* includes safety tips, an A-to-Z glossary of cooking terms, a quick guide to the laws of *kashrut*, and summaries of Jewish holiday customs.

Mark Stark, head pastry chef at the Getty Center in Los Angeles, is a graduate of the California Culinary Institute. Although this is only Mark's first cookbook, or perhaps *because* it is his first effort, he has hit upon a delightful format which is notably gender-nonspecific and which really might be used by mother and son, father and daughter, husband and wife, or just friends.

For those out there who have never been taught the difference between beat, blend, combine, fold, or mix, Mark Stark has drawn you a picture. You can't miss! This is another great candidate for a gift.

April 1998

Jewish Gardening Cookbook among the most original and unusual books in the category

ONE CAN IMAGINE the difficulty Michael Brown, author of *The Jewish Gardening Cookbook*, along with his publishers, faced in naming what must be one of the most

The Jewish Gardening Cookbook
Growing Plants and Cooking for
Holidays and Festivals

Michael Brown
Jewish Lights, 1998   224 pages

unusual and original books this department has seen in a decade. It is definitely not a cookbook, yet there are some excellent recipes, all vegetarian (one reviewer has commanded us to "forget corned beef, lox, and bagels. Here is a sampling of real Jewish food: the stuff our ancestors ate in Biblical days.").

It is much more than a gardening guide, yet if one wishes to pursue the creation of a garden that will provide the traditional fruits and grains to add something special to our holiday preparations and celebrations, Brown gives us chapter and verse on how to procure, plant and tend the traditional seven species (*shivat haminim*), which are fig, grape, wheat, barley, date palm, pomegranate, and olive (growing a date palm is not advised in many climates, nor on the terrace of a Florida condominium apartment).

The novice gardener will find detailed instructions on the creation of a garden which will provide the appropriate traditional fruit or grain to enhance our traditional holidays and festivals, thus tying our observance in with the seasons that dictated our forebears' lives and created the context for their celebrations.

Back in my U.S. Navy destroyer days, my family moved into a tiny house in Rhode Island and were surprised to find a healthy stand of bamboo growing next to a back bedroom window. The house came with instructions for keeping the plants from freezing in winter. It seems that the man who built the house had enjoyed many years of service in the Far East, and found it restful and nostalgic to hear the slapping and rustling sound of the bamboo in the summer breeze.

The author, in this case, returning to America after almost ten years in Israel, found that among the things he most missed about Israel was the land and the connection between what grew there and the history of the Jewish people. (One might interject that he had better get back to Israel before they pave over the entire country.) As an avid gardener and as an educator, he adds to his unique book Biblical references, poetry, songs, prayers, commentary, and if you never knew but would like to know how to conduct a *Tu-bishvat seder*, it's in there.

One reads and hears a great deal these days about an increasing search for spirituality, for greater meaning in our lives. Each year we are pleased when our children connect with our history by learning to bake matzo. Green takes it further; he shows us how to grow the wheat, separate the kernels from the chaff, grind it into flour, and by so doing identify with our past in a meaningful way. He concludes that the planting of a Jewish garden provides a place where we can rest on Shabbat, or, in the manner of Rabbi Nachman of Breslov, the 18th century Hasidic scholar:

> *Master of the Universe*
> *Grant me the ability to be alone;*
> *May it be my custom to go outdoors each day*
> *among the trees and grasses*
> *among all the growing things*
> *and there may I be alone,*
> *and enter into prayer*
> *to talk with the one*
> *that I belong to.*

Each year we grate our horseradish for Passover. For years I have tried to grow my own. Horseradish is supposed to grow like a weed and care is recommended lest it take over the garden. Mine have always failed. But I have learned from this marvelous book what I was doing wrong. And whether or not we celebrate next year in Jerusalem, we hope to celebrate with incredibly strong horseradish grown in what we hope will be our Jewish garden.

Could this simple act open us up to the possibilities of our faith?

April 1999

A great gift at Chanukah time

**Chocolate Chip Challah
And Other Twists on the
Jewish Holiday Table**
Written and Illustrated by Lisa Rauchwerger
UAHC Press, 1999   127 pages

NOT A YEAR PASSES that I don't get a *geshrei* from the editor-in-chief—"Thanksgiving is here already and where is your review?" And of course, publishers and producers simply don't give us enough time to take a real good look at what is out there to buy for Chanukah. So here's a kind of quick look at what's on the shelf waiting for a good look.

This interactive family cookbook uses the Jewish calendar as the framework for the preparation by parent and child of tasty treats while involving the children in activity pages for each holiday and introducing them to the calendar itself. We won't discuss the latke recipe; the one in the book is fine, just not mine! But the Big Apple Applesauce, the Maccabee Mushroom Burgers, and the Carrot Soup are not your ordinary fare and, although the recipes are uncomplicated, not a can of cream of mushroom soup is in sight. The dishes appear to be edible. And if there are no children around the house, these can be tried with your significant other.

December 1999

Gefilte Variations in time for Passover seder

"I NEVER EAT any kosher food," she said. "It's loaded with salt and fat." Loaded with salt and fat; until recently, a pretty fair assessment. And then came the thrust toward diversity; kosher Mexican, kosher Chinese, kosher Thai, French, Italian, you name it.

The *Va'ad Ha'kashruts* of the world found the new mother lode, sending forth the incorruptible *mashgeachim* to supervise and approve the newest salsa, the latest soba noodle, the currently most popular Bar Mitzvah hors d'oeuvre—sushi (no more of those greasy, heavy *knishes* for me, nosirree, and alas).

> **The Gefilte Variations**
> **A Kosher Cookbook**
> Jayne Cohen
> Scribners, 2000   416 pages

Of course, the kosher Italian was not the classic cuisine cooked by the Jews of Rome or Venice for centuries.

Which is why we are eternally thankful to Jayne Cohen, creator of *The Gefilte Variations*, who reminds us that "Ha-Cha Salsa" may be kosher, but it's not Jewish.

So what does this author of the best new Jewish and kosher cookbook we have seen in years mean by "Jewish food?" Cohen recognizes that Jewish food cannot be defined merely as food cooked by Jews. Nor is Jewish food limited to *cholent, haroset*, chopped liver, and brisket. Yet the Russian *blini* is clearly identified (possession is 9/10's, etc.) in America as the Jewish *blintz*, so let's not kid ourselves, kiddo—whether from Ashkenazi or Sephardi origins, we know what Jewish food is, and it ain't pasta primavera!

This book will teach you plenty about the world of Jewish cuisine. Have you noted that the latest rage in those restaurants identified in the guides as having $$$$ prices are salads with bits of pomegranate? Well, Jayne Cohen shows us that the pomegranate is worked into the floor mosaics of 5th century synagogues. I say "shows" because wherever there is a chapter end with a few inches of space we are treated to a two-inch black and white cut of a 19th century cookie cutter or an 18th century kiddush cup. Not a lot of space devoted to beautiful photographs of food, in fact none at all. This book is authentic, yet innovative, taking off on traditional recipes with flights of rare creativity. Thus Gefilte Fish becomes Salmon Gefilte Fish Poached in Fennel-Wine Broth with Ginger-Beet Horseradish (pareve) and beef, potato and fried onion kreplach are mouthwateringly tempting, made with wonton wrappers. And brisket takes on new life and new importance as we hear more from Jayne about why Jewish cooks learned to do so much with the tougher cuts of meat that were permissible.

We begin with Braised Brisket With Thirty-Six Cloves of Garlic (Is this where Emeril Legasse learned to cook?), progress to Aromatic Marinated Brisket with Chestnuts, and conclude with Eggplant-Stuffed Brisket Braised with Tomatoes, Saffron and Honey. This last recipe pays homage to the eggplant, termed "Jews" food in mid-19th century Florence. Sephardim learned to eat eggplant in Arab Spain, but the meaty vegetable became a favorite in the Balkans, Romania, and wherever it would grow in Russia.

Jayne Cohen must have looked into the hearts of many young cooks afraid to tackle the classic recipes. Her instructions are instructive. This is no paltry collection of recipes. This is a cookbook. Whether you hanker for *mamaliga* (cornmeal porridge, akin to polenta) described herein as Sautéed Chive Mamaliga with Feta-Yogurt Cream or Duck and White Bean Cholent, Cohen takes you through it step by step, giving little hints, offering small variations, teaching, teaching all the time.

The Gefilte Variations is available just in time for Passover, and not just for Seder meals. There are menus for the rest of the week as well. Similarly wonderful menus are given for other holidays and festivals throughout the year.

The glossary, too, differs from the customary, offering a definition of *ongepotchkeh* and a comparison with *potchkeh.* A bibliography of cookbooks is included, among which are many reviewed in this column. Such classics as Faye Levy's *International Jewish Cookbook,* and Joan Nathan's *The Jewish Holiday Kitchen* are listed. They are classics, but to this writer's mind, Ms. Cohen's non-coffee table book is a "must-own," not for the novice, but for the serious cook-aspirant who seeks to learn the difference between a *hamantasch* (a three-cornered cookie) and a *hamin* (from the Hebrew for Hot—long simmering Sabbath stew—*cholent* or *dafina*).

Regular readers of this column know that cookbooks which omit the use of modern kitchen appliances, such as the microwave oven, usually receive short shrift here. Exceptions must be made for two reasons. First, there are serious problems of kashrut observance, even more so than in conventional ovens. Second, with a few exceptions, the recipes in this wonderful book seem to work better using older methods. But the matter should be addressed in later editions, as high tech kitchens go far beyond the simple microwave (which itself made its first appearance 40 years ago), to convection ovens and now even more sophisticated equipment.

Pardon me, but I can visualize and can almost smell the parsnips in the tangy Russian cabbage soup with pot roast-beet kreplach...

April 2000

Lots of memories in this wonderful book

Customer (at the famous Lindy's restaurant in NYC): "How come the rice pudding with raisins cost one dollar and the rice pudding without costs a dollar and a quarter?"
Lindy's waiter: "It costs us twenty-five cents in labor to take out the raisins."

SOMETIMES WE GET kind of confused when we talk about "cookbooks" and "food books" and the many permutations and commutations thereof. There are the great seminal works, like *The Joy of Cooking* and *Mastering the Art of French Cooking,* as well as others which actually teach you how to cook by James Beard, Julia Child, Craig Claiborne, Jacques Pepin, Joan Nathan, Barbara Kafka and many, many more. Then there are the "cookbooks" which are collections of recipes, some of which are valuable to the amateur chef because of their regional nature, like the cooking of Provence, the Caribbean, or Tuscany, for exam-

---

Arthur Schwartz's New York City Food
An Opinionated History and More Than 100 Legendary Recipes
Stewart, Tabori & Chang, 2004   400 pages

---

ple. And then there are the generally dreadful collections created by clubs and institutions like Jaycee ladies, the Governor's First Lady, or Temple Sisterhoods (Didn't you always want to know "A Hundred and One Ways to Make a Great Noodle Kugel"?).

In the Navy, we often wondered how the ship's menu, followed by all ships and stations, meal for meal, day for day worldwide, contained so many seemingly archaic dishes. We eventually learned that the menus were created with the well-meaning assistance of the Navy League wives during World War I, and were adhered to for almost 50 years.

Well, Arthur Schwartz's *New York City Food* is not a cookbook; it is a food book in the best sense of that genre. It is a history of food in New York City from 1624 to the present, couched in terms of what we ate and eat, what we remember and what we currently crave, along with 100+ very special recipes. Beginning at the beginning with what the Native Americans ate, and then the Dutch, Schwartz chronicles the gastronomic contributions of the Irish, Italians, Germans, Jews, and Chinese, as well as those restaurants which came under the category of "feeding the people."

One of the great treats of my childhood was eating at Child's, a 25-restaurant chain famous for its chicken croquettes and corned beef hash (this writer never had a piece of "intact" meat at Child's); Schrafft's, which catered to "ladies who lunch," was noted for its cheese bread (the term "low carbs" was more than half a century away); and the incomparable Horn & Hardart Automats, where nickels pushed into slots delivered chicken pot pies (whose mother ever made chicken pot pie?) as well as other marvels one never had at home, and what seemed like a mile-long steam table filled with wonders including a panoply of beautiful vegetables (a five-veggie plate for a quarter). This writer's mother was less enthusiastic about the automats themselves than about the Horn & Hardart retail outlets from which she brought home the all time best creamed spinach, Harvard beets, and macaroni and cheese. If memory serves, the dining rooms were furnished with lots of marble and each table was crowned with a condiment centerpiece of ketchup, mustard, vinegar, salt and pepper. It was not uncommon to see a down-on-his-luck person making "depression soup" by adding all those condiments to a free cup of hot water.

> Customer: "I haven't come to any roast beef in this roast beef sandwich yet."
> Waiter: "Try another bite."
> Customer (taking a huge bite): "Nope, not yet."
> Waiter: "You must have gone right past it."

The famous restaurants from the Gay Nineties to the recently demised temples of taste—Delmonicos, Leon & Eddies, 21, La Cote Basque, Le Pavillion, Le Cirque—as well as the current successes of Daniel Boulud, Danny Meyer and their contemporaries are all there. But we Jews from New York will love the chapter, "The Jews," for

> one can safely say that some of the most quintessential New York City foods are of Eastern European Jewish origin: bagels (and lox), pastrami on rye, corned beef, pickles, cheesecake, matzoh balls, knishes and egg creams.

Even the humble hot dog, which was really German, became the food of the people through the entrepreneurial efforts of Jews like Nathan's of Coney Island.

And finally, although great delicatessens like the Second Avenue Deli and Katz's still exist, who among us would not kill for an old-fashioned "appetizing store" (basically a *dairy* deli) with its array of half a dozen kinds of herring, belly lox, nova, pickled lox, lox fleagles, sable carp and baked (hot smoked) salmon and barrel sauerkraut and pickles and oil cured olives and great loaves of halvah (that they cut to order—with a lox knife!), and, and, and...?

Schwartz is all over the place, covering almost all bases (and he's almost large enough to do so). But I wish he had time and space for more of the old Hungarian/Romanian restaurants and their specialties—the Moscowitz & Lupowitz kind of place with the potted lambs' tongues, *lungen* stew and stuffed *miltz*. (And where's the Charlotte Russe?)

> *Customer in a Jewish restaurant: "Waiter, what is that fly doing in my soup?"*
> *Waiter: "The backstroke!"*

True story: Way back in the 1940s, my mother ordered a piece of strudel for dessert at Sammy's Roumanian Restaurant. It arrived at the table kind of broken up. Mom complained. The waiter said, "Lady (long pause), it may not be so *fency* (short pause), but it's good!"

Schwartz even has an article explaining why Jews like Chinese food. ("What do Jews do on Christmas day? They eat Chinese food and go to the movies.") As a kid I figured it out for myself: it tasted good and it was cheap. And, of course, the following takes place in a Chinese restaurant:

> *Jewish Customer: "Waiter, come over here and taste this wonton soup."*
> *Waiter: "I can't."*
> *Jewish Customer: "What do you mean, you can't?"*
> *Waiter: "No spoon."*
> *Jewish Customer: "Ah hah!"*

This is a wonderful book; you'll love it; and it makes a great gift. (Wanna know how to make *Black & Whites*, anyone?)

August 2005

Three cooking perspectives

FOR YEARS we found ourselves buying Waterford goblets and Wedgwood china as wedding gifts for couples who would ultimately order in pizza. Now it seems as though most of our wedding shopping has been through the online registries at such emporia as Bed, Bath, and Beyond and Crate & Barrel. We are still not certain, however, just how much at-home cooking is taking place.

In the case of *kashrut* observers in Tidewater, it is a different matter. There just aren't enough places to eat out in or order in from. And just as kosher food doesn't come cheap, neither do *fency* kosher cookbooks. Here's news of a few new entries.

LAURA FRANKEL, author of *Jewish Cooking for All Seasons*, is executive chef and co-owner of Shallots, reputed to be one of the top restaurants in Chicago and one of the best kosher restaurants in the United States. More than an anthology of recipes, Frankel's culinary *oeuvre* is driven by a passion for locally grown, organic produce and high quality ingredients throughout.

What the reader will *not* find are recipes for what might be considered typically Jewish dishes. If you are looking for recipes for brisket, gefilte fish, kugel, or *tsimmes*, this is the wrong book. While all the recipes follow *kashrut* guidelines, annotated for dairy, meat or *pareve*, Frankel does not attempt to compete with Bubbe's recipes. Neither does she serve such dishes in her restaurant. What Frankel does attempt, with great success, is to provide recipes that are mouthwateringly delicious just to anticipate.

Jewish Cooking For All Seasons
Fresh, Flavorful Kosher Recipes for Holidays and Every Day
Laura Frankel
Wiley Cloth, 2006   272 pages

Whether it is Passover dishes like Torte with Chocolate, Spring Vegetable Soup with Basil Pistou; Roasted Duck Breasts with Cherry-Red Wine Reduction for Shavuot; or Chocolate Opera Ganache for Rosh Hashana, *Jewish Cooking* considerately includes make-ahead instructions, tips to ensure success, and serving ideas. There is a Basic Recipes section for spice mixes, stocks, and garnishes which can be made in advance, a sensible guide to equipping your kitchen, and a source directory for products not locally available.

This is truly a cookbook, one which many of our local kosher caterers would be wise to acquire. Imagine Muhummarah-Crusted Halibut with Saffron Broth and Ivory Lentils at your next *simcha* celebration. Laura Frankel will introduce the experienced or neophyte cook, kosher or not, to a whole new world of Jewish cooking.

NECHAMA COHEN learned she had type 1 diabetes in 1985, has shared her "enlitened" approach to a healthier lifestyle with thousands, and is currently founder and CEO of the Jewish Diabetes Association. *Enlitened Kosher Cooking* seeks to combine cutting-edge nutritional planning with haute cuisine. Thus each of the 250 "Good-Carb, Healthy-Fat, Sugar-Free" recipes contain a nutritional chart, dietary exchanges and food values for calories, fat, carbohydrates, protein, sodium, cholesterol, calcium and fiber. Like Frankel, Cohen

Enlitened Kosher Cooking
Nechama Cohen
Feldheim, 2006   419 pages

also includes tips for making condiments, some of which can be stored for months in the freezer and can be refrigerated for up to two weeks. Whether your fish dish needs *S'chug, Hilba, or Matboucha,* you can find at least one way of making each, and sometimes a quick method as well as the classic recipe.

It may be thought that *Enlitened Kosher Cooking,* with its emphasis on low-carb, low-fat, sugar-free recipes appeals solely to families with a diabetic member; not so! With so many already in what is termed a pre-diabetic condition or hereditarily at risk, Cohen's beautiful book provides a useful alternate for the homemaker willing to delight the family with healthful, somewhat sophisticated, and excitingly delicious meals once or twice a week.

THE FINAL COOKBOOK features recipes from the Culinary Arts Department of Hadassah College Jerusalem. A much more modest publication, this 163-page collection is peppered with information about the origin of dishes and includes sections on appetizers, soups, eggs and dairy, fish, chicken and desserts. This rather humble paperback volume has an important advantage over the above-mentioned glamorous volumes: it is spiral bound and when opened lies flat on the cook's counter, a practical plus that overcomes the occasionally clumsy translation and the assumption that the user really knows how to shop and cook and merely needs the recipe. Thus the recipe for "spicy beef patties" simply calls for "finely ground meat," and "beef stew" calls for "2 pounds meat..." Instructions can be as simple as "Be careful so fish won't fall apart."

What's Cooking at Hadassah College?
Recipes from the Culinary Arts Department
Hadassah College Jerusalem, 2006   165 pages

Nonetheless, *What's Cooking* pays tribute to the non-Jewish culinary contribution to what is now regarded as Israeli cooking, a cuisine which takes from Ashkenazi and Sephardic sources (heavily Arabic at times). While Israeli German Jews will eat Moroccan and Yemenite foods and Israelis of Yemenite background will eat Indian, Vietnamese and Thai foods, *What's Cooking* cleaves mainly to what we recognize as Israeli food. Although there is little difference between Moslem Iraqi food and Jewish Iraqi food, the adherence to *kashrut* and the festivals creates a distinction. Thus, *What's Cooking at Hadassah College* can be mainly characterized as Middle Eastern food, and their students' collection, annotated for dairy, meat and *pareve*, would be a worthwhile addition to any Jewish kitchen. *(Contact a local Hadassah chapter, or call 800-928-0685, or e-mail rmays@hadasssah.org to order this book.)*

Note: As a parting footnote from this reviewer (a point raised in other reviews), it is indeed odd that none of the above books acknowledge in any manner the existence of microwave and convection ovens and the essential role they play in the modern kitchen, worldwide. – H.S.

October 2006

Simple, healthy and delicious

LEVANA KIRSCHENBAUM has been associated with upscale Kosher dining through her restaurant, her library of successful cookbooks and her online blog. She refers to this book, *The Whole Foods Kosher Kitchen*, as the "culmination of my life work." This reviewer's curiosity was piqued by the words "Whole Foods" in its title, now that the famous food emporium Whole Foods is coming to town. I was certain there was some connection, but, alas, it was not meant to be. However, in perusing the book, some intriguing recipes were noted

The Whole Foods Kosher Kitchen
Glorious Meals Pure and Simple
Levana Kirschenbaum
Levana Cooks, 20011   399 pages

that I really looked forward to trying (intriguing enough to overcome everything that annoyed me about the book).

First, let's get all the annoyances out of the way:

1. The book weighs about 3 pounds and promises to be a huge pain-in-the-kitchen to maneuver.

2. On the back cover is the notation that this is the "gift edition." I asked the publicist about the "non-gift edition," hoping that there was a simple ring-bound version that a serious cook could lay out flat on a kitchen counter (and minus the "gorgeous" but totally unreal looking photos of finished dishes). He replied that the non-gift edition had been withdrawn by the author as not of sufficient quality.

3. Granting Kirschenbaum her point of view that "whole foods" and efforts to cook from "whole ingredients" are better for us, it is understandable that not every home freezer has the capacity to store gallons of soups, stock or other items made in bulk for future use.

4. The author's textual sermons have a kind of harping tone, and she is sometimes just mistaken. For example, the cook is enjoined from heating large containers of soup in the microwave lest the outside get scorched before the inside gets hot. Kirschenbaum should know that microwave ovens heat food *from the inside out.*

5. It is okay to have strong opinions, but to dismiss iceberg lettuce, that wonderful, crunchy, never bitter salad green without which we would never have a wedge salad, smacks of outright snobbism.

6. So the author wanted "gorgeous" and gorgeous she got: A heavy, super glossy, deluxe, forty-buck coffee table book with photos of dishes that don't look real and that serious cooks may never use.

Now that all of that is off our chest, let's look inside:

Fully agreeing that no bottled salad dressing comes anywhere close in quality and flavor to homemade dressings, I love Kirschenbaum's use of anchovies (which she calls "a blessing if disguised"), Dashi (Hondashi) powder, capers and ginger. There are a dozen and a half excellent recipes.

Ever true to her Moroccan roots, Kirschenbaum's wonderful soups also pay homage to Asian influences using a Japanese miso base and Thai touches, Ashkenazi (Unstuffed Cabbage [not listed under soup] and Quick Borscht) and Indian recipes.

We tend to avoid using frozen fish. However, our love of sashimi, which we understand requires the use of frozen fish due to health regulations, has led us to wonder why good frozen fish would not be satisfactory. Kirschenbaum, while insisting that fresh is best, believes that frozen, vacuum packed fish is excellent, and much less expensive as well. Similarly, one senses that she is correct on using frozen, unprocessed fruits and vegetables in dishes where appearance doesn't matter—purees; soups; sauces; coulis. She offers two great lists of food groups—one that lists foods that *Need to Be Organic* and one for foods that *Need Not Be Organic*. Her overarching emphasis is on unprocessed or minimally processed food.

The Whole Foods Kosher Kitchen is so strong on the use of whole grains in salads, vegetable and other dishes that one expects to find a recipe for whole wheat water! Therefore, it is understandable if the author is a bit weak in the "meat" section; perhaps she has covered meat dishes more thoroughly in her other books.

In keeping with Kirschenbaum's stated purpose, offering upscale kosher recipes that eschew such no-no's as schmaltz, organ meats, and well-larded steaks, every dish is conceived with an eye toward healthy eating. As stated, lots of grains are used, and cross-referenced are Passover-friendly recipes and gluten-free adaptations. The author's passion for wholesome foods may indeed inspire the reader to change cooking and eating habits in an effort to eat one's way to good health without sacrificing enjoyment.

I love her attitude about eating out. You can't lose weight eating out. Eat home more. And never give up something you love.

Finally, the book came with a wonderful DVD in which Kirschenbaum demonstrates the preparation of simple, healthy and delicious Shabbos and Passover feasts.

July 2012

Four on food — briefly noted

FOR MONTHS this beautiful and practical cookbook (covered in plastic so food and liquid stains can be easily wiped off) was among this year's best kept publishing secrets. Virtually unreviewed, it was talked about and passed on by word of mouth to friends and relatives, its recipes traded online. Finally it was picked up by the major food book critics and is now a bestseller. And it should be.

Jerusalem, a Cookbook
Yotam Ottolenghi and Sami Tamimi
Ten Speed Press, 20013   320 pages

Chefs Ottolenghi (author of *Plenty*) and Tamimi, partners in the eponymous London restaurant chain and the high-end restaurant Nopi, "return" to the Jerusalem of their youth to explore the distinctive foods of its diverse Jewish, Muslim, and Christian populations. Their selections include traditional, age-old dishes, cooked traditionally, just as they should be. Others benefit from the authors' poetic license, updated to suit current times and sensibilities.

Shakshuka, for example, is Tunisian in origin, but everywhere I have eaten this hugely popular dish claims to have invented it. In Israel it is claimed by Iraqis, Yemenites, and Moroccans. My Persian *machatunim* are masters of the dish: a rich tomato, onion and sweet pepper-based sauce (ideally cooked in a *paella* pan) in which eggs are poached. I haven't made Ottolenghi and Tamimi's version yet, but it looks fantastic—the alpha and omega of *Shakshuka*.

One wishes these recipes had been around years ago, as the upscale thinking of the authors might have taught us what we have had to learn the hard way. For example, I have probably read at least fifty recipes for *latkes* over the years and so have myriad other cooks. So why do so many good cooks make bad *latkes*? Wrong ingredients? Poor technique? How many decades did it take me to discover Yukon Gold potatoes that don't discolor as you prepare the *latkes*?

Jerusalem, a Cookbook does not attempt to offer recipes from every diverse culture in Jerusalem, but those it does offer are superb. We have made the Roast Chicken with Clementines, Fennel, & Arak and taken pleasure in the cries of "encore."

Not just a collection of recipes; there are valuable cooking lessons here.

T*AGLIT-BIRTHRIGHT ISRAEL* sends Jewish adults between the ages of 18-26 to Israel to strengthen individual Jewish identity. The program has been a very successful partnership between the government of Israel, private philanthropies and Jewish communities around the world (United Jewish Federation of Tidewater and Tidewater Jewish Foundation are significant supporters).

Israel To Go
Look and Cook Book
Edited by Lara Doel
Lunch Box Press, 2013   119 pages

The *Look and Cook Book* is a small, beautifully illustrated pocket culinary tour through Israel featuring twenty specially selected kosher recipes (including *Shakshuka*!) designed to be fairly easy for a home cook to follow. Included are Blintzes from *Tzfat*, Bedouin Pita and *Hummous*, and Braised Lamb Shank. It was interesting to learn what our Birthright generation (ages 18-26) found to be the best food in Israel.

THIS AUTOBIOGRAPHY is a wonderful photo album of a New York City landmark, plus a few dozen pages of text covering the famous deli's beginnings and the various twists of ownership and management over five generations dating back to 1888 (125 years ago!). As is the case with Russ and Daughters, there was a time when there was a Jewish delicatessen on every block of the Lower East Side and competition was fierce—but few survived the Jewish exodus from the neighborhood after World War II. Katz's is famous for their "Send a salami to your boy in the army," promotion during the war; they sent over 100,000 salamis and still ship hundreds of pounds of their meats weekly. Each

Autobiography of a
Delicatessen – Katz's
Photographs by Baldomero Fernandez
Text by Jake Dell
Bauer & Dean, 2013   383 pages

week they corn (pickle) and smoke twenty-five to forty thousand pounds of meat and serve two to five thousand hot dogs, along with eight to fifteen thousand pickles (sour and half-sour).

Author Jake Dell, a fifth-generation owner who gave up going to medical school because he loves the business, reminds us of the origins of corned beef and pastrami. They are, respectively, pickled brisket and pickled smoked belly and were created in the *shtetls* of eastern Europe as a means of turning cheap cuts of beef into tender and delicious food, as well as a method of preserving the meat where there was no refrigeration.

Although Katz's is a habit for regular customers, it is an iconic tourist attraction: tourists arrive by the busload. Up to 4,000 customers are served daily and all meat is hand-cut by cutters whose families have been working at the deli for three generations. There is a photo gallery of every category of employee, from cookers to cutters to servers to cleaners.

Katz's remains a favorite of celebrities from the worlds of sports, theater, and politics. And, of course, everyone recalls the famous scene in "When Harry Met Sally" with Billy Crystal and Meg Ryan in Katz's, where a customer sitting nearby exclaims, "I'll have what she's having!"

We are not certain if there has been a book about some of Katz's famous neighbors, such as The Original Yonah Schimmel Knishery, or Gus' Pickles, or Sammy's Romanian. Gone are such legendary restaurants as Moskowitz & Lupovich, Glucksterns, and Ratners (a dairy emporium). In a sense, they are replaced by restaurants of the new immigrants, from Russia, Poland, Greece, Korea, and Vietnam.

Don't expect any recipes in this book. *The Autobiography of a Delicatessen – Katz's* offers methodology rather than recipes. It is rewarding to see Katz's gain the recognition of other famous delis like the Carnegie Deli and the Second Avenue Deli. For more on this subject, the reader may wish to read Arthur Schwartz's *New York City Food,* published in 2004.

WHAT ARE Anthony Bourdain, Oliver Sacks and Martha Stewart in total agreement on? You got it! Russ and Daughters is one of New York City's greatest living institutions. Very good! Next question: What was a basic difference among an Italian grocery, a German delicatessen, and a kosher deli?

Russ and Daughters
Reflections and Recipes from the House that Herring Built
Mark Russ Federman
Foreword by Calvin Trillin
Schocken, 2013   205 pages

It's this: Italian grocers sold mortadella and capicola as well as parmesan and mozzarella cheeses; German delicatessens sold liverwurst and bratwurst as well as bergkase and cambozola cheeses; A kosher deli couldn't sell cheese or creamed herring: dairy products could not be sold in a store that sold meat. So "*appetizing stores*" were invented.

Therefore, on the Lower East Side of New York City, if you wanted a pastrami or corned beef sandwich or to "Send a salami to your boy in the army," you might have gone to Katz's Delicatessen. But if you wanted a "half a quarter belly lox," or a nice schmaltz herring, or a *shtikel* vegetable cheese, you could get the best deal at Russ & Daughters, now being run by the author's daughter, the fourth generation to run this century-old business.

Up from a pushcart selling herring to immigrants to "J. Russ, Cut Rate Appetizing," to its present emporium (definitely no longer cut-rate), the family business has been nurtured by scores of brothers, sisters, sons, daughters, children and in-laws, all of whom put in their "sweat" time. Even when going to college, law and medical school they were expected to return on weekends and summers to "help out" in the store. Author Mark Russ Federman has contrived to tell the family's story ("sliced thin"), throw in a few good recipes and sprinkle it all with wonderful family photos. *Russ & Daughters* is a good read, especially if you're interested in learning about fifteen different kinds of herring.

October 2013

HISTORY MATTERS

'An important book' for all readers

I HADN'T PLANNED on reviewing this book. Not that it wasn't important, but rather because the publisher ignored our request for a review copy.

Then, I read Professor John A. Garraty's review in *The New York Times* Book Review (Nov. 26, 1989) and Professor Julius Lester's somewhat more knowledgeable review in *The Boston Sunday Globe* (Nov. 26, 1989), and realized that these two esteemed scholars, each in his own way, had somehow failed those who look to such endorsements as serious guidance as to what should be read, and who should read what.

First, it should be stated that this is not a book for scholars, although the

The Jews in America
Four Centuries of an Uneasy
Encounter: A History
Arthur Hertzberg
Simon & Schuster, 1989   424 pages

scholar might benefit from the philosophical thrust of Rabbi Hertzberg's work. There are no footnotes and scant chapter notes. It is, moreover, an easy read, so much so that I was first deceived into thinking it superficial, a mere gloss of Jewish history

in America. That, of course, is the genius of the author: to distill acres of books, lectures, documents, etc. into a single volume capable of challenging all the Jewish professionals in the country (rabbis included), all the *balabatim* in all the Jewish organizations, yet able to attract and retain the interest of a full gamut of readers. It is, simply put, a great one-volume survey.

Of course, there are problems. Some areas, such as the inaction of America, and particularly FDR, during the Holocaust, truly demand greater detail. But then, we have Weidman's *Abandonment of the Jews*. Some have chided Hertzberg for devoting too much space to historical exegesis and not enough to "a fuller description and analysis of the creative tension and excitement within American Jewry today." Well, that's the problem with books that start to get written in 1982 and finally get published late in 1989. This writer's view is that *The Jews in America* is Volume One of a two-volume work, the first by Hertzberg and the second by Charles Silberman (*A Certain People: American Jews and Their Lives Today*).

It is possibly heretical to mention both authors in the same breath. Rabbi Hertzberg is a professor of religion and has had a world of experience both as a congregational rabbi for four decades, and as president of the American Jewish Congress in the 1970s. Silberman, on the other hand, is one of our foremost "journalist-scholars," and there is considerable uncertainty as to the real difference here, except for the analysis which differs greatly. If Hertzberg argues that those elements which American Jews have embraced in order to distinguish ourselves as a group, i.e., folk-Jewishness, unconditional support for Israel, and fear of anti-Semitism, are ephemeral and nearly spent, then Silberman concludes that despite this, "the end is not at hand." Hertzberg concludes that failing to bring about a spiritual revival, not merely among a small group of ultra-orthodox, but among the mainstream of American Jews, will result in American Jewish history becoming merely part of the American memory as a whole. Silberman reads the same documents and concludes that contrary to the fear of many Jews, even a few years ago, Judaism as a religion has never been stronger than it is today in this country.

It is probably unnecessary to take sides, as in true pejorist fashion we fear the worst and hope for the best. Hertzberg offers some chilling insight, a very readable discussion, an important book for Jew and non-Jew alike. Certainly his choice of expression, "uneasy encounter," is more than apt; it gets at the very marrow of the matter. I wish I could order you to read it.

April 1990

Emotional terrain of immigrants

TAKING HIS TITLE from his grandmother's diary, where she wrote, "The lonely days were Sundays, Sundays when I watched the town people going to church, while we stayed upstairs in our apartment. Then I would feel like an outsider in this little community," Evans navigates the "emotional terrain of the immigrant generation of Jews who arrived in the small towns of the South in the eighteenth and nineteenth centuries." The phrase, he says, " ... serves as a psychological backdrop for the ongoing and undulating American drama ... including the history of Jews in the South and the impact of Israel and the Holocaust on Jewish and human history, as well as my own family story."

The Lonely Days Were Sundays

My Life and a People's Struggle for Identity

Eli N. Evans

Harper San Francisco, 2002   460 pages

After reading Eli Evans' eloquent collection of essays, an informed potpourri which reflects his unique perspective of Southern Jewish life and which ranges widely among issues of civil rights, international (particularly Middle Eastern) politics, Israeli, Southern, Jewish and American history, I picked up the phone and placed a call to him. This Jewish author is fond of quoting the exchange between Henry Kissinger and Golda Meir: "I am an American, Secretary of State, and a Jew, in that order," Kissinger is supposed to have told Golda Meir. "That's all right," she is said to have replied, "We read from right to left."

Thus one might opine that Evans is a Jewish son, a poet, and a Southern historian, in that order. The reason for my call was not so much to thank him for sharing his professional insights on the Jewish communities of the South, nor his journalistic insights on the Kissinger Shuttle or the Clinton-Gore campaign, but for the more personal window he opened into his life and that of his family.

I called, specifically, to mention a book reviewed here about a year ago, *Where They Lie*, by Mel Young. I had remembered a grim statistic which revealed that more than half the Jewish soldiers from North Carolina who had fought and perished on the side of the Confederacy in the Civil War, had actually died, not on the battlefield, but of pneumonia, as they suffered through a cold upstate New York winter, in a Union prison camp, literally days before the surrender at Appomattox. Evans, born and raised, as a classmate of his recalls, on the right side of the tracks in Durham, N.C., had a serious interest in such matters. His father, Emanuel J. "Mutt" Evans, served as mayor of Durham for 12 years, a Jewish Southern liberal, who perforce "shepherded his city through the difficult years of desegregation, successfully integrating the schools, public accommodations, the fire and police departments, and city agencies."

As we spoke, we both acknowledged a mild irony in the fact that this Yankee, this New York Jew who came to Norfolk 40 years ago, who put down roots and had three generations living here, and who directs a Jewish charitable foundation, was reviewing a book by a southern Jew with roots going back three generations, but who now lived in New York, directing a charitable foundation established by a Jew (The Revson Foundation).

Evans himself had been to Norfolk many years ago as a Jewish Book Fair speaker in connection with his book, *The Provincials: A Personal History of Jews in the South*, which, I am advised, is happily still in print and still selling. His connection goes much deeper, for his mother, whose death in 1985 inspired Evans' final and most moving essay, was a prominent local, regional and national leader of Hadassah, who counted among her dear friends and Hadassah cohorts Miriam Kroskin, of blessed memory. Evans recalls "the visits to Durham of the national leaders—women ... such as ... Miriam Kroskin of Norfolk—fabulous women, really, who in the pre-feminist era of postwar America channeled all their love and energy into Hadassah."

We spoke briefly about the lack of a comprehensive history of the Jews of Norfolk and Tidewater-Hampton Roads. With no disrespect intended for Irwin Berent's marvellous series in the *Renewal* magazines of several years ago (Berent himself would be the first to admit that without a thorough archival effort he was able merely to scratch the surface), it is unfortunate that we are in danger of losing our history before it can be set down.

The appearance of this work which combines the author's "knowledge of his region and of his Jewish heritage" and which "brings to his writing the unique perspective of one who has grown up Jewish in the Bible Belt," is more than good reading. It is also a timely reminder that if, in Eli Evans "the Jews of the South have found their poet laureate," we in this community are still looking. Perhaps after reading *The Lonely Days Were Sundays*, others will agree and will persuade him to return to our town.

September 1993

An exceptionally well-written book

Jackie Mason once quipped, "If Jewish civilization is 6,000 years old, and Chinese civilization is only 4,000 years old, where did the Jews eat on Sunday for 2,000 years?"

O N THE EVE of World War II, Shanghai, the economic capital of China, which had been home to a small Sephardic community of Jews, became the only city in the world that Jewish refugees could enter without a visa. Despite the reality of the Japanese occupation of most of Shanghai following its invasion in 1937, Jewish immigration was permitted, even in defiance of Nazi pressure. Herded into a ghetto by the Japanese, thus resisting Nazi demands that they be exterminated, over 20,000 European Jewish refugees managed to escape the Holocaust and lived out the war under Japanese rule in mainland China.

Escape to Shanghai
A Jewish Community in China
James R. Ross
The Free Press, 2007   298 pages

Escape to Shanghai is a dramatic account of this little known subplot on the big worldwide stage of WWII, and a fascinating one at that. The arriving Jewish refugees, for the most part, had little money and no connections. Shanghai's foreign community had a well-established social and economic hierarchy, near the bottom of which were the European Jews. The Sephardic community, which had originally come from Baghdad about 100 years earlier, enjoyed great wealth, and were near the top of society. The British, of course, were the pinnacle. Somewhere down the list was a fairly sizeable community of Russian Jews who had first settled in Manchuria and subsequently fled to Shanghai. There were a few well-to-do furriers and importers among them, but most worked at lower middle class occupations and some even took menial jobs.

Author Ross, accessing as he did the considerable documentary material available, has created a really good account of Jewish life during a period of great stress and adversity. He has focused on a few individual Jews in telling his story, from which it is possible to generalize on the experiences of the whole community.

The transformation of this compelling story to the motion picture screen has a far smaller chance of fulfillment than did *Schindler's List,* which is a pity, as the cinematographic values of this city with its teeming millions and its polyglot foreign community are breathtaking to contemplate. Since it ain't gonna happen, *Escape to Shanghai,* exceptionally well written, should be on the list of all who have read and been captivated by Thomas Keneally's now-famous novel.

March 1994

A book to please baseball fans

IT IS APPROPRIATE that author Nicholas Dawidoff begins his thoroughly enjoyable reconstruction of a life best described by a phrase from the Cold War, "a mystery wrapped in an enigma," with a prologue entitled, "Who Was Moe Berg?" Moe Berg played baseball for the Chicago White Sox, the Washington Senators (remember them? "Washington: first in war, first in peace, and last in the American League"), and the Boston Red Sox from 1932 to 1939.

How a nice Jewish boy, educated at Princeton (where he is considered, to this day, the best baseball player in the school's history), the Sorbonne, and a graduate of Columbia Law School, a man fluent in half a dozen languages, chose baseball as his career is one of the subjects of Dawidoff's exploration. Hank Greenberg, the handsome, second-generation Detroit star, had turned back the anti-Semitic accusations that Jews were unathletic. Berg, a third-string catcher and then coach, was great copy for a legion of sports writers who found in him a rare intellect, full of great material for those days when there wasn't much to write about.

The Catcher Was a Spy
Nicholas Dawidoff
Pantheon Books, 1994   352 pages

Much has been written about Berg's assignments for the OSS during World War II, and archival material at the CIA headquarters which is on public display confirms the relationship. *The Catcher Was A Spy* deals in great depth with the complete scope of Berg's assignments, particularly that extremely important and sensitive effort to determine Germany's atomic-bomb capability. There is no doubt that the man, of whom it had been said, "... could speak a dozen languages but couldn't hit in any of them," had found an arena to exercise his idiosyncratic style. The difficult task undertaken by the author has been the separation of what was merely apocryphal from the factual. Berg rubbed shoulders with so many people of prominence in the intelligence field that his mystique only deepened.

This was partly due to what Dawidoff describes as the "Bohemian" nature of the OSS as organized by General Donovan. "He hired 'Circus King' Henry Ringling North, John Ford, assorted Vanderbilts,

DuPonts, Mellons and Morgans, as well as members of Murder, Inc.; ... John Birch, Tolstoy's grandson and Toscanini's daughter;... we had all kinds of ego-maniacs and crazies."

In 1945, when the OSS closed down, there were 13,000 employees on its rolls: 1,500 stayed on and became part of the newly formed CIA. Moe Berg was not one of them, and his life took on an inscrutability that almost defies belief.

This magnificently various and fascinating man reminds Ken Burns, director of "The Civil War" and "Baseball," of what a complete metaphor the game of baseball offers our complicated republic. During this summer of the dreaded strike, Nicholas Dawidoff's sympathetic and witty treatment of a truly unique life is superb reading.

September 1994

Moshe Arens' diary chronicles 1988-92; arrives at time which 'tries men's souls'

DID THE BUSH [H.W.] administration intervene in Israeli politics "in an undisguised attempt to bring down the democractically elected government of Israel?" *Broken Covenant*, based on Moshe Arens' diary, chronicles the period from 1988 through 1992, when he was first foreign minister and then defense minister in the Shamir Likud government.

Although memoirs of this type tend to be inordinately self-serving, Arens' book, which clearly presents a "conservative" perspective, is no *apologia pro vita meo*. He accuses the Bush administration of repeated leaks to the press which grossly misrepresented to the world the nature of meetings held with Arens regarding the Arab-Israeli Peace Process; of promising more than they could or intended to deliver in terms of America's promises to protect Israel from Iraqi missiles during the Gulf War; of repeatedly refusing to supply Israel with adequate intelligence information; of using the threat of withholding the $10 billion loan guarantee desperately needed to help resettle *olim* from the former Soviet Union as a means of discrediting the Likud government and of unduly influencing the peace process.

Broken Covenant
American Policy and the Crisis Between the U.S. and Israel
Moshe Arens
Simon and Schuster, 1995   303 pages

The U.S. is not the only subject of his criticism. Arens lashes out at British Prime Minister John Major, then foreign secretary, who told Arens, "the problem with Israel is that it is growing."

Arens' book is very timely, arriving at a moment which "tries men's souls." Recent terrorist attacks have provided Likud members with their strongest argument against the Labor government, and although the survival of a nation may be at stake, it is not impossible to believe that even here party politics is "business as usual."

Which is not to say that Arens would play politics in this situation, but it is his conviction that, were his party in power, it could reverse what appears to be an inevitable withdrawal from Golan and the territories. His belief that the pendulum which swung against Israel's interests during the Bush administration has swung the other way and that President Clinton's problems with Congress and his favorable disposition toward Israel creates an environment in which Rabin could take a harder line.

Arens fears the perception, on the part of those who would harm Israel, that Israel is faltering in its resolve, such that her great strength will ebb and she will be unable to resist Arab aggression. "What fills me with apprehension," he writes, "greater than any I felt even during the difficult years I have described [in this book] is the thought that when the day comes when even the most dovish of Israelis will refuse to submit to further demands, Israel weakened by territorial concessions may then not be strong enough to defend itself."

This writer is always hypnotized by the glimpses into the workings of politics and international diplomacy that such memoirs provide. Anyone interested in one side of the argument, as it were, will wish to read *Broken Covenant*. Which is not to say that its main premise will hold much water. The danger does not come from weakness caused by territorial concession. The greatest danger confronting Israel is the result of weakening autocratic Arab governments, soon likely be overthrown by massive fundamentalist movements. Egypt, the largest Arab nation, is led by an elite which hasn't a clue to the countering of Islamic militancy, and President Mubarak survives at the pure discretion of his military commanders.

How long that will last is uncertain, but the Israeli movement toward peace, with territorial concessions, may be the last slim chance for Mubarak's survival. Israel may be strong enough to turn back any attack, but the heroes of 1948 through 1973 will not be in command for much longer and it is doubtful that Israel is ready to pay the price in blood that a future war will exact.

April 1995

Elise Margolius' history of Ohef Sholom Temple 'an occasion for celebration and consideration'

THE "REISSUE" of Elise Margolius' history of the first 125 years of Ohef Sholom Temple, in conjunction with that indomitable lady's sesquicentennial update covering the years 1964–1994, is an occasion for celebration and consideration.

Although Jews have resided in Tidewater since the late 18th century, most studies brush lightly over the 19th century. Serious details do not appear until about 1900, at which time the major congregations of Ohef Sholom, Beth El and B'nai Israel were fully established and the organization of a diverse Jewish community began.

Our First Century and A Quarter, 1844-1969

Our Sesquicentennial: The Past Twenty-Five Years, 1969-1994

Elise Levy Margolius
Ohef Sholom Temple

Great appreciation is due the careful recording of names and events, of presidents and staffs, of *simchas* and passings. But perhaps more important is the thread which weaves itself through this too-brief history of a congregation struggling to maintain its traditions while confronting the need for change on all fronts, as well as its need to "deal with the competition of the myriad of Jewish organizations."

In the first volume, which incidentally benefitted from very high quality printing with clear and uniformly reproduced photographs not replicated in the new volume, author Margolius reports on Ohef Sholom's growth. The congregation moved from the Cumberland Street building (which in 1880 became the home of the newly organized Beth El) to the former Methodist church on Church Street ("The Pepper Box") to a new building on Freemason and Tripoli Streets, hailed by *The Virginian-Pilot* as one of the most beautiful church [sic] buildings in the South."

Margolius' effort to summarize over a century of development in just a few pages of the first volume, although notable, leaves undone the task of "filling in the details... as an ongoing project of the community." Historian Irwin Berent said as much and expressed his hopes that someday we would go beyond the details of who did what at such-and-such a time and place. So too, with the

110

current volume. The author touches upon important changes within the temple: changes in the prayer book; changes in ritual; the addition of Bat Mitzvah; discussions concerning the wearing of a yarmulke; the organization of a communal supplementary school; the decision to organize a separate Temple school; and so on. A careful reading of the comments of past presidents as to the major accomplishments of their administrations reveals, *inter alia*, the bass notes against which the life of the Temple is played out, in the context of what issues and matters were the concern of other congregations and organizations in the community.

Thus, matters of intermarriage, funding, Israel and the day-to-day events in the life of Jews and the impact Ohef Sholom has on their lives and on the community at large is vaguely revealed to the perceptive reader. There are so many names mentioned which bring back a flood of memories even to a relative newcomer. Who will tell the story of the individual Jews?

Over the years others have tried their hand at setting down part of the history of our Jews in Tidewater. Rabbi Malcolm Stern, Irwin Berent, and others have, with Elise Levy Margolius, made a beginning. Is it not time for a professional historian to gather up all the pieces and at last compile the encyclopedia of Tidewater Jewry which this vibrant, growing and changing community richly deserves?

May 1996

Singularity of Jewishness speaks from pages of enjoyable book

THE FROMMERS, who have taught oral history and who have published *It Happened in Brooklyn* and *It Happened in the Catskills,* have at once a tremendous story to tell us and yet nothing to say. Nothing to say, because they let the people in *Growing Up Jewish in America,* those whose ancestors fought in the Civil War, and those who emigrated from Europe, those who are young (22) and those who are old (99), speak to us instead.

This is a story with a cast of dozens: rabbis, baseball players, tailors and teachers, writers, scientists, musicians and grocers. And what a story emerges from the accounts of those who made the leap from poverty to prosperity in the golden land.

Growing Up Jewish in America

An Oral History

Myrna Katz Frommer and
Harvey Frommer

Harcourt Brace & Co., 2007   254 pages

We have made it a point to record the oral histories of Holocaust survivors, aware that the passage of time will leave us largely dependent upon those histories for our clearest understanding of their journey. Similarly, the very success we have enjoyed in America leaves us a bit nervous, not fully trusting traditional methods of passing knowledge and experience from one generation to the next.

The authors' subject is Jewish childhood across America during this century. Most of my contemporaries wish we had asked more questions about our parents' childhood, those who were children in this country. I have so often regretted not asking my grandfather, who was born in 1878, what his life was like as a boy in America before the turn of the century.

The principal value of this book, other than the sheer joy of reading it, is the dynamic of the lives of the players against a background of the major events of the 20th century. In some respects, the "coming-of-age America" story, so often encountered in our literature, from Steinbeck to Dreiser, from Hemingway to Cather, is echoed in these pages. But in another sense, the Jewish experience is unique, played out as it was through interaction with a frequently hostile gentile world in the context of the immigrant-first-second generation tensions.

There are some great photographs—well, not great as photographs (grainy, faded, what one expects from old photos), but great to look at.

It made me want to get out the old family albums and do the major job of cataloging and captioning I have been promising myself I would do for the past

20 years or so. But the Frommers have, in a way, done the job for us. This is about our *mishpocha*.

Yitz Greenberg: "There were no Republicans in Borough Park. It was a version of the Biblical injunction: 'If I forget thee O Jerusalem...'—'If I vote Republican, let my right hand wither...'"

Sylvia Skoler Portnoy: "There was a branch of our family that lived in New York, and it seemed to me that they had the real Judaism while we in New England had to cope with a Christian world. I thought they felt part of the world in general while we felt apart."

Sol Breibart: "I was bar mitzvahed in the little shul in Charleston in 1927. My family had some friends over to the house and served wine and that was that."

Steven Soldneer: "I'm from the generation that was born in the Depression, grew up during the Holocaust, and experienced as children and teenagers the birth of the State of Israel and its first years of struggle. That's of our memory."

Growing Up Jewish in America is about Jews from small midwestern towns, large southern cities, from orthodox, conservative and reform backgrounds. The clash between the secular and spiritual life, between entrepreneurs and the social reformers—it's all there. And the singularity of the Jewishness of the 100 interviewees is what speaks out loudest from the pages of this enjoyable book.

May 1996

A dramatic example of abuse of power by the church

THE CURRENT SPATE of apologias from Christian authorities is credited in part to the influential research and publication of works such as the best-selling *Hitler's Willing Executioners*. Certainly not all the research is being done by Jewish scholars. However, the recent publication by David I. Kertzer of *The Kidnapping of Edgardo Mortara* represents a dramatic example of the gross abuse of power by the Church and the ultimate and acutely embarrassing admission of abject powerlessness by the Jews of Italy during that period of the mid-19th century we recognize as the *Risorgimento*.

In June of 1858, a six-year-old Jewish boy was taken by force from his home in Bologna by a police squad. As the family watched in horror, unaware that this family tragedy would play a role in altering the course of European history, the boy was spirited to Rome. The kidnapping, prompted by the accusation that the family's Catholic serving girl had secretly had him baptized,

> **The Kidnapping of Edgardo Mortara**
> David I. Kertzer
> Knopf Books, 1996   298 pages

was not unusual in a papal state which featured institutions for the conversion of Jews. What was unusual was the battle over this particular six-year-old which ended in the collapse of the pope's political power and the emergence of the Italian nation-state.

How could the story of an illiterate servant girl, a grocer and a little Jewish child from Bologna have altered the course of Italian and Church history? We are indebted to author Kertzer, himself an award-winning professor of social science, anthropology and history at Brown University, for rescuing this dramatic story from the "ghetto of Jewish history." That Church historians should avoid illumination of this singular example of the Church's mistreatment of Jews is not surprising, especially after the Holocaust. After all, "who was it who developed the tradition in Europe of requiring Jews to wear colored badges... who for centuries taught that any contact between Jews and Christians was polluting to Christians and should be punishable by force?"

The legal questions of the validity of the child's baptism notwithstanding, the struggle by Edgardo's father to reclaim his son, the ensuing involvement of Camillo Cavour, deemed the "father of modern Italy," and the sad story of Edgardo's joining the ranks of the *castrati*, ends finally with Edgardo's death in 1940 as an elderly (88) monk in an obscure monastery.

What is striking about this case is that finally, the world at large took an interest, and finally others rose in protest. The Mortara affair marked a beginning of the end of Jewish institutionalized helplessness. From this incident arose the creation of national and international Jewish self-defense organizations in both Europe and the United States.

Written in brisk style with a flair for the dramatic, *The Kidnapping of Edgardo Mortara* is an extraordinary story which will reward the reader's attention. Kertzer, himself the son of the late Rabbi Morris Kertzer who served as a U.S. army chaplain in Italy during World War II, rarely ceases to fascinate.

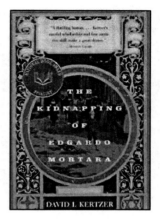

August 1996

Reviewer stops 'to laugh, to cry' and remember

THIS HAS BEEN one of the most difficult books I have ever read. Not because it isn't charmingly written. But at almost every page I have had to stop, to laugh, to cry, to deal with the flood of memories of my own childhood summers in the "country," of my meeting Annabel (my wife) in the Catskills, whose father was athletic director and whose mother was bookkeeper and who, herself, was a counselor at the day camp of Skliar's Hotel, and where, in Monticello, N.Y., we applied for and received our wedding license. The Catskills are in my soul, from the *kochalayns* of White Lake, to the splendor of the Concord, and every kind of place in between. I loved them all.

You will understand, then, and forgive this reviewer for his lack of objectivity. Any book about what was at one time the largest resort area in the nation is bound to engage my attention. The warmth and humor that Cissie Blumberg (a regrettably unmet contemporary of mine at Syracuse University) brings to

Remember the Catskills
Tales of a Recovering Hotel Keeper
Esterita "Cissie" Blumberg
Purple Mountain Press, 1996   292 pages

her treatment of the struggles and achievement of two generations of Catskill Mountain hotelkeepers elicits sincere gratitude on my part to my friends Stan Raiff and Dr. Howard Coron for supporting Cissie's effort and for sending me a copy.

Monuments, the more than 500 hotels were monuments to Eastern European hospitality, prescient models for the Club Meds of today where families find a complete vacation for adults and kids, with food, recreation, entertainment and, very importantly, people like themselves.

It was the women who made the whole system work. Where the women didn't cook, they supervised the cooking, the housekeeping staff and generally handled that most exacting of tasks, the selling of rooms, the negotiating of price, the settling of complaints. They were most often the front line to the customers, who seldom interacted with the men of the family.

The essential ingredient to the success of the whole enterprise was that it was cheap! Those working class immigrants who crowded the Lower East Side of New York at the turn of the century, finally won, through the union movement, the long-dreamed-of vacation with pay. They fled the heat and pollution of the city and found fresh air, gorgeous scenery, food over which to fantasize, and it was cheap; cheap because the gruelling labor of the family, 12 to 14 hours a day, seven days a week throughout the entire 10-to-12-week season, was thrown in free, as it were.

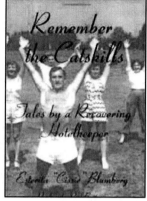

In the mid-thirties, my mother and I stayed the whole summer, for $25 a week, including my father's weekends. By 1950 the rate was still only $10 to 12 a day, including three-and-a-half meals. As Cissie tells it, there were seasons when the waiters took home more than the owners.

It's pretty much all there in *Remembering the Catskills*, including an excellent index of hotels. You may find one you remember. Some will get their kicks from reading about the legendary entertainers who started their careers in the Catskills and who had a lasting impact on the entertainment industry in the United States and around the world. To the long list of such as Danny Kaye, Jerry Lewis, Sid Caesar, Red Buttons, Alan King, Jackie Mason, Milton Berle, Buddy Hackett, Billy Crystal and Robert Klein are those who became major powers in the studios of Hollywood and on Broadway, such as Moss Hart, Dore Schary and Don Hartman.

There is even a tribute to what might be called the equivalent of the circus roustabouts, those men of shadowy origins who put up and take down the great tent. The hotels had their mysterious, usually hard-drinking, jacks-of-all-trades who set the place up each spring and took it down each fall and kept the pumps working and the "lagoons" (cesspools) perking. I remember a raspy voiced, stone-handed, gruff-looking man named Oakie, presumably from Oklahoma, who was at least part native American. Oakie repaired my water pistol and let me ride among the garbage cans in the horse-drawn wagon that he dumped in a clearing of the woods behind the hotel. He made me look away when the wagon passed lovers "communing with nature" in those same woods. Oakie was one of the kindest gentlemen I ever knew.

Inevitably, the great annual invasions of mostly Jews into the traditional havens of anti-Semitism where the Ku Klux Klan was alive and well led to a kind of anti-Semitic code: thus the sobriquet, "Borscht Belt" was born. It kind of played well against "bible belt." Route 17, old Route 17, where unlucky motorists were soaked a dollar a quart for water as their cars overheated on the Wurtsboro Hills, was termed the "Derma Road." And we held our breath driving through Tuxedo, craning our necks to spot the "shamus" on the motorcycle, lying in wait for unsuspecting city drivers.

Cissie Blumberg "set out to tell the story of a special time and place, to present the Catskills as they really were, to applaud the achievement of those who labored there (who baked those little onion rolls for Sunday morning

– the ones we ate with the baked herring?). Our immigrant fathers were not angels, but they had the courage to found, the vision to build, and the strength to maintain a resort industry and a vacation haven—and they did it against odds," she reminds us.

What remains? The beauty of the mountains. What will become of the Catskills? It can never be the same. Of course not. What can be the same in a century in which so much was lost? What remains are the *meises*, Cissie Blumbergs and the stories of all those who lived there, worked there, and vacationed there.

November 1996

Two of interest to the Jewish reader

AS AN UNDERGRADUATE studying Shakespeare 50 years ago, I recall spending much of the first semester studying Elizabethan belief systems, cosmological, epistemological, teleological and whatnot. How else to understand what the playwright was saying; how else to understand what the audience was understanding?

But we never talked about Jews. We more or less skirted the issue. In retrospect it does seem rather strange that the millennia-old question of what is a Jew or who is a Jew, in the context of what or who was an Englishman, was allowed to just slide, unaddressed.

Shakespeare and the Jews
James Shapiro
Columbia University Press, 1996   317 pages

James Shapiro, Professor of English and Comparative Literature at Columbia University (and associate chair of that department) has written a thoroughly researched text, rich with material culled from little known sources. Not an easy read, although the extensive footnotes are blessedly at the back of the book, *Shakespeare and the Jews* goes far beyond the important, yet in some ways superficial, query as to why, if there were only a few hundred in England during Shakespeare's time, there was apparent hatred and fear of the Jews?

As a cultural historian, Shapiro has been more interested in exploring how and why various historians have disagreed with each other in their narratives of the Expulsion of the Jews from England in 1290 and their readmission in 1656. That the direct documents, including the parliamentary minutes, are missing, only adds to the mystery and fuels centuries of exaggerated claims.

Incredible as it may seem, Shakespeare's England was obsessed with questions about Jews. The absurd legends involving Jews in ritual murders raged through the times, but the literature abounds with concerns over how to recognize the Jew, and how to deal with the converted Jew. Shylock's famous insistence on the similarity of Jews and Christians carries its own double entendre wherein a Christian is the antithesis of a Jew, and yet may not be distinguishable from one.

There are even concerns expressed that the Jew may even be, worst of all, a Catholic in disguise. Shapiro gets beyond the rhetoric and reveals the important role these few Jews played in the developing English Renaissance. No matter how many generations went by, the few Jews of England, because of the intertwining of the roots of Christianity, remained an uncanny source of brooding and importance.

IN STARK CONTRAST to their brethren in England, be they tens, hundreds or thousands, the Jews of Germany, and particularly those of Frankfurt, locked in a ghetto, subjected to unending humiliations and punitive taxation and, from time to time, massacred and plundered, nonetheless multiplied and represented about ten percent of the population of Frankfurt in the 14th century.

Founder
A Portrait of the First Rothschild and His Time
Amos Elon
Viking Press, 1996   208 pages

Born into this oppressive ghetto in 1744, clearly beneficiary of the Enlightenment that was sweeping Europe, Meyer Amschel Rothschild became one of the richest men in Europe. He founded a dynasty so powerful that there were those who thought the winds of revolution which were about to sweep Europe in the mid-19th century would come to naught. "There will be no war in Europe," Guttle Rothschild, Meyer's widow wrote in 1847: "My sons will not provide the money for it."

A great deal has been written of the legendary Rothschild clan, yet this is the first biography of its founder, and we are grateful that a writer of Amos Elon's ability has undertaken the task. Not a definitive work (although it certainly defines its subject—but that term has come to imply finality and ultimateness), *Founder* portrays Meyer Amschel as an extraordinary man and portrays as well his times, the condition of the Jews, and the state of Germany until the collapse of the old order brought about by Napoleonic conquest.

Publication of *Founder* this month corresponds neatly to the current exhibition at the Jewish Museum in New York, "From Court Jews to the Rothschilds: Art, Patronage, and Power, 1600-1800." How ironic indeed that this celebration of "kosher Baroque" has a counterpart in the story of a man whose legacy includes not one trustworthy painting. Elon, a master, struggles to unblur Meyer's silhouette.

November 1996

Two books share pain and joy of Jewish women with Black husbands

THIS REVIEWER was initially drawn to James McBride's well-crafted tribute from a black man to his white mother by the fact that his mother was the daughter of an itinerant orthodox rabbi and by the circumstances of her childhood in Suffolk, Virginia, during the Great Depression.

Loaned to me by a friend, *The Color of Water* is a moving example of a growing genre within a growing genre. Interracial families are finding the voice with which to express, admire or deny their fears, hate, shame, love, suffering and joy. Jewish-black families within that category provide a particular spin to the stories for all the obvious reasons.

The Color of Water
James McBride
Riverhead Books, 1995   230 pages

The odyssey of Ruth McBride Jordan, who was born Rachel Deborah Shilsky (Rachel Dwajra Zylska), in Poland in 1921 and whose family immigrated to America when she was two, is told with great narrative skill by her son, a writer and musician of considerable success, who, along with his 11 brothers and sisters, has amassed a shower of undergraduate, graduate and professional degrees.

Rachel's escape from drudgery and sexual abuse as a child was the cause of her abandonment of the forms of her Judaic upbringing and her subsequent denial even of her racial heritage. Yet even when embracing Christianity with a whole heart, and co-founding a successful African-American church, Rachel/Ruth has lived her life through her relentless drive to educate her large family. Unable to depend upon her immigrant mother's well-established family in New York, she nevertheless, in a way, understood and forgave them.

"Mameh's sisters were more about money than anything else, and any hurts that popped up along the way, they just swept them under the rug. They were all trying hard to be Americans, you know, not knowing what to keep and what to leave behind."

Natives of Tidewater will recognize the names of Jewish families from Suffolk; they're in the book: Aubrey and Frank Sheffer, Gerry Jaffe (whose meat-packing plant is prominently mentioned), Helen Weintraub and Aubrey Rubenstein. And they will remember, too, the family of Rabbi Fishel Shilsky, his wife Hudis, their son Sam (killed in Korea), Gladys, and of course Rachel.

McBride's technique of interspersing personal lifetime reminiscences of his family life with flashback chapters of his mother's life helps create a dramatic tension in the book and creates a kind of docu-novel in which pieces of the mystery of Rachel/Ruth's fascinating journey are revealed little by little, much the same as they were discovered by the author, who had to coax the story from his mother.

The Color of Water reveals hard realities from hard times; it is at once a study in race relations, family and religion – not always pleasant, but always hopeful.

JANE LAZARRE'S *Beyond the Whiteness of Whiteness*, the memoir of a white mother of black sons, while equally extraordinary, is as different from *The Color of Water* as, shall we say, black from white.

The author is director of the Jewish Writing Program and Professor of Writing and Literature at the Eugene Lang College, at the New School for Social Research, and she has published several novels. The dust jacket proclaims that she has crafted a compelling narrative; compelling it is, but without the narrative drive of McBride's work.

This book is more about choosing, because one must. "I am Black," Jane Lazarre's son tells her. "I have a Jewish mother, but I am not 'biracial.' That term is meaningless too me." The author has difficulty with those who don't see that she is no longer an ordinary white woman. "The whiteness of whiteness," she exclaims, "is the blindness of willful innocence. It is being oblivious, out of ignorance or callousness or bigotry or fear, to the history and legacy of American slavery, to the generation of racial oppression continuing; to the repeated indignities experienced by Black Americans every single day ..."

Beyond the Whiteness of Whiteness

Jane Lazarre
Duke University Press, 1996   140 pages

That her son knows when he is in a group of people who are white, Jewish or not, that he is a Black man, celebrating his Black culture and not secure in his Jewish culture, is not totally shocking. Although part of this feeling is related to racial "comfort," one can only wonder what might have been his feelings had his mother been other than an unreligious, essentially unobservant Jew.

It is too easy in a brief review such as this to oversimplify and thereby do a great injustice to what is a great gift, this personal gift of Jane Lazarre. Yes, it is sometime difficult to come to grips with the fact that after 14 generations of slavery in this country, and only four or five of "freedom" without any semblance of equality, we are coming to the close of the first generation in our history following the Equal Rights Amendment of 1964.

That this millennium should end with our society so divided still is probably the greatest disappointment of my life. But as James Baldwin has said, "This world is white no longer, and it will never be white again."

It seems basic that just as you "don't have to be Jewish to enjoy Levy's Rye," you "don't have to be Black to realize that African American thought and experience is essential for all people to learn if we want to understand the truth of what happened to this world over the last few centuries ..."

Jews are very sensitive to the use of the term "Holocaust" to describe anything but the Holocaust. We mustn't trivialize what happened to us. So use a different word. What matters is that what happened to us happened because we were Jews. What happened to Africans who came to our land in chains happened to them for no other reason than they were black. How shameful to trivialize what happened to them. These two slim volumes help us to confront the racism that has shaped our society and which remains our harshest tragedy.

September 1996

Author weaves stories of five families covering a span of nearly a century

LIKE MOST OF US, Jonathan Kaufman was knowledgeable about the Holocaust, but knew little about the Jews who remained in Eastern Europe. How did they and their traditions survive the past half century of Communist rule. And if they did, why?

A Pulitzer Prize-winning reporter and recipient of the National Jewish Book Award (*Broken Alliance: Turbulent Times Between Blacks and Jews in America*), author Kaufman weaves the stories of five families over a span of nearly a century. He aptly anchors his timeline to the ninth of November, a connection which results from conscious planning or one of the most fateful coincidences in his story. The abdication of Kaiser Wilhelm following the first World War, the founding of the ill-fated Weimar Republic and Hitler's unsuccessful Munich beer hall putsch in 1922, all on November 9, may well account for the selection of November 9 for the infamous Kristallnacht which shattered for once and all any hope of a life in Germany for Jews.

A Hole in the Heart of the World
Being Jewish in Eastern Europe
Jonathan Kaufman
Viking Books, 2007   328 pages

But did it? The aftermath of the next great November 9th event—the collapse of the Berlin Wall in 1989—shed a new light on Eastern Europe and the Jews who remained. For those in Germany, East or West, the question they faced was profound: "Was it possible, after the Holocaust, after the Nazis, to live as a Jew in Germany?"

For a short time after World War II, there was hope. Throughout Europe, the synagogues were reopened and the institution of democratic process led the remnant remaining to dream of a Jewish future.

It is necessary for Kaufman to drag us, with his five signal families, through their mental and physical suffering, through their triumphs and disappointments, in order to understand the true phoenix-like rebirth, literally from the ashes, of a persistent, small in numbers, but again large in influence, Jewish community in the post-Nazi, post-Communist Europe. This despite the terrorist bombings and neo-Nazi nationalist movements.

Through the lives of the Gysis, a prominent Jewish family in East Berlin; Estrongo Nachama, a West German Cantor and Auschwitz survivor who makes his way in East Berlin; Sylvia Wittman of Prague, Barbara Asendrych of Warsaw, and Tamas Raj of Budapest, Kaufman reveals the buried heritage they uncover.

One can criticize the author's tendency to be repetitive where the five different story lines share common historical backgrounds, but finally can only empathize with those who, under terrible pressures, made human decisions and compromises, and frequently refused to compromise. Those familiar with the evolution of Edward Serotta's photographic experience over the past 20 years will sense a parallel evolution, just as Jewish visitors to Eastern Europe have seen the Jewish milieu there change from a dying and rapidly aging remnant, to a growing, politically and culturally active Jewish community. We rejoice at the survival of Jewish life in Eastern Europe, and stand awestruck that Judaism lives and fills a hole in the heart of that world.

February 2007

Ellis Island to Ebbets Field is a 'homerun-slam-dunk-k.o.' gift

"**J**EWS HAVE STEREOTYPICALLY been considered people of the book rather than people of the jump shot, right cross, or home run." Thus we have read numerous books about this or that Jewish oddity, the "Jewish athlete."

Most know about Sandy Koufax, who refused to pitch on Yom Kippur. It was a big deal, but until I read Peter Levine's authoritative book, I didn't know that while Sandy was in shul praying, Don Drysdale was out on the mound getting shelled. As he was knocked out in the third inning of the game, he is reported to have said to his manager, Walter Alston, "I bet right now you wish I was Jewish, too?"

Ellis Island to Ebbets Field
Sport and the American
Jewish Experience

Peter Levine

Oxford University Press, 1992   290 pages

Today, nobody cares; it is just assumed that a Jewish athlete may not show up on this or that holy day.

Of course, today there are many fewer professional Jewish athletes. In the '30s and '40s, for example, there averaged about ten Jewish major league baseball players at any given time; four or five in the '50s and '60s; about two now. And therein lies part of the fascination of *Ellis Island to Ebbets Field*; the progression of Jewish sports role models, few in number, but powerful in influence, is measured against the social and economic progress of our people in America, which, for better or worse, impacted so severely upon the Jewish presence in professional sports.

Before I received my review copy I purchased one as a birthday gift for a friend. "Thanks a lot," she said. "My two favorite subjects: sports and Jews!" And so it is a real treat to read about the legendary heroes and those who just missed, the anecdotes, the marvelous stories, the interviews; some of the material doubtless apocryphal, but most meticulously researched and supported by primary sources.

My grandfather used to tell me about Benny Leonard, the world champion boxer who lived in his neighborhood. Levine's coverage of the Jewish boxing greats of the '20s and '30s, in the context of destroying "the theory that the Jews are physical cowards," is a must-read for any young person raised in the era of the "Super-Jew" represented by the Israeli conquerors in the Six-Day War. For not to understand the nexus of our existence in a society where we were thought to lack physical courage, is to be unable to understand why American Jews of the '40s did so little to prevent the Holocaust.

But enough of such serious thought. This book has its delightful side and the interviews with such as Phil Weintraub, Mel Allen, Marty Glickman, Allie Sherman, Goody Rosen, Danny Schayes and others balance a nostalgic dimension against one of sharp immediacy. The author tells us that some of these interviews connected him with his own past. For me, it was like a 50th anniversary high school reunion.

This is not a paperback *Who's Who of Jewish Jocks*. Nor is it an easy skim. The few photos are great, but what an opportunity lost not to have included more. I think, too, that more and lengthier excerpts from the media of the time would have been welcome. Yet, how ungrateful must I appear to be? If you have a friend who is serious about sports as well as serious about Jewishness, Peter Levine's book is a homerun-slam-dunk-k.o.; any such friend, including your husband or wife, will thank you for this Chanukah gift.

December 2007

Book on Amazon fascinates and frustrates in equal measure

FOUR YEARS AGO I had an itch to explore the Amazon River, *efsha*, and without much difficulty persuaded my 15-year-old grandson, Jonathan Anderson, to join me. We flew to Iquitos, Peru, the most isolated city in South America and one of the three most isolated cities in the world (the other two being Lhasa in Tibet and Timbuktu in the Sahara desert). I confess to having been totally unaware of the existence of a community of Jewish *Mestizos* living in what amounts to a remote rain forest.

Jews of the Amazon
Self-Exile in Paradise
Ariel Segal
Jewish Publication Society, 1999   340 pages

Ariel Segal, a native of Caracas, Venezuela, well credentialed in both Jewish studies and Latin American History, now makes his home in Israel, but *Jews of the Amazon* is the outcome of four months spent by the author in Iquitos in 1996, studying the descendants of Jewish men who, over a hundred years ago, left such places as Morocco, Gibraltar, England and Alsace-Lorraine, and traveled into the heart of the Amazon. Seeking fortune and adventure, many married or otherwise cohabited with indigenous Amazonian women, and created a culture which combined elements of both groups.

Segal's book fascinates and frustrates in equal measure, being part narrative, part personal memoir, part historical review, and part scholarly analysis. Suitable for the general nonfiction reader, his effort to syncretize, to reconcile and unite essentially antagonistic systems of philosophy requires a sturdy set of appendices and notes, making up almost one third of the volume.

Lest these Jews, highly assimilated in many respects, be readily dismissed as just that, assimilated Jews with only marginal ties to their faith, Segal finds profound similarities to the circumstances of the Marranos of the Iberian peninsula. Of course, strictly speaking, this would not apply as the Jews of Iquitos were not forcibly converted to Catholicism on pain of death, yet the establishment in Peru of only one legitimate religion prevented, from a practical sense, the open observance of Judaism. Thus we find the Jewish Mestizos "dwellers of a no-man's land between two faiths." James Ramsey Ullman, in the 1930s, described Iquitos as a "city without a country," and reported that "virtually all its business and commerce is in the hands of Europeans—and not only Europeans but European Jews. The list of its principal merchants reads like the roster of the Zionist organization."

Many of the first Jews to settle were *conversos*, Jews forced to convert to Christianity by agents of the Inquisition, and they worked as *caucheros* (literally, rubber man), *mercachifles* (peddler, vendor) and importantly as *regaton*, traders who traveled through the rivers bringing merchandise from the cities to villages in the jungle, bartering it for among other things, native products and rubber. In fact, during the rubber boom they actually chartered steamships to stop in at the plantations and transport the rubber.

So what we are faced with here is indeed a syncretic group, thoroughly assimilated not only in the Christian culture, but in the Amazonian native culture as well, yet desiring to preserve their Jewish ancestors' culture. A few families have emigrated to Israel, others are waiting for permission. The Israeli ambassador and some prominent Lima Jews have shown an interest in the remnants of this Jewish community, which, incidentally, continues to contribute money to the State of Israel.

There is no question that the group has survived as an organized, self-proclaimed Jewish community, and recent work with DNA testing has introduced fascinating new means of determining "who is a Jew?" The new inclusivity, perhaps demanding new *halacha* (if such is not an oxymoron), may be just that new and powerful idea which will save us in the long run from becoming the anachronism predicted (incorrectly) by the Arnold Toynbees of the last century.

This blend of history, anthropology, philosophy and personal recollection, despite its prolixity, is sufficiently fascinating to warrant the reader's attention. How I wish I knew then what I now know. My visit to Iquitos would have been differently organized. And it's a long way back.

May 2000

The American Jewish Plymouth Rock?

DESPITE THE FACT that Jews made beginnings in America, disembarking in Philadelphia, Boston, Baltimore, Norfolk, Charleston and Savannah, as well as New York, "the Lower East Side has become the American Jewish Plymouth Rock," standing "for Jewish authenticity in America for a moment in time when undiluted eastern European culture throbbed in America."

Hasia Diner is the Paul S. and Sylvia Steinberg Professor of American Jewish History at New York University, and this slim volume (182 pages of text, with detailed notes following), really an easy-to-read scholarly monograph, examines the way American Jews, most of whom have never seen the Lower East Side, nor can trace an ancestor there, have made it the place of their memories, their common heritage, regardless of where they live at the outset of the 21st century. Histories of Jewish communities, from Buffalo to Los Angeles, from Hartford to Denver, and from Brownsville in Brooklyn (which had a greater percentage of Jews than did the Lower East Side—95% Jewish in 1905 vs. 50% on the Lower East Side), have established the Lower East Side as a sort of benchmark, an index against which to legitimize their experience.

Lower East Side Memories
A Jewish Place in America

Hasia R. Diner

Princeton University Press, 2000 219 pages

Of course there had been a major Jewish presence on the Lower East Side before the great influx which began in the 1880s. B'nai B'rith, the oldest continuing Jewish organization in modern history, was created there in 1843. But within a decade of the start of the 20th century, many Jews had moved to locations in Washington Heights (upper Manhattan) and the Bronx. One is reminded of what we have seen in Pardes Katz, Israel, where many of the *olim* of the 1950s, from Yemen, Morocco and Iraq have succeeded a generation later in relocating to Petah Tikva, Ramat Gan and even Ranana and Shoham. It only takes another generation before the privations and hardships are forgotten, and our collective memories recall happier times than even the present. Pious elders spoke of rebellious children, but memory speaks of hope and opportunity. Ethnic separation among Sephardim and Russians mirrors that of the Lower East Side immigrants from Germany, Russia, Hungary, Rumania, Galicia and Poland.

One's personal memories go beyond the steaming sweet potatoes purchased from a pushcart (it was a matter of discussion when the price went up in the late 1930s from 2 to 3 cents), beyond the potted lamb's tongues at Moskowitz and Lupowicz; or the *pirogen* at Ratners. In my childhood, the place to buy Czechoslovakian crystal, fine linens or majolica vases was the Lower East Side. And today, despite the tremendous inroads on the area by the Asian community, there is a major "discount" shopping area, where charges are accepted but where cash is king. In my pre-teen years, when Sunday was spent with Mom and Dad, we drove down to the Lower East Side at least monthly. I remember my Dad ordering a piece of strudel for dessert, and when it came, broken up, my Mom complained to the waiter, who replied, "Lady, it may not be so *fency*, but it's *gut!*"

Nowadays the word *maven*, used in everyday American parlance to mean expert, doesn't quite evoke the picture of the original greenhorn, needing to buy a suit and having insufficient funds to pay for it, enlisting the services of a maven who took him into the clothing store on East Broadway, coached him into the perfect suit and paid for it. The transaction went something like this:

The suit had no price tag, but used a simple code. Take off the first and last numbers and read it backwards. Thus a suit marked 600517 cost $15.00. The maven laid out the money and the greenhorn paid him $2 a week for 10 to 20 weeks, depending on the degree of avarice involved.

I remember buying suits in this store, except we knew the owner and the code.

Readers of *Lower East Side Memories* will appreciate the exploding of some myths and the factual analysis of others. Diner's research is impressive, and her exploration of children's stories, novels, movies, museum exhibits, TV shows and delis reveals how the Lower East Side became awash in a kind of "memory culture." It is a pity that the maps reproduced are barely legible without a magnifying glass, but Diner's interesting work of historical scholarship leaves us with the understanding that although the facts of the history of the Lower East Side deviate substantially from our collective memories, those memories are in no way diminished, for the Lower East Side is a worthy icon of the entire immigrant Jewish experience.

November 2000

A fresh, caring, engaging approach to the Cuban-Jewish journey

THIS WRITER AND HIS FAMILY were stationed for two years in the United States Naval Base, Guantanamo Bay, Cuba, during and just after the revolution which brought Fidel Castro to power in January 1959. Although the small community of Jewish personnel on the Naval Base held Shabbat services and celebrated holidays and festivals together, it never occurred to any of us that there were Jews in Cuba, much less in Guantanamo City, just a few miles from the base, or in Santiago, the nearest "big city."

Cuban-Jewish Journeys
Searching for Identity, Home, and History in Miami
Caroline Bettinger-Lopez
Foreword by Ruth Behar
University of Tennessee, 2000   277 pages

Sadly, the approximately 3,500 Cuban Jews who fled the new totalitarian government (the old totalitarian government of Fulgencio Batista, interestingly, permitted the free practice of religion), were confronted by the same ignorance on the part of the organized Jewish community of Greater Miami.

Caroline Bettinger-Lopez did the bulk of the research presented in *Cuban-Jewish Journeys* for her senior thesis while an undergraduate student of anthropology at the University of Michigan. Her precocious thesis, elaborated and reflected upon, became the book; thus, from time to time the reader will need to overlook a scintilla of youthful researchers. This will not be difficult, for at the outset it must be said that her work is marked by a fresh, caring, and engaged approach to one of the bittersweet sagas of the perennial diasporic Jewish condition.

If the 1950s saw unprecedented prosperity for many Jewish Cubans, the decade of the '60s saw them joining the wave of Cubans crossing the 90 miles across the Florida Straits to be greeted as "temporary refugees." Some Cubans relocated to New York, Puerto Rico and Latin America, but tens of thousands chose South Florida, creating in Miami the largest Cuban exile center in the world.

It is at this point that the reader must come to grips with the manner by which we define the exiles, how they have defined themselves, and how that definition has been transformed over time. For just as Jews have variously been classified as Jewish-Americans (much the same as African-Americans, or Italian-Americans) and American Jews (Americans who just happen to be Jewish), author Bettinger-Lopez goes to considerable lengths to inform the reader that the 90-mile journey across the Florida Straits pales beside the journey these "temporary refugees" faced in transforming themselves from Jewish-Cubans to Cuban Jews.

It was a matter of supreme irony that Ashkenazim from Eastern Europe and Sephardim from Turkey and the Levant, frustrated in their effort to reach the Land of Opportunity by the legislation of 1924 which effectively closed America's doors to further mass immigration, settled in Cuba. "Look how things turn out," offered a Cuban-Jewish leader in Florida. "Our fathers stayed in Cuba because it was the country closest to the United States. We came to the States because it was the country closest to Cuba."

Cuban-Jewish Journeys, then, sifts the contemporary documents, books, articles dealing with the 40 years of life in South Florida, and overlays upon this distillation revealing and touching interviews with Cuban-Jews of varying backgrounds and lifestyles. Bettinger-Lopez has done what is most difficult for an anthropologist; by allowing herself to penetrate the lives of her subjects, she has taken on their problems, their successes, their joys and heartaches.

The immigrants' perception is that they were not welcomed by the American Jewish community which mistakenly looked upon them as having money, not in need of help and not likely to remain. Yet we learn that many left everything behind; and the professionals among the refugees weren't licensed to practice until much later, following the establishment of special licensing schools. (On a personal level, I know of Cuban-Jewish dentists working as dishwashers in a Polynesian restaurant owned by friends of my family.) With the exception of one synagogue, the Conservative Temple Menorah in Miami Beach, the religious community failed to reach out to the newcomers, and the Greater Miami Federation, despite latter-day efforts which have successfully integrated the Cuban Jews into the communal structure, basically took the position that "... we must try to persuade Cuban-Jewish refugees that they have no future in Miami..."

Bettinger-Lopez devotes considerable effort to make clear the cultural barriers which had to be overcome. For example, the traditional (orthodox) Sephardic Cubans spoke no Yiddish; therefore, the American Orthodox Ashkenazi Jews simply couldn't believe they were Jewish. Of particular interest is the mixed reception given to, and the ultimate integration within the earlier arriving Cuban-Jewish community, of Mariel boat people two decades later.

The eponymous *Journey* fascinates. The success of this community is legend, and well documented by Bettinger-Lopez. But the more subtle changes are skillfully revealed as the next generation, warm to its Cuban heritage, joins prior immigrant groups in the intensive assimilation they have enjoyed and yet decry. The story is the same, yet importantly different in one respect. This is a diaspora which has faced two migrations in less than one century, two sets of challenges, two sets of cultural allegiances. The 21st century Cuban-Jew, self-described by the younger set as *Jewbans* or *Jubans*, are exuberant participants in American life who cling to their multiple heritages, deal with changing gender roles (a major issue when viewed from a Latino perspective), and look to their synagogues as the center of social and political life, perhaps even more than their religious life. And somehow, amidst the turmoil of these past 40 years, there has been time to rekindle a great love and support for Israel, especially among the youth.

One wishes this book could have been printed in larger type, with more and better photographs, while at the same time being grateful for having it at all. There are few among us who have any first-hand remembrances of places like Belz or Riga, yet the *shtetls* are imprinted in our collective memories and hearts. How much more recent and more poignant for Caroline Bettinger-Lopez' subjects must be remembrances of Havana, Camaguey, and Santiago, and the lives they built there from nothing, only to do it all over again in Miami?

April 2001

Impressive collection of photographs

FROM 1881 TO 1921, a great flow of more than two million Yiddish speaking immigrants arrived in New York harbor. For the most part, they were dirt-poor, spoke little or no English and had no idea of the grinding poverty they would face in the *goldena medina*.

In 1882, Abraham Cahan arrived from Vilna, Lithuania, an old-line socialist on the run from the czar's secret police. Cahan quickly learned English, earned his spurs on the Hearst and Pulitzer papers and became one of the founders, in 1887, and subsequently the editor of the most successful newspaper written in the language of the old country. *The Jewish Daily Forward,* better known to its readers, writers, editors and typesetters as the *Forverts,* in its heyday had a circulation of 250,000, larger than the *New York Times.*

A Living Lens
Photographs of Jewish Life
from the Pages of *The Forward*
Edited by Alana Newhouse
W. W. Norton, 2007   352 pages

The *Forverts,* along with other successful Yiddish newspapers, accomplished the task of assimilation all too well. The American children of the immigrants were able to speak Yiddish, but soon lost the ability to read Yiddish, and by the 1930s, only a trickle of Jews made their way to New York, and the Yiddish language edition barely outlived World War II.

In the mid 1990s as the newspaper, now an English language weekly, prepared to celebrate its 100th anniversary, staff members discovered the metal filing cabinets which comprised the archives and which had been moved from the *Forverts* building on East Broadway to a storage room in the paper's new home on East Thirty-Third Street. Thus another precious legacy, a collection of more than 40,000 photographs that spanned the entire 20th century, was rescued.

As Irving Berlin put it in his song, *The Easter Parade,*

The photographers will snap us, And you'll find that you're in the rotogravure!

The *Forverts* collection, edited for us in this impressive collection, *A Living Lens,* relies heavily on the special Sunday supplement known as the rotogravure, which refers to the process by which the photos and captions were engraved into metal plates for printing. Readers will appreciate the expected classic photos of Lower East Side pushcarts, shops, school kids and Yiddish theater personalities. There were travel photos of major Jewish cities and contributions from readers who were encouraged to send in photos, as well as important contributions from well-known photojournalists such as Roman Vishniac.

Lest the reader think of this collection as one limited to the very dusty past, be assured that the collection covers the last half of the twentieth century as well, beginning, to my surprise, with a photo of our own beloved Chaplain Samuel Sobel (of blessed memory) conducting Sabbath service for the Second Marine Division, aboard the USS *Rockbridge* in 1952. They are all there: the Hollywood producers, the Jewish baseball stars, the presidents, the New York politicians, the Israelis, the whole *mishpacha*.

Excellent commentary throughout is provided by Leon Wieseltier, J. Hoberman, Roger Kahn, and Deborah Lipstadt, among other well known historians and intellectuals.

June 2007

From an esteemed local author

WITH THE CREATION of the Commodore Uriah P. Levy Center and Jewish Chapel at the Naval Academy at Annapolis, it is perhaps time to review once again what remains as the definitive short biography of Commodore Levy, written by another intrepid sailor, Captain Sam Sobel, U.S. Navy (retired).

Uriah P. Levy's apprenticeship to the sea, his service in the United States Navy, culminating in his elevation to flag rank, despite enduring six courts martial, his most memorable humanitarian achievement in the abolition of flogging in the Navy, and finally, the Levy family's saving

Intrepid Sailor
Samuel Sobel
Cresset Publishers, 1980   121 pages

of Monticello and subsequent gifting of it to the American people, spell out in a nutshell the substance of this slim volume. These events, occurring as they did during a period of great turmoil in our history, are surrounded by such interesting circumstances as would whet the appetite of a scholar such as our own Sam Sobel, who, among his many services to our country for which he has been highly decorated (Legion of Merit with Gold Star, Bronze Star Medal with Combat V, Navy Commendation Medal and Purple Heart Medal), is recognized as the spiritual architect of the beautiful Commodore Levy Chapel on the Norfolk Naval Station.

Sobel's research and lucid biographical portrayal reveals the young Levy, shipping out as a cabin boy, but stipulating that he be permitted to return home to Philadelphia in time for his bar mitzvah, a not inconsiderable feat at the dawn of the 19th century. The youthful Lieutenant Levy, when offered a captaincy and command of a new 60-gun frigate by the emperor of Brazil, politely declined, adding "Sir, I would rather serve as a cabin boy in the American Navy than as captain in any other service in the world!" All the while fighting off anti-Semitic challenges, Levy served until his death in 1862, having spent 60 years at sea and over half a century in the service of his country.

Much of the remainder of *Intrepid Sailor* is devoted to Levy's struggle to have his gift of Monticello, along with his estate, accepted by the federal government or the Commonwealth of Virginia. Not until 1915 did Congress finally enact legislation making the transfer of Thomas Jefferson's home possible. A final and important chapter involves the creation of the Levy Chapel in Norfolk, one which involved the Tidewater Jewish community and with which the community has an ongoing and important relationship.

It is not, therefore, surprising that Jewish leaders in Tidewater have been at the forefront in raising funds for the new facility at the Naval Academy, more than just a chapel, but a study center to be used by all midshipmen, a fitting legacy to our "intrepid sailor," and an appropriate time to take another look at the life of service of our esteemed author, Captain Samuel Sobel.

August 2007

A definitive work

THE COLLECTION OF INTELLIGENCE, domestic or foreign, military, political or industrial, its analysis, dissemination and operational application is the stuff of wildly popular fiction and even more dramatic and gripping non-fiction. We tend to misuse the term "spy" when, for example, we refer to "spy satellites," which are after all not covert, but right up there in plain view. Our own national experience has been that disaster awaits us when intelligence organizations get too involved with operations, as evidenced by the CIA's Bay of Pigs fiasco and more recent operation of interrogation stations outside of the United States.

> **Gideon's Spies**
> **The Secret History of the Mossad**
> Gordon Thomas
> Thomas Dunne Books, 2007   616 pages

Having said that, one must accord Israel's elite Mossad high honors for its largely successful combining of the collection of intelligence and the conduct of operations. Gordon Thomas details some of Mossad's catastrophic operations, as well. The abortive 1997 effort to assassinate Khalid Meshal, a Hamas leader living in Amman, is a case in point. Prime Minister Netanyahu was determined to exact immediate revenge for the deadly suicide bombing of a Jerusalem marketplace.

Over the objections of Mossad leadership, who thought it unwise to attempt an assassination in the capital city of a peaceful neighbor, Netanyahu insisted on doing it "here and now." The botched operation was a huge embarrassment to Israel and forced the Prime Minister to release even more dangerous terrorists in exchange for captive Mossad agents.

Thomas walks us once again through some of the early operations, tracking down and assassinating various terrorist murderers of women and children and suppliers of weapons to terrorist organizations. The background on how the Mossad was created and how it functioned on a minute budget, mainly through the use of a small, but totally dedicated and well trained *katsas* (case officers and agents), augmented by more numerous *safanim* (lay or semi-professional units to target PLO), is rendered in fascinating detail. The eponymous Gideon, of course, is the biblical hero who saved Israel against superior enemy forces because he had better intelligence. Thus the Mossadniks are dubbed latter-day Gideonites.

Gordon Thomas has updated his 1995 classic and the reader may be somewhat surprised to find heretofore unreported commentary from an Israeli perspective on the politicizing of both the CIA and the British MI6 which resulted in tainted intelligence leading up to the Plame affair, the spurious documents indicating that yellowcake ore had been secretly sold to Iraq.

Gideon's Spies is a big fat book, far more interesting than any three espionage novels placed end to end, and Thomas has generously provided us with a glossary of political and tradecraft terms, a brief Arabic glossary, notes on his impressive list of sources, a selective bibliography and a comprehensive index. In a way this account of Israel's secret intelligence service is a history of Israel itself. Israel has had to defend itself for almost 60 years and its first line of defense in large measure has been the knowledge provided by the Mossad. While no one book can possibly tell the whole story, particularly about an organization whose work has been cloaked in secrecy (although of late Mossad has been more open about releasing information about its *kidon* [assassination] units—as a deterrent), Gordon Thomas has given us what is the definitive work on this legendary service—for now.

August 2007

HOLOCAUST

Two by Tec

MANY OF US SAT, transfixed, between Rosh Hashanah and Yom Kippur, by the incomparable production, *The Civil War,* aired on public television.

Memories flooded back from my childhood, and once again I watched the Decoration Day parade down the then-glorious Grand Concourse in the Bronx. I was seven, eight, or nine years old, and remember the parade led by the old veterans of the Spanish American War, followed by those of the Great War. Seated in front of the reviewing stand were some really old gents, bemedalled, bearded, leaning on canes and crutches, the few survivors of the Grand Army of the Republic.

When Light Pierced the Darkness
Nechama Tec
Oxford University Press   262 pages

Dry Tears
Nechama Tec
Oxford University Press   242 pages

For most of us, the most compelling feature of the television series was the juxtaposition of the memoirs, the letters of the "ordinary" people, with the photography of the *Shoah*. For *Shoah* it was, from the staggering thought of six million enslaved for 250 years (how many lifetimes of suffering does that add up to?), to the execution of the Andersonville death factory commander who went to the gallows declaring that he was just following orders! The memoirs of the dead and survivors alike, preserved in attics and basements, as well as official archives, moved us to tears.

Nechama Tec, Professor of Sociology at the University of Connecticut, and the author of *Dry Tears: The Story of a Lost Childhood,* will visit our community on Yom Hashoah. A Holocaust survivor who lived in Poland for three years during World War II, passing as a Christian, Tec was unable to deal with her memories for 30 years. But then, in 1984, her poignant story of a Jewish girl who was eight years old when the war began, and 14 when it was over, became part of the what we have recognized as a whole new generation of memoirs, not blunted, but in many ways sharpened, by the passage of time. Tec was one of the fortunate few who survived World War II by passing as a Christian. She was sheltered by Christian Poles without whose help she would have died.

Her book, and particularly the Oxford University Press edition, with the invaluable Epilogue added, illuminates more than just the long struggle for survival, and the attitudes of all the helpers, righteous and otherwise. For here is a case wherein the survivors found themselves, for a time, in a highly favored position during the immediate postwar period when Tec's father was running a prosperous factory. But by the end of 1945, Poland was still unsafe for Jews, and the Communist rule was particularly distasteful. The family fled to the West.

Citing the Anne Frank case as an example in *When Light Pierced the Darkness*, Nechama Tec directs our attention to the sharp contrast between the almost universal familiarity with the Anne Frank story, and the lack of knowledge by most about the Frank family's Christian benefactors and how they fared. The social scientist returned to Poland to ask social scientist-type questions, but returned with a very human and moving body of knowledge, at once systematic, scrupulous, and thoughtful: poignant and reverent.

Tec's investigation into this special angle of Holocaust research centers around three questions:

First, what was it like to "pass" and hide among Christians? Second, describe the paid Christian helper. Describe the anti-Semitic Christian helper. Finally, what were the motivations of the "righteous helper"?

Her examination of such interesting corners is foreshadowed by the questions themselves. An anti-Semitic "righteous" person? Well, not righteous, as defined, but a helper nonetheless. And for those who wonder why so few were helped, there is the fascinating perspective shed on the typical Polish Jew of that era—such that we understand that the Jewish fugitive was as obvious, in most cases, within the Polish milieu, as the runaway slave in America. For in the Poland of the 1930s, when 75 percent of the Jews were urban dwellers and 75 percent of the Poles were rural dwellers; and where less than 10 percent of Polish Jews could be considered assimilated; and where Jews didn't even speak an acceptable Polish; there simply was no chance to "pass" for the vast majority.

The reader may be somewhat put off by the statistical analysis. But you are urged to get past that, for this is not really a book of statistics. It is decidedly anecdotal, and filled with the memoirs, the primary source material of the time. We look forward to having Ms. Tec visit our community this spring, and the best preparation for that visit would seem to be a look into the works reviewed herein.

Her latest work, *In The Lion's Den*, will be reviewed when received. We would do well to read upon Ms. Tec before her visit.

December 1990

'Nonfiction' novel *In the Lion's Den* deserves space in personal libraries

WE HAD HOPED to receive a review copy of *In The Lion's Den* in time to report on it before Nechama Tec's visit to Tidewater in connection with the community's observance of Yom Hashoah. Well, we almost made it, or just made it, depending on when you get and if you read your newspaper. But this is the Week of Remembrance, and this is the book her growing "fan club" has been waiting for.

In The Lion's Den
The Life of Oswald Rufeisen

Nechama Tec
Oxford University Press, 1990 279 pages

Recent Holocaust literature, as we have mentioned, perhaps ad nauseam, tends to focus upon a particular aspect of the Holocaust. The struggle for survival and the effort to resist has been a major theme of late, impelled by the desire to dispel the unwarranted but unfortunately common belief that the victims went meekly to their fate, like sheep into the slaughter pens.

Another stream, feeding into the welling body of literature, has been the one dealing with the "righteous Christian," the term "righteous," of course, is itself capable of being split into several tributaries.

And now, author Tec has given us a novel novel, rivalling the work of Tom Clancy, differing in this respect; it is nonfiction, based on meticulous research, and I couldn't put it down. Oswald Rufeisen represents part of what was not even a tributary, but a mere trickle, a select group of Jews, who, while passing as Christians, used their connections against the Nazis for the benefit of potential victims. At this point in time, there is such a short list that they can be numbered on one hand.

In *When Light Pierced the Darkness*, the point was made that in the Poland of the 1930s less than 10 percent of Polish Jews could be considered fluent in Polish. "Rufeisen," therefore, as one of few who could speak fluent German, and as a youth of 17 years, fled Poland ahead of the German army. His ability to pass as half-Polish and half-German led him to a position as translator and personal secretary to the German head of police. Living in constant fear of discovery, he nevertheless managed to pass information along about Nazi plans, and actually sabotage these plans and others. His arming of the Jews of the Mir ghetto and the organization of their escape, is but one of the fascinating episodes of *In The Lion's Den*, an appropriate title, inasmuch as Rufeisen, when denounced, found asylum in a convent, converted to Catholicism, and is known as Father *Daniel*.

We will leave to the reader the task of determining whether in the end Oswald Rufeisen, whose Hebrew name was Shmuel, is a Jewish Christian or a Christian Jew. His life's work now is building bridges between the two ideologies. This Pulitzer Prize nominee is part of our Holocaust Memorial Library, however, it deserves a place in the reader's personal library.

April 1991

The Transfer Agreement tells story of pact between Jews and Third Reich

PICKING UP THIS HEFTY paperback, a new and updated edition of the best-selling (1984) dramatic story of a pact between the Third Reich and Jewish Palestine, one asks oneself, "Is it possible that I never read this book, and know nothing about the entire matter, or is it just that I have forgotten? And if I have forgotten, haven't most readers? And isn't it time for a wake-up and a reminder?" For in truth, the details of the agreement by which Zionist movement leadership arranged the transfer of some 60,000 German Jews and about $200 million to Jewish Palestine in 1933 in exchange for the halting of the worldwide Jewish-led anti-Nazi boycott which threatened to topple the Hitler regime at a time when it was most vulnerable, boggles the mind and compels our attention.

The Transfer Agreement

Edwin Black

New Dialog Press, 2000 430 pages

Author Edwin Black, the son of Polish Holocaust survivors, recaptures the drama of the story in highly readable prose without sacrificing the attention to detail resulting from five years of investigation by a team of researchers and translators in the U.S., England, Germany and Israel.

Out of the 35,000-plus documents uncovered comes much more than just the story of this fabled transaction. For in the course of detailing the intensely controversial negotiations between Jews and Nazis, Black provides an insight into what was going on in 1933 in Jewish circles, Zionist and non-Zionist, worldwide. Activities in Jewish Palestine, relationships with moderate and hard-lining Arabs and the political struggles among left, right and center groups of Jews in Israel and around the world, are brought back to life.

And what turmoil surrounds the passion of Chaim Arlosoroff and his brutal assassination, Sam Cohen and others involved in the incredibly complex financial arrangements surrounding the Transfer Agreement? For as the Zionists doubled their efforts for what they perceived (correctly) be a "now or never" operation. Hitlerism was spreading to every country housing people of German heritage. By this fateful summer of 1933, the Nazi menace was achieving global proportions. In Austria, Jewish quotas in professions and colleges were being debated. In Mexico the Confia, an organization of Nazi sympathizers, asked the government to consider Jewish businessmen foreigners and to levy punitive taxes on them. Anti-Jewish incidents, ranging from student protests to the banning of newspapers, occur in Czechoslovakia, Rumania, Canada, Hungary, England, and the United States.

Although *The Transfer Agreement* created a considerable stir when it first appeared, that was because, according to the author, "...the book's topic was ahead of its time."

"The World," he adds, "was not ready to comprehend complicated asset transfer discussions between the Zionists and the Nazis, two groups whose relations were not widely known at the time."

But with a gun to the head of the Jewish people, Zionists did undertake the Transfer Agreement. Abe Foxman, Director of the Anti-Defamation League, agrees, as "Desperate situations, hard choices, agonizing possibilities and the debates between rescue and relief have filled my world since infancy."

If we weren't there, faced with heartbreaking decisions, how can we judge? Yet, thanks to the timely reissue of this terribly interesting chronicle of the era of burgeoning Nazi power, these choices can be viewed in a new light. Certainly, none can suppose that the world, despite the early success of the Jewish-led boycott, was prepared to save the Jews who weren't able to save themselves.

June 2000

A conservative view

THAT POPE JOHN PAUL II, the first Pope to enter the Great Synagogue of Rome in 1,900 years and the first Pope to ask forgiveness at the Western Wall in Jerusalem, could now be criticized for promoting the canonization of Pope Pius XII, is perhaps at the source of efforts to demonstrate that Pius XII was a true philo-Semite, responsible for saving thousands of Jewish lives during the Holocaust.

The Myth of Hitler's Pope
How Pope Pius XII
Rescued Jews from the Nazis
Rabbi David G. Dalin
Regnery Publishing, 2005   209 pages

Rabbi David G. Dalin, professor of history and political science at Ave Maria University in Naples, Fla., has set out to accomplish two things with this book: first, to refute the thesis of John Cornwell's *Hitler's Pope*, that Pius XII was in fact a collaborator of the Nazis; and second, to focus attention on Hitler's real cleric, Grand Mufti Hajj Amin al-Husseini, who established residence in Berlin and advised and assisted the Nazis in carrying out the "Final Solution."

Eugenio Pacelli, a career Vatican diplomat who was considered by the Nazis to be a "Jew-loving" cardinal before being elevated to the papacy as Pius XII, was vilified after his death in a play called *The Deputy* for his "moral cowardice and inexcusable silence as Europe's Jews were being murdered by the Nazis." Even worse, he is accused of being a Nazi collaborator.

Rabbi Dalin's research reveals the pronouncements of generations of popes, from Innocent IV, Gregory X, Martin V and Paul III, rejecting and condemning the ritual blood libel responsible for so many murderous pogroms. Numerous documents are quoted in which a series of papal pronouncements ordered that Jews be allowed to live in peace and worship in their synagogues. It is even implied that the Spanish Inquisition was fostered and promoted by the royal courts of Spain and Portugal, rather than the Church itself. The author sternly takes to task John Cornwell as well as Daniel Goldhagen (*Hitler's Willing Executioners* and *A Moral Reckoning*), and James Carroll (*Constantine's Sword*) for repeating every discredited accusation and for omitting "all mention of the countervailing traditions of tolerance" within Roman Catholic thought, past and present.

One need not get buried in the thousands of documents now available to scholars of every persuasion to know that, despite papal pronouncements of love for the Jews over the centuries, Jews were herded into ghettos (not closed in Rome until 1870), forced to wear the yellow star of David on their clothing (a papal invention later adopted by the Nazis), and allowed barely to exist as distinctively second-class citizens. As late as 1928, Pius XI condemned unreservedly "hatred against the people *once chosen* by God..." (italics mine).

Moreover, Rabbi Dalin tips his hand in the very first chapter as he rails against the "liberal media" and "liberal Catholics." His epithetical use of the "L" word 16 times in the first chapter alone is unfortunate to say the least, coloring and, in this writer's view, weakening his argument.

The author successfully argues that Eugenio Pacelli was not anti-Semitic and certainly not in collaboration with Hitler. In 1936 Pacelli played a major role in silencing the infamous American hatemonger Father Coughlin, and in 1938 while Vatican secretary of state, he declared "it is impossible for a Christian to take part in anti-Semitism. Anti-Semitism is inadmissible; spiritually we are all Semites." In point of fact, Germany did not send a representative to Pacelli's coronation as pope, and it is important to understand that he did act to protect most of the Jews of Rome.

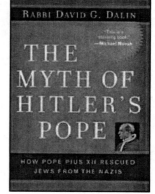

But questions remain unanswered. Certainly Cardinal Faulhaber, Archbishop of Munich, publicly "deplored the Nazis' persecution of Jews and other non-Aryans." But Faulhaber failed to protest officially, seeing the preservation of the Church as his central task. Similarly, it is theorized that Pius XII, whom the Nazis had threatened to kidnap, feared protesting the Germans' anti-Jewish actions lest that trigger reprisals against the Vatican. Yet, that silence persisted when Hungary began the deportation and execution of its Jews in June of 1944, when Rome and the Vatican were already under the protection of Allied troops. Silence prevailed even in the face of the pronouncements of the Primate of Hungary, Monsignor Seredi, who declared that "we have no objection to the measures taken...we do not protest against the elimination of the noxious influence of the Jews."

It is one thing to defend the reputation of a much-maligned pope; it is another thing entirely to mount a diatribe against all the voices within the Church seeking further change.

Rabbi Dalin breaks no new ground with his chapter on *Hitler's Mufti: Muslim Anti-Semitism and the Continuing Islamic War against the Jews*, but it does serve as a useful counterpoint to his defense of Pius XII. For while some might have wished for the Pope to do more for Jews during the Holocaust, a powerful Muslim cleric was frequently closeted with Hitler and repeatedly called for the destruction of European Jewry. Grand Mufti Al-Husseini, welcomed by German Muslims as the "Führer of the Arabic World," characterized the Jews as "the most fierce enemies of the Muslims" and an "ever-corruptive element" in the world.

The latter part of the 20th century was witness to groundbreaking strides in drawing Jews and Catholics together. The revolutionary work of Popes John XXIII and John Paul II brings Catholics and Jews face to face, each with their own valid covenant. There is every reason to hope that Pope Benedict XVI will continue this effort. However, it is one thing for popes to proclaim and another thing for Christians to accept. Clearly, all of the philo-Semitic proclamations of popes through the centuries did little to save Jews from degradation, torture and death. Thus, there seems to be a place for the so-called liberal media to continually illuminate and question.

October 2005

MEMOIRS

Not a 'kiss-and-tell' book about Kirkpatrick

IN MY YOUTH, I seldom danced with a lady after being stood up by her for a date. In 1985, having had Jeane Kirkpatrick cancel her appearance at our United Jewish Fund gala (ironically, Alexander Haig, who was fired as Secretary of State following months of intramural tussling with Kirkpatrick, appeared in Norfolk in her place), my ardor for that particular lady cooled measurably. Yet, having visited the United Nations with a group of campaigners on a Mission to New York, and having been thoroughly depressed by the concrete realization of Israel's virtual isolation there, one must admit that Kirkpatrick's sage and gutsy fulfillment of her mission contributed greatly to the restoration of American credibility at the U.N., and, more particularly, to the non-abandonment of Israel by the United States when the State Department was a shaky and somewhat reluctant supporter.

The Kirkpatrick Mission
Allan Gerson
Free Press, 1991   311 pages

Unusual for works of this nature, it is not a kiss-and-tell book, and Allan Gerson, a key member of the Kirkpatrick team, avoids the kind of self-serving we have come to expect. With history being rewritten in one-year rather than one-century cycles these days, the perspective of as little as five years does much to render this memoir insightful and useful to those who tuned the U.N. out when Arthur Goldberg left.

To understand the importance of Jeane Kirkpatrick's "mission" and her tremendous contribution as a public servant, one need only remember the nature of our "missions" to Washington during the years of her tenure in New York. In those days, we used to run UJA Study Missions to Washington as the second best way of upgrading commitments to the campaign ("missions" to Israel being the best, of course). Customarily, we flew our prospects up in the morning, briefed them at AIPAC, at the Israeli Embassy, at the Pentagon and perhaps at one other place, ending the briefings, always, at the State Department. The negativism towards Israel (pre-George

Schultz), the pro-Arab apologism, the consistent unevenhandedness, made the State Department briefer an unwitting tool for the Campaign. Our missioneers were so infuriated and frightened by what they heard, particularly by the answers to their questions, that our caucuses, held immediately following, were invariably successful.

The U.N. team couldn't always come down on our side, but they exhibited, under Dr. Kirkpatrick, an evenhandedness seldom matched in Washington. Allan Gerson's absorbing account of the political intrigue and the pre-session sessions at which the real battles took place is more than illuminating: it is dramatic, exciting and absolutely first class.

August 1991

Tidewater prepares for Elie Wiesel's return

TIDEWATER PREPARES for the laureate's return; his third visit. In timely fashion we have the second volume of his memoirs (volume one, *All Rivers Run to the Sea*, was published five years ago) to refuel our interest in one who has been considered, against his wishes, a symbol. "Symbols can be repudiated or even erased with impunity. Man is something else, a human being, not a symbol," avers Elie Wiesel.

Wiesel's first appearance in the late '60s as part of the Jewish Forum (we really didn't know from "Tidewater" in those days) was at Ohef Sholom Temple. The sanctuary was packed to hear this great artist discuss the Holocaust in the context of his early works (or was it his early works in terms of the Holocaust?).

And the Sea Is Never Full
Memoirs, 1969
Elie Wiesel
Knopf, 1999   410 pages

Even then he had difficulty accepting the terms used to describe what was to him indescribable: Holocaust; Shoah; Auschwitz; Birkenau. Despite the fact that "the Holocaust defies language and art," even if language and art "are necessary to tell the history that must be told," and because at that time there was little (Primo Levy and a few others) articulate testimony, Wiesel was the witness, but one at a crossroad in his personal and professional life. For the writer and journalist, marriage and parenthood, academic appointment, and elevation to the level of icon was all just ahead of him.

And it is more or less at this point in his and our lives that *And the Sea is Never Full* begins.

The titles, from Ecclesiastes *(All rivers run to the sea, and the sea is never full; ...All things are full of labor, man cannot utter it; the eye is not satisfied with seeing; nor the ear filled with hearing)* foreshadow the next three decades of work: 24 works published since 1970; militancy on behalf of Holocaust survivors, yes, but for all disenfranchised everywhere. During the midpoint of these years he received the Nobel Peace Prize (1986) and returned to Norfolk to help us celebrate our Federation's 50th anniversary.

What he said then is clear in my mind today and far more understandable in the light of this new volume of his memoirs. He packed them in at the JCC's "old" gym, and remarked that "if anyone had told me years ago that there would be a vibrant, strong State of Israel, such as exists today, I wouldn't have believed it.

And if anyone had told me that I wouldn't be living in that state, I wouldn't have believed that either." What emerges from this life is the too-familiar theme of the determined religious observer/scholar/writer/lecturer/cause champion/husband/ father/brother—everything—torn, especially between Israel and its need for his championship (particularly during the era of universal delegitimization and isolation of Israel) and Wiesel's inability to expect any less of Israel than its maintenance of the moral high ground, even when fighting for its very existence.

Of course, even the most self-serving autobiography, if written by one who has been the advisor to, confidant of, and spirited opponent of heads of state, foreign ministers, national chairmen of UJA and presidents of CJF, would be of great interest. Given the opportunity to be the fly on the wall during historic confrontations, Wiesel seldom tries to sugarcoat his actions, even when unpopular. He does simply give his reason and, in retrospect, expresses either regret or satisfaction with the results.

What makes this autobiography far more appealing than most, what one critic has called a "delight," what another calls "highly revealing," is to this reader found in its ambiguity. The sea is never full; the work is never done. Every pleasure in life is accepted with suspicion. Is it deserved?

What cruel price must be paid? If Wiesel, the survivor, was appointed (by self, by history, by his fellow inmates, even) to speak and demand justice on behalf of all those who can't, he has done that and more.

Is it necessary that he continue, on behalf of every vital cause? Of course. Thus, we have Wiesel and Reagan (remember Bitburg?); Wiesel with Mitterrand; Wiesel with Gorbachev; with Lech Walesa; Nechama Lifschiti (former prisoner of conscience); the Dalai Lama and Radovan Karadzic; with Bill Clinton and Yitzhak Rabin.

We have Wiesel in the breach for the past half-century, and particularly the 30 years covered by his not delightful, but compelling, not so much highly revealing as consistently penetrating memoirs. And soon we will have Wiesel in Norfolk once again in celebration of Congregation Beth El's 150th anniversary. Elie Wiesel is a great man, a great personality, probably one who will be cheated—as his Nobel Peace Prize will doubtless mitigate against the well-deserved award of the Nobel Prize for Literature. What will be his message to us next month? If his memoirs and his past is prologue, then his message must clearly be that we continue what it is we do.

To save the life of a single child, no effort is superfluous. To make a tired old man smile is to perform an essential task. To defeat injustice and misfortune, if only for one instant, for a single victim, is to invent a new reason to hope. Elie Wiesel may wish for others to take over. But he gives us hope, embracing the future without abandoning the past And with the Holocaust itself on trial in England, neither his nor our task is completed.

Today I Am a Boy treats readers

DAVID HAYS, A VETERAN of Broadway, having designed sets and lighting for more than 50 plays, musicals, and ballets (for George Balanchine at the New York City Ballet), decided some years ago to recount his and his son's adventures sailing a small boat around Cape Horn. The result was a *New York Times* bestseller. At the age of 66 he decided to become a Bar Mitzvah.

His membership in a Connecticut synagogue whose congregation was "only 48% Jewish," and his relationship with the young rabbi ("younger than my kids") led him to join a group of eight twelve-year-olds studying together for their Bar and Bat mitzvah. The result is a witty, wise, and warm story of a mature man's search for God and for meaning.

Today I Am A Boy
The Bar Mitzvah Journey
of a Grown Man
David Hays
Touchstone Books, 2001   255 pages

Hays' hijinks with the group he calls the "Hormone Hurricanes," as he struggles to learn Hebrew and the ancient rituals of the faith, form the bedrock for his wrestling match with the deeper mysteries of life and belief.

Throughout we are present as he recalls his parents and his dealing with their final needs, as he remembers departed friends as well.

Not at all a gloomy book, there are laugh-out-loud parts, self-directed humor, some classic jokes, like the one about the accordion player who stopped for coffee after a gig, locking his accordion in the back of his car. When he returned to the car, to his dismay he found the rear window smashed in, and someone has deposited a second accordion in his car. Or the one which asks the difference between a violin and a viola? (When someone walks into a bank with a violin case everyone is afraid it will contain a machine gun and he will take it out and use it. When someone walks in with a viola case everyone is afraid it contains a viola and he will take it out and play it.)

Despite his worry lest he embarrass himself and his family, Hays gets through his Bar Mitzvah creditably, offering a brief but sentient sermon:

> "*Today I am a boy. On the brink of manhood, to be sure, with my beloved classmates.... Looking back over a long life, I now understand that everything that I've done that has been fine has been done in the spirit of that boy; and everything I have done that has been mean has been done in the spirit of the man that once, so long ago, I thought it desirable to become.*"

This is a beautifully written, thoughtful book which was a delight to read.

A personal story enmeshed in American Jewish history

RABBI ARTHUR HERTZBERG, the Bronfman Visiting Professor of Humanities at New York University, professor emeritus of Religion at Dartmouth College, Rabbi Emeritus of Temple Emanu-El in Englewood, N.J., renowned Jewish scholar and Zelig-like participant in six decades of Jewish history, has written a memoir which is at once touching, impressive, instructive and at times infuriating.

Son of a Hasidic rabbi, profoundly learned in Jewish texts himself, his youth, begun in a railroad flat on Third Street on the Lower East Side of New York, Hertzberg evokes the description recently reported on in Weidman's *Fourth Street East*. He describes his parents as different from most immigrants in that they did not seek to "fit in" to the American mold, but brought their Eastern European world with them. Hertzberg spent his life adhering to the principle that total assimilation would not bring happiness and success to Diaspora Jewry in the long run. "I became an American by refusing to assimilate," he declared. And he never wavered from the conviction that "Jews, and other minorities, cannot bet their future on changing the hearts and minds of the majority. They will find their place in society by using their power in the public arena to force change."

A Jew in America
My Life and a People's Struggle for Identity
Arthur Hertzberg
Harper San Francisco, 2002   460 pages

Hertzberg, as early as the late 1940's, was presciently asking if "hatred of the 'other' is endemic in Western culture ...was the Holocaust a unique expression of that hatred?"

Early on he learned that "the lasting danger to humanity is the uncompromising defender of the faith—any faith."

Rabbi Hertzberg, the student, seems always to have been taken on as a project by his professors, or perhaps it was the other way around. Whether at the Jewish Theological Seminary, Harvard or Columbia, he would be found taking walks with the leading scholars under whom he studied. Yet, grounded as he was in old world culture, he remained, in his own mind, the outsider. As rabbi of a conservative synagogue in post-WW II Nashville, he had difficulty dealing with the Christian world, his Jewish congregants and the segregated culture, feeling himself to be "thrice an alien."

As the memoir moves further away from its "coming of age" phase to

Hertzberg's transition to member of the Jerusalem scholarly elite, free-thinking leader of Diaspora Zionist groups, and president of the American Jewish Congress, he seems more and more to be the contrarian voice, refusing to go along with the conventional wisdom. Thus, when we were all flush with excitement over Israel's successes, proclaiming, "we are one!" Hertzberg was denouncing the thin Zionist clichés, declaring "we who have not lived hour by hour with radio broadcasts, hoping to be reassured that our children had not fallen in battle, are not one with Israelis who have hardly ever known a day of peace. We can sympathize; we can help—but we are not one." For half a century he has asked for sympathy and compassion for the enemy, an unpopular dovishness in its day, but somewhat prescient as we belatedly reexamine the failed "greater Israel" policies of the '70s and '80s.

Whenever Rabbi Hertzberg was forced to step back, slightly wounded in the unceasing Jewish political battles, both in the United States and Israel, he seems to have found refuge in scholarship and teaching, be it at Columbia, Dartmouth or New York University. Whenever a reasoned voice was needed, in the matter of Black-Jewish relations, U.S.–Israel policy, or in the byzantine world of Israeli politics, he seems always to have been called out of his academic shelter to be "at the head table," with the great players.

In retrospect, it is not so much that his story is so enmeshed with our history as a people over the past 60 years, although it certainly is, nor that more often than not he was more right than not, but rather his perspective as an American Jew. Arthur Hertzberg, in *A Jew In America*, charts a course between religious fundamentalism and pure secularism, between ethnic arrogance and religious indifference. At times inspirational, at other times provocative, at all times a compelling and pivotal life.

January 2003

Escape from an intolerable destiny

THAT WOMEN ARE in some societies in the 21st century regarded as men's chattel is not news. After all, it is only recently in the great span of time that it has not been so in America. And although American Jewish women of this writer's generation were really the first to break the chains of time-honored custom, American women, Jewish or otherwise, of Farideh Goldin's era can barely fathom that there was a time it was not so.

Wedding Song, then, is a shocking wake-up call, albeit a hauntingly beautiful one.

One is shocked not so much by the heartbreaking recital of what appears to be the cruel imposition of a closed community's values upon its members, male and female, but by the reminder that this memoir, literally torn from within, of a time a quarter of a century ago, could be written, word for word, in other languages and with other players by millions of Farideh's and our sisters this very day.

Wedding Song
Memoirs of an Iranian Jewish Woman
Farideh Goldin
Brandeis University Press, 2003   218 pages

One early reviewer has said, "I read *Wedding Song* with great pleasure." That is akin to saying that listening to Beethoven's *Ninth Symphony* is relaxing. This reader read *Wedding Song* in awe and with some pain; awe because one who has been known to us for so many years has demonstrated such talent as a marvelously gifted writer; pain because her portrait of the artist as a young girl and woman and of her struggles for self actualization evoked more than sympathy. Knowing and admiring Farideh for so long, one can only suffer along with her—not a pleasure, but a privilege.

Wedding Song, from its opening revelation of the author's father, angrily burning the books she had squirreled away in various corners of the house in violation of his command that she not "corrupt herself, giving all of us a bad name," to her recapturing of the fragrance of her first piece of chocolate, is an exotic feast of stories, not all of them sad, and opens a window for the reader into a society and a culture closeted from view until revealed by her light. Her memory of events and people and customs and colors and smells and tastes is simply remarkable.

That most of the acts which we may perceive to be cruel and degrading were prompted by love and the desire to avoid criticism from within the Iranian Jewish community and the Iranian Moslem community is not to be overlooked, and Goldin's ultimate joy at her escape from an intolerable destiny is tempered by her respect and love for the suffering of her mother, grandmothers and great-grandmother, from whom she had to depart, but for whom she never ceased to yearn. What couldn't be known as she schemed and fought to return to Virginia was that virtually the entire Jewish community of Iran was doomed to form another Diaspora, as the post-Shah politics of the 1970s wreaked havoc on all non-Moslem Iranian cultures.

Grateful as we must be for the gift of this beautiful collection of stories, we may be forgiven if we hope that Goldin has not honed her considerable skills just for this singular cathartic effort. At midlife, she is revealed as a rare talent and readers of *Wedding Song* will surely wish to hear from her again.

September 2003

A rewarding journey

ONCE AGAIN, your reviewer must apologize for just getting around to this moving autobiography by Israeli author, Amoz Oz, winner of the Israel Prize for Literature in 1998, the Goethe Prize in 2005, and a repeat candidate for the Nobel Prize in Literature. Born Amos Klausner in Jerusalem to "pioneers of Israel," albeit not the drain the swamps and make the desert bloom sort of pioneers, but intellectuals of the right-wing Revisionist Zionist stripe.

A Tale of Love and Darkness
Amos Oz
Translated by Nicholas de Lange
Harcourt, 2005   538 pages

His uncle, Joseph Klausner, ran against Chaim Weizmann for the presidency and chaired the Hebrew literary society at the Hebrew University of Jerusalem, while his father, Arieh Klausner, who entertained hopes of a professorial appointment, lived with his disappointment as a librarian and writer.

But the darkness of Oz' memoir has its roots in his mother's frustration and unhappiness with her life as a homemaker in an almost impoverished home, while she, too, entertained hopes of an intellectual career. Tragically, she committed suicide when Oz was 12, and at 14 he became a Labor Zionist and joined Kibbutz Hulda, changing his name from Klausner to *Oz* (Hebrew for "strength"). Imagine the child, torn between intense resentment over the fact that his mother didn't even love him enough to say goodbye, and his dismay at not being worth living for. That Oz and his father never, not once in the 20 years between her death and his, as if she had never lived, discussed his mother, is indicative of the unremitting pain they suffered.

And the darkness does not end there, for the transformation of Israel in Oz' eyes from the dream of the socialist-Zionists to its present state is mourned as deeply as the death of his mother.

Oz' IDF service was in the kibbutz-oriented Nahal, with a tank unit in the Six-Day War and in the Golan Heights during the Yom Kippur War. By the time he was 22 he began publishing the books and stories—18 books and about 450 articles and essays—which made him a household word as one of the most influential and highly regarded intellectuals in Israel.

Oz' childhood recollections of the arrival of the first wave of Holocaust survivors, of the daily goings-on during the early years of the state of Israel and of what it is like to live in a country constantly under threat, are given focus and purpose through his masterful wordplay and analysis of the painful relationships between and among individuals, families, Arabs and Jews.

A Tale of Love and Darkness is at once funny, tragic and touching. Those familiar with his novels come to expect a "spareness" to his prose, a quiet reaching for intimacy in portrayal. Here we have a larger canvas, with broader brushstrokes, and the laying on of layers of paint, through a denser prose. Not until halfway through the book do we learn of his mother's suicide, and at the very end of the book is a beautiful chapter detailing the events leading up to and following her death. From his childish recollections of the interaction among friends and family, to his adult ruminations on the state of the Israeli state, to his final pages, is a fairly long but infinitely rewarding journey.

September 2005

Cantonese and Yiddish

THIS IS ONE of a number of books that have been staring at me from my cluttered desktop for several months, accusing me of neglecting my promise to read and review.

Jack Botwinik was raised in a culturally rich, yet non-religious home in Montreal, Canada. His mother is an Italian Jew, and his father, a Polish-born Yiddishist, while certainly not observant, would countenance neither inter-dating nor intermarriage.

Belinda, a Cantonese, left Hong Kong for Toronto as a foreign student. She had never met a Jew while growing up. While there were remnants of Buddhist practice in her home, little explanation of the rituals were passed on to her and her attendance at a Catholic primary school was dictated mainly because it was the best school available to Belinda at the time. Her early opinion was that all religions were hoaxes.

Chicken Soup with Chopsticks
Jack Botwinik
Paper Spider, 2005   224 pages

We are led to believe that as the relationship grew more serious, Botwinik's and ultimately Belinda's quandary was simple: The Torah forbids intermarriage. The Torah might actually be the word of God. Neither partner would countenance a conversion of convenience merely to satisfy the requirements for marriage. From Jack's point of view,

> *"Confronted with an ancient, rich, and fascinating Chinese tradition I knew nothing about, and which threatened to eclipse my own, I was challenged to identify what was ultimately unique and special about my Jewishness. I was forced to differentiate the essence of my Judaism from its cultural echoes in which I had been immersed my entire life."*

Thus commenced a four-year period of soul searching with its concomitant emotional turmoil, severe enough to affect the couple's health.

> *"We read voraciously on different spiritualities. We attended Chinese churches, Buddhist and Taoist temples; took part in Jews for Jesus, Reform, Conservative and Orthodox Jewish synagogues and events; visited a Sikh Gurdwara; a mosque; and toured Israel for a month."*

Although the narrative in *Chicken Soup with Chopsticks* (clearly one can't eat chicken soup with chopsticks—but they work for matzo balls and won ton) moves along briskly enough, Botwinik feels it necessary to intersperse more than personal reflections, thus it occasionally becomes somewhat didactic, and generally assumes little or no background on the part of the reader.

Belinda's ultimate conversion into Orthodoxy (she is now known as Bina Ester, and their harmonious marriage is blessed with two toddlers) does not prevent the family from embracing both parents' cultural background. "Our children speak Cantonese and Yiddish. Chinese and Jewish foods, songs and books are an integral part of daily living."

Belinda and Jack's ordeal is told basically from his point of view; the reader would welcome more of her voice, and of course, without prying into areas of privacy, we would have welcomed some sign of a romantic life that went beyond hand-holding from this 29- and 25-year-old couple. Perhaps there was none— but perhaps there was some important chemistry which held them together during the four year struggle.

The author concludes that "Judaism can demonstrate its validity and relevance to us if only we investigate and challenge it."

January 2006

Rare moments of sunshine

1939, ON THE EVE of Hitler's invasion of Poland and on the heels of the enactment of cruel legislation stripping German Jews of their civil rights and their property, 10,000 children left Germany by way of the Kindertransport.

Seven-year old Edith Milton, née Cohen, daughter of Dr. Helene and Bruno Cohen of Karlsruhe, Germany, along with

---

The Tiger in the Attic
Memories of the Kindertransport
and Growing Up English
Edith Milton
University of Chicago Press, 2005   242 pages

---

her teenage sister, is one of the very fortunate Jewish children rescued from the impending Holocaust and sent to live with the kindest of families in England, who took these children in and raised them as their own throughout the six years of World War II and the austere postwar years thereafter.

Edith's mother, by means of a miraculous instinctive change of plans, sacrificed all her earthly goods to take a different route out of Germany (her husband Bruno having died earlier from an infection), made it safely to the United States, scrubbed floors to make her start, and ultimately passed her exams enabling her to practice medicine once again. But the gates to Jewish immigration had essentially closed, and it would take a decade before mother and daughter would be reunited.

Therein lies the rub and sets the stage for Milton's brilliantly written coming-of-age memoir. Ideally, Edith lives out the war in England—the same England which sent thousands of its children to temporary homes in the United States during the war—emerges as a teenager, emigrates to America, rejoices in her reunion with her mother and rediscovers her Judaism.

But in the end, things play out quite differently. The wonderful family that took the Cohen girls in and created a loving home for them were solicitous about their religious upbringing, inquiring of their mother as to her wishes. Helene, the most peripheral of Jews, affected no concern and so little Edith attended church with the Harvey family. She grew up English and Christian.

The reader is treated to a wonderful picture of an upper-middle-class English family coping with the realities of WWII: the rationing of food, the nightly visits to bomb shelters during air raids, the taking in of other children from time to time—all through the eyes of a keenly observant and remarkably literate child. This child from whom the father she loved was taken, and from whose mother she was separated, in some ways was able to find the emotional security she needed with the Harveys and their extended family, all of whom she came to love and was loved by in return.

"Uncle" Bourke, head of household, was for Edith, the prototype of everything manly, everything fatherly, and his gentle, blithe demeanor created the image she sought as an adult in a romantic prospect. "Aunt" Helen and all the other "aunts," "uncles" and "cousins" provide a wonderful *Masterpiece Theatre* setting, charming beyond belief, until the anticipated and dreaded day Edith is granted a visa to America and must come to grips with the reality of her Jewish mother and relatives and their poultry farm in Vineland, N.J. It would be more than 20 years before the teen-aged Edith and her somewhat dour, determined mother would reach a kind of peace between them and come fully to terms with each other.

Eventually, Edith visited Karlsruhe and her father's grave site, as well as the clusters of markers for Karlsruhe's Jews not buried there, perished at Auschwitz or some other death camp. She departs, never to return, strangely dissatisfied with her visit yet not truly knowing what she expected to gain from it.

Edith and her sister, now in their seventies, do not speak of Karlsruhe at all, but continue to shake their heads "over the marvel of being pulled away from a world drowning in chaos... a rare interval of inexplicable astonishing sunshine at the very moment when you are least expecting it."

March 2006

Well-researched and inspiring

A DECADE AGO, *Escape to Shanghai,* written by James R. Ross, a journalism professor at Boston's Northeastern University, was reviewed in this newspaper. Based on first-person accounts of "Shanghailanders," it was a compelling account of the struggles of this small Jewish community that by dint of individual foresight or just plain luck, got out of Germany and Austria in the nick of time.

Fifty-five years after leaving Shanghai, Berl Falbaum, Michigan journalist, author, college teacher and public relations executive, launched his project to compile an anthology of individual stories of Jewish survivors of the Holocaust, the remnant of some 20,000 who overcame severe hardships to get to Shanghai and to endure there throughout the war. Sadly, memories have faded and many survivors, including Falbaum's own parents, have passed away.

As is generally the case with Holocaust memoirs, there are many similarities, yet each is unique in its own way. In *Shanghai Remembered,* Falbaum and 23 other former refugees, the "Shanghailanders," relate their experiences in the paradoxically unwelcoming Chinese community: unwelcoming to "foreign devils," yet a country requiring no entry visa.

> ## Shanghai Remembered
> Berl Falbaum
> Momentum Books, 2006   229 pages

It was, thus, the last hope for Jews shut out by the cruelly indifferent Evian Conference held in France in 1938 just a few months before *Kristallnacht.*

Who were these 20,000 who made the decision to flee from impending extermination? For the most part, they were economically comfortable professionals and small business owners, well educated and with the means to book passage for the voyage (generally from Italy, but some traversed Europe and Siberia overland). Despite having to leave most of their assets behind (the Nazis had enacted laws which required Jews to sell their businesses and belongings at a fraction of their value), most arrived in China able to make a start, frequently with the help of earlier arrivals. It was not easy—but they established schools, synagogues, cafes, sports teams and became a community.

The subsequent occupation of Shanghai by the Japanese changed everything for the worse, as all "stateless people" were restricted to a ghetto in the Hongkew district, an area of extreme poverty and total lack of sanitary conditions. Unable to leave on a regular basis, they were unable to work and from 1943 until the end of the war, the Shanghailanders suffered terrible privations including death and injury when the ghetto was bombed by the U.S. Army Air Corps.

Certain themes run through each individual testimony. The mother or the father (or both) saw the handwriting on the wall and made the decision to leave at all costs. Close relatives said they were crazy to go, that things would not be so bad. The naysayers were soon murdered by the Nazis. Virtually every memoir tells of the bridge between the ghetto and the mainland over which the Jews were not permitted to pass without special permission, and of a sadistic Japanese official who inflicted insults and occasional beatings on those who applied. (Not mentioned by the author is the fact that the Nazis continually suggested to the Japanese that they exterminate these Jews immediately, a suggestion the Japanese never adopted.).

At the end of the war, the departure of the Japanese and the relative prosperity of the Jews, working for the most part for the American liberators, did not last long as the triumphant communist armies brought a new reality to Shanghai. Thus, each family had to choose whether to return to Europe, immigrate to Australia, or take advantage of legislation which permitted almost universal immigration to the United States by German and Austrian refugees. The majority came to America, generally in 1947 and 1948 to begin yet another life after a decade in China. Most did well and became proud and grateful American citizens.

We stand in tribute to those survivors, who despite the injustice and pain, endured and did so with integrity and compassion for others. The author's daughter, in a moving foreword, concludes that, "I am in awe that goodness perseveres and lives on in my father and others despite the unbelievably difficult life they endured."

The accompanying photos enlighten Falbaum's well-researched and assembled book.

August 2006

Reads like a novel

DALIA SOFER'S NOVEL, *Septembers in Shiraz*, was more than loosely based on her family's experiences surviving in and fleeing a despotic society ruled by corrupt and cruel ideologues. Lucette Lagnado, a senior special writer and investigative reporter for the *Wall Street Journal*, has given us a memoir of her family's privileged life as upper middle class Jews in Cairo until their forced departure in 1962 and their subsequent travails as "wandering Jews." We witness the circumstance by which they declined, suffered, endured. It would be warming to conclude that they ultimately prevailed—but such was not to be the case.

The Man in the Sharkskin Suit
My Family's Exodus from Old Cairo to the New World
Lucette Lagnado
Harper Collins, 2007   332 pages

The Man in the White Sharkskin Suit reads like a novel, encompassing as it does almost an entire century during which the corrupt Egyptian monarchy, propped up by the entrenched imperial British army, offered its substantial Jewish minority the chance to live freely, to succeed financially, educate their children in the best schools, enjoy a rich social life while at the same time practicing their faith without interference. The post-World War II departure of the British led to the forced abdication of the decadent King Farouk at the hands of a revolutionary coup led by Gamal Nasser. These events foreshadowed the marginalization of Egypt's Jews, and their ultimate emigration, a modern day Exodus, became a reality following the creation of the State of Israel in 1948 and the Suez War of 1956.

Leon Lagnado, a tall, handsome bachelor known for his impeccable appearance, usually attired in the eponymous white sharkskin suit, was a hardworking, synagogue-observant boulevardier. His daily routine included morning and evening prayers, some sort of not clearly explained, but very lucrative, brokering business, dinner with his mother, and a late evening of gambling and dancing in the upper-class clubs frequented by British officers and Egyptian nobility. Still a bachelor at age 42, he met, quickly wooed and married the beautiful 20-year-old Edith.

Warm, generous, and protective (perhaps overly protective) of his family, Leon's other face was that of the typical male-chauvinist middle-eastern patriarch, whose sons came first (to be treated like princes), daughters next (to be totally indulged but denied training in any utilitarian skill), and the wife last (to manage the house). When their fortunes changed, however, and the staff of servants and porters which tended to everyone in the family could no longer be afforded, then the wife was to do all the work—shopping, cleaning and cooking. Under no circumstances could any wife have a serious career.

Leon and Edith's marriage was not a happy one despite the presence of four children. By the time the family was forced to leave Egypt, Leon and Edith were no longer sharing the same bed, due largely to his return to the old evenings-out lifestyle of his bachelor days. Leon's behavior was not atypical in his culture.

Forced finally to emigrate from their beloved Cairo, leaving behind his wealth, Leon, suffering from a badly mis-healed broken hip, and his family arrived in Paris with only $200. His pride, his flawless British-accented English, impeccable demeanor and manners, and obvious middle eastern chauvinism did little to endear the family to the Hebrew Immigrant Aid Society (HIAS) professionals in France (as well as later in the United States), forcing the family to linger in Paris until at last cleared to leave for America. The main concern of HIAS was that in his semi-crippled condition, Leon would not be able to find a job and the family would be a long-term welfare burden in the United States. Sadly, the concern was more than justified.

The Lagnado family failed to realize the American immigrant dream. The streets were not paved with gold and Leon couldn't really hold a job. Neither would he permit Edith to work. They suffered a penurious existence with Leon, shattered by his immigrant experience, vainly attempting to force his three oldest children to remain fully observant of Jewish law. Ultimately, they were driven off—eventually to find success on their own.

The author, Lucette, dubbed "Loulou" by her French-speaking family, though a young child and ill during the emigration, is left at home to grow into adulthood with her declining father. Her nearly terminal illness and lengthy treatment for Hodgkin's disease brings the reader almost too quickly to the sad ending of Loulou's memoir. One might have wished for a more balanced and detailed portrayal of her success as well as that of her siblings. The photographs, mostly unearthed by the author's eldest brother Cesar, are exceptional and very touching.

The clash of cultures resulted in the inability of a handsome, cultured man, fluent in French, Italian, Hebrew and English (but who spoke only Arabic to his Syrian mother), to adapt to life away from his circle of experience in Cairo. Leon, and to a lesser extent Edith, were lost in America.

Loulou's eventual visit to Egypt confirmed the essential fact of Egypt being *Judenrein*, but at least enabled her to achieve a kind of closure to her father's sad ending.

The Man in the Sharkskin Suit plays out against the reality of the forced exodus of about a million Jews from Arab lands and is a wonderful blending of disparate worlds, poignantly written.

A minor masterpiece

THE RELEASE OF Robert Clary's autobiography, initially published in 2000, in a quality paperback edition has provided a welcome opportunity to experience a minor masterpiece of Holocaust literature. Lacking the literary style of Primo Levi's memoir of Auschwitz, or Elie Wiesel's terrifying account of the death of his family, the death of his innocence and the death of his God, Clary's account of his passage through hell has its own eloquence and merits attention.

Born Robert Max Widerman (pronounced *veederman*) in Paris in 1926, Clary is best known for his six years as Corporal Louis Lebeau on the hit television series *Hogan's Heroes,* which

From the Holocaust to Hogan's Heroes
The Autobiography of Robert Clary
Robert Clary
Taylor Trade Publishing, 2008   209 pages

is airing still in reruns around the world. The final half of his book is devoted to the story of his struggles and eventual success in America as a nightclub performer, Broadway show singer, dancer and actor, and occasional movie personality. This writer saw him in his breakthrough show, *New Faces of 1952.* Immensely energetic and talented, this diminutive Frenchman gave no hint of the horrors of his young life. It wasn't until more than three decades later, when he came to Tidewater to speak at a Federation gala dinner, that I understood fully who this man was.

It is Clary's description of his childhood in Paris, in the security of a large working-class Orthodox family of tailors, meat-cutters, department store clerks and bakers, all émigrés from Poland, that provides a rich mosaic of Jewish life in pre-World War II Europe. The German occupation of France in 1940 and Clary's subsequent dramatic deportation in 1942, at the age of 16, to the infamous transit camp Drancy begins his testimony. This is Clary's deeply personal account of two and a half years of horror.

Clary's survival, the reader will conclude, is part luck, part deftness and part personal fortitude. Small in stature (at 16 he looked 14), he just made the cut, and was initially selected for work rather than the gas chamber. Clary recounts his incarceration in four Nazi concentration camps: Ottmuch, Blechhammeer, Gross-Rosen and Buchenwald. Protected and cared for by fellow prisoners, whom he helped in return, Clary had the courage to sneak out of the barracks at night, crawl into the pigsty and steal scraps of pig food to augment the starvation diet. Thus, he had the strength to survive the 14-hour work days, the unending hours-long roll-calls, and the freezing marches to and from the work sites.

In April 1945 he was liberated from Buchenwald by the Allies. His joy turned to grief when he learned that his parents, two sisters, two half-sisters, and two nephews had perished in the Nazis' genocidal campaign.

Clary's Holocaust testimony, *From the Holocaust to Hogan's Heroes,* takes a back seat to none I have read. It is right up there with the most gripping. As a Hollywood star memoir, the autobiography of Robert Clary is also right up there with the best. Written by him, without the customary amanuensis, Clary's experiences as a Jew during the Holocaust colors his description of his 50-year career as actor, singer and in later years photo-realist painter, with an honest recognition of life's often-horrific reality. His memoir is thus greatly distinguished from those by most other show business personalities.

March 2009

A tale of remarkable courage

D R. HALEH ESFANDIARI, a 66-year-old Iranian-American national, returned to Tehran in December 2006 to visit with her 93-year-old mother as she did several times a year. Raised in a Shia Muslim family, she was born in Tehran, grew up in Austria and has lived in the United States since 1980 with her Jewish Iranian husband, Professor Shaul Bakhash, and their daughter. Esfandiari left Iran at the time of the 1979 Iranian Revolution.

On December 30, enroute in a car to the Tehran airport to return home after her visit, Esfandiari was robbed at knifepoint by uniformed thugs, threatened with death and her luggage and purse with both U.S. and Iranian passports were stolen. From the beginning, she suspected that this was a planned rather than a random robbery. Her suspicions were further raised when, upon applying for new passports and travel documents, she was denied permission to leave the country and subjected to several weeks of daily intensive interrogations at the Ministry of Intelligence.

My Prison, My Home
Haleh Esfandiari
HarperCollins, 2009   223 pages

On January 18, 2007, Esfandiari's mother's apartment was raided by Ministry personnel and her laptop confiscated, along with other items.

On May 8 she was taken into custody and imprisoned in Tehran's infamous Evin Prison. Official and unofficial efforts on the part of a broad segment of academicians, politicians and both foreign and domestic diplomats to secure her release were ongoing throughout her confinement.

On August 21, after more than three months of imprisonment, she was released on $333,000 bail. The deed to her mother's apartment was kept as security.

On September 2 she flew to Austria.

Those are the bare bones of Haleh Esfandiari's season in hell. And while it is true that although she was fairly well treated in prison, neither beaten nor tortured, although humiliated and terrified, this memoir brings to mind Dalia Sofer's poignant novel, *The Septembers of Shiraz*.

Esfandiari's past work as a teacher of Persian literature and language, as a journalist and frequent lecturer on Iranian affairs, but principally her service as director of the Middle East Program at the Woodrow Wilson International Center for Scholars in Washington, D.C., set her up as a target for the Ministry of Intelligence in Iran. Their objective: to browbeat her into confessing that the Wilson Center was a tool of the CIA and the American government, and was being used to foment a "velvet revolution" aimed at bringing about regime change in Iran. It appeared inconceivable to Iranian intelligence functionaries that Lee H. Hamilton, a former U.S. Representative and former vice-chair of the U.S. 9/11 Commission, could segue into the presidency of the Wilson Center and remain independent of the U.S. government.

Throughout her incarceration, Esfandiari exhibits remarkable courage in the face of potentially real danger, for if actually charged and forced to trial, she would undoubtedly be convicted and sentenced severely. Despite fears and constant worry over the strain being placed on her frail elderly mother, she gives nothing to her inquisitors, careful to be consistent in answering and re-answering the same questions. She controls her contempt for the interrogators, refusing to eat prison food, relying mainly on fruits and vegetables purchased or sent in by her mother, and spurning all prison medications even when denied access to her own. She loses one fifth of her body weight and realizes that, if not freed soon, she may not live.

Ultimately, the worldwide pressure of diplomats, scholars and politicians, plus the unceasing efforts of her husband, Shaul, in the United States, are successful and she is released. Relationships with Iran having further deteriorated since 2007, one can only wonder what her fate might be today.

Ever the teacher, Esfandiari utilizes alternating chapters to provide the reader with summaries of historical background in Iran, from the British hegemony through WWII to the see-sawing relationship with the United States. A patriotic American, a person true to her heritage and the nostalgia she felt for her childhood, the author is not reluctant to show where the United States may have made some poor decisions regarding Iran, thus engendering mistrust and suspicion. However, she comes down hard on the prevailing theocracy and her disgust is ratified by her horrifying experience.

My Prison, My Home is very timely reading when one considers what is taking place in Iran, both from the standpoint of its nuclear research and of the dissatisfaction of Iranians with its autocratic rulers.

December 2009

POLITICS

Book expands on Buckley's controversial article; 'cuts through much of the smoke'

RECENT ADDITIONAL CONCERN about Americans' anti-Semitism, neo-Nazis and the Black-Jewish rift, manifested locally by the appearance of Abraham H. Foxman at the Old Dominion President's Forum, compels this department to encourage readership of Buckley's timely study of a timeless issue.

The featured interview of Foxman, national director of the Anti-Defamation League, in *The Virginian-Pilot* (Nov. 29), and the *UJF Virginia News* (Nov. 27), report on the national poll on American attitudes toward Jews, revealing a hard-core group of about 20 percent embracing a range of stereotypes about Jews.

In Search of Anti-Semitism
William F. Buckley
Continuum, 1992   198 pages

Thus Buckley's book, an expansion of his controversial article in *National Review* and the unprecedented response it provoked, is point and counterpoint to any statistical/anecdotal study, for it cuts through much of the smoke and we are indebted to the author for what he has done. As Professor Jacob Neusner aptly puts it, "Instead of assuming 'we all know' what anti-Semitism is, he undertakes the burden of sorting matters out. This he does with wit, insight, and common sense and unfeigned affection for the Jews and what the State of Israel stands for."

The hurt, the sense of betrayal felt by us following the sound bashing lately received at the hands of black intellectuals and reflected in such works as *The Secret Relationship Between Blacks and Jews* should by now have opened our eyes to a disturbing turn of events. Anti-Semitism, which exists on the right, flourishes on the left.

It is, ultimately, important for us to understand that while "anti-Zionism" is often a code word for anti-Semitism, as developed by Alan Dershowitz in his best-selling *Chutzpah*, opposition to this or that Israeli policy is not necessarily anti-Semitic.

Buckley has organized his work into two sections; the first, the original essay which addresses four allegations of anti-Semitism involving Joseph Sobran, Pat Buchanan, the *Dartmouth Review* and the *Nation*. The second is a collection of comments to which Buckley responds. This includes a letter from William Pfaff, as well as letters from Irving Kristol, Norman Podhoretz, Alan Dershowitz,

Robert Novak, Edwin Yoder, Jr. and others. Finally, Buckley adds a thoughtful and reflective conclusion.

Unquestionably, treatment of the subject in this book takes on some added moral status, coming, as it does from a recognized high priest of conservatism. Thus, it is possible to criticize Buckley, at times, for giving us a blinding glimpse of what we might consider to be the obvious.

Buckley asserts that it is not his intention to offer a social profile of the American Jew, but to distinguish between what is wrongfully thought of as anti-Semitic and the ways in which anti-Semitism shows its face "in the influential world in which Mr. Buckley and his fraternity live: in opinion magazines, in publishing houses, in the op-ed pages, in syndicated columns, in TV talk shows. One might add the boardrooms, and be grateful that a writer and thinker with the author's wit, even-handedness and thoroughness has chosen at last to wear the "grey flannel suit."

December 1992

Writer details Hussein's arms build-up

FOR A FEW MONTHS after the triumph of Operation Desert Storm, questions remained. What was Saddam Hussein's residual military capability? Where did Iraq get the armaments to provoke the Persian Gulf War? Now, a year after the operation, thanks significantly to investigative works such as *The Death Lobby*, we are privy to the details of the Iraqi arms build-up. The blame lies squarely in the laps of the Western countries which supplied weapons to Saddam.

Timmerman's book, although published soon after Operation Desert Storm, does not appear to be typical of those works rushed to the printer full of egregious errors in order to take advantage of the topicality involved. Moreover, the author, who writes for *Newsweek*, *The Wall Street Journal* and the *International Herald Tribune*, while providing a great deal of new (to us) information of the events leading up to and including the Israeli bombing of the Osirak reactor, is not an Israel basher! Without overlooking Israel's role as a sometimes U.S. intermediary in arms deals in the region, he treats the matter in its proper perspective.

The Death Lobby
How the West Armed Iraq
Kenneth R. Timmerman
Houghton Mifflin Co., 1991   443 pages

The Death Lobby is the result of extensive travel and interviews with those who have been at the fore of Middle Eastern strategic weapons programs, as well as first-hand interviews with the makers and merchants of the arms themselves. It is no secret now that the Gulf War could not have been mounted by Saddam without the active involvement of Western governments at the highest level. But for a detailed understanding of the methods used by front companies—with the tacit approval of governments, including ours, who were paying lip service to the various technological and armament embargoes—the reader will wish to dig into this book. How ironic to learn, at this juncture, when the matter of loan guarantees to finance Israel's monumental refugee settlement task is the occasion for outrageous linkage with issues of

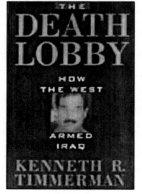

new settlements, that as recently as 1989 our government was making unsecured loans of $500 million to the Iraqis. These loans, ostensibly to finance agricultural and industrial projects, were sucked up as part of Saddam's multibillion-dollar armament scheme.

Would that lessons could really be learned from this and similar exposés of U.S. and Western greed. Regrettably, the sale of arms continues—not merely guns and bullets, but sophisticated missiles and their control technology, hither and yon—to any wild-eyed kook with the funds to buy.

March 1992

Book documents personal account of one who walked the darkness of Soviet history

IN A MANNER not unlike the proliferation of Holocaust memoirs, there is a growing literature of moving and highly personal accounts by former prisoners of conscience, whose struggle to maintain some semblance of dignity while surviving under atrocious conditions of punishment, demands our interest and attention.

Beginning with Alexander Solzhenitsyn's famous *A Day in the Life...*, *The First Circle* and *Gulag Archipelago*, and, to my view, culminating with the riveting *Fear No Evil* by Natan Sharansky, these works, besides documenting the struggles of innocents and activists alike (for the desire to leave the Soviet Union was clearly not an innocent wish), foreshadow the demise of a bureaucracy so bloated and so tunnel-visioned as to defy its own survival.

Memoirs of 1984
Yuri Tarnopolsky
University Press of America, 1993 239 pages

With the publication of *Memoirs of 1984*, Yuri Tarnopolsky has now joined the pantheon of those who have walked through the darkness of recent Soviet history. Senator Paul Simon (D-IL), author of the foreword to the book, has judged it a living testament to the power and force of freedom and a tribute to those who, by their very sacrifice and dedication to human values, perpetuate the ideals of freedom and democracy throughout the world.

The reader is reminded of the late Paul Cowan's self-description as an "orphan in history," by this memoir of a man who lived in Russia for 50 years, and for most of which he felt himself a stranger in his native land. The very real period of incarceration aside, this book of essays and recollections are by a man who felt he had endured 50 years of both accidental and voluntary captivity, all the while carrying on an "arduous attempt to understand my native country and myself and the place of both in the world."

Recognizing that discrimination against Jews in the Soviet Union, as it had been often throughout history, was the *a priori* foretaste of impending social disaster, nominally patriotic Russian Jews learned that formerly downtrodden friends and relatives (who left by the thousands until the doors were slammed shut in 1979) had found jobs, earned enough money to buy houses and cars in countries where everyone had color TVs and where the stores were stocked with toilet paper.

Tarnopolsky's point is that we should take former inmates' descriptions of Soviet prison life with a grain of salt. For him, "it was just a little bit harder than being free." The trial and sentencing of eminent and active refuseniks (like Sharansky) to labor camps, or to exile (like Sakharov and Solzhenitsyn) created martyrs. In the case of Jewish activists and refuseniks, they created Jewish martyrs, thus sealing their fate. The author reflects with unusual candor on refusenik motivation.

> "Some American Jews were disappointed to find that most Russian immigrants were driven neither by Zionism nor by the desire to practice Judaism. Most were not attracted by political freedom, either. It was not a positive ideal that put them in motion. It was the same expelling force of poverty and hopelessness that had brought to America the previous waves of immigrants from Ireland, Poland, Italy, and Russia."

The chapters describing the author's experiences in prison and his jousting with the authorities are written as well as those of his more illustrious predecessors. Yuri Tarnopolsky is, after all, a poet, as well as a scientist. His works represent an important addition to this growing body of refusenik literature. It is in his conclusions, however, that the reader will find great satisfaction. Tarnopolsky fell in love with America, and finally came to understand why Orwell's prediction of the world's succumbing to the disease of totalitarianism by 1984 failed to come about, mainly because, as he put it, "George Orwell has already immunized the world's reason, as well as my own mind, against it."

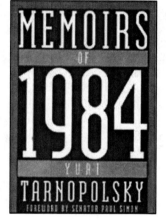

The book concludes with a long list of names of people and organizations in Russia, the U.S., Israel and in Europe, literally dozens who had a hand in keeping this refusenik's hopes alive, then in getting him safely out, and started in his new life. One feels a pride—for this story has been replicated frequently, although not always so eloquently described.

And one cannot be taken on such a deeply personal journey without being touched by feelings of equal depth.

Yuri Tarnopolsky, Former Soviet Refusenik

YURI TARNOPOLSKY was born in Kbarkov, the Ukraine, in 1936. With a master's degree in chemical engineering and a Ph.D. in organic chemistry, he worked as a professor in Siberia until he returned to Kbarkov in 1977. In 1979 he applied for emigration. When his family was denied visas, he became a refusenik activist. In 1983 he was arrested and sentenced to three years in a Siberian labor camp. Finally granted permission to exit the U.S.S.R. in 1987, he emigrated to Chicago, which made him an honorary citizen, and then relocated to Rhode Island.

Tarnopolsky is the author of a book of poetry, several U.S. patents and numerous scientific publications. He is the recipient of the Liberty Award (*Prix de la Liberté*) of the French P.E.N. Club (1985) and the Gimprich Award to a Distinguished Refugee Scientist (1992).

Tarnopolsky lives with his wife, Olga, in Narragansett, Rhode Island, and they have one daughter. He is currently working on his next book and on his invention in chemical separations.

October 1994

Extraordinary personal experience details 'dark heart' of neo-Nazism

THE "DEFENSE" ORGANIZATIONS are dependably aggressive in their continued outcries and warnings of the hidden strength beneath the small waves of neo-Nazism and other blatant forms of anti-Semitism. Even the better informed among us, those who have seen and digested the ADL coverage of the recent neo-Nazi rampage at Buchenwald (Response) or its preview a year ago of the underground work of Yaron Svoray, are tempted to ask ourselves, "How big a deal is this, a few lunatics on the fringe; could this be an over-reaction on the part of ADL and the Wiesenthal Center to keep the contributions coming?" If we are tempted, imagine what the purveyors of hate are actually saying. As Simon Wiesenthal himself puts it:

"In the final analysis, the future will be determined not by how many Nazis there will be—or fascists or extreme nationalists or white [or black] supremacists—but how many anti-Nazis there will be to confront them."

The basic "plot" involves Yaron Svoray, an Israeli journalist who met a "skinhead" while travelling in Germany in 1992. The young man, unaware that Svoray was Jewish, introduced him to the semi-secret world of German neo-Nazism. The saga of this kibbutz-born child of survivors and his operation, undertaken by the Wiesenthal Center, under the cover of Ron Furey, right-wing journalist, now appears in definitive form.

In Hitler's Shadow

Yaron Svoray and Nick Taylor
Doubleday, 1994   275 pages

This extraordinary personal report details Svoray's penetration during four trips into the dark heart of a movement which bears part of the responsibility for what has been the greatest outpouring of violence against non-Germans in Germany since the 1930s. There are really two stories here. First, of course, is the "truth is stranger than fiction" adventure itself. The undercover operation, which was fraught with real danger, commands our interest and attention as would any novel of international intrigue. *In Hitler's Shadow* is a gripping reminder of the tenacity of sickness, racism and hatred. It should signal authorities and those of us who tend to dismiss anti-Semitic attacks as the work of a few maniacs. When the old Liberty Lobby sought to discredit the United Nations because it flew a blue and white flag, "the same color as the communist zionist Jew flag of Israel," how far a stretch is it for some to discredit a candidate for the U.S. Senate because he is endorsed by gay and lesbian groups which have

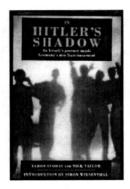

a "sinister Jewish influence"?

We have learned that the label "defense" is politically incorrect when referring to the Anti-Defamation League or the Wiesenthal Center. Preferable these days is the term "human rights organization," or some such. Forgive me for being old-fashioned. I rely on these agencies for my defense, and am grateful to our authors for giving us a major trove of information, nay, ammunition, to use in our unending war against the Nazi legacy.

October 1994

'Love to hate or hate to love' book excellent but could have been great

THIS IS A BOOK you will love to hate or hate to love. Prepublication enthusiasm for *Jewish Power* has been such that J.J. Goldberg, a contributing editor of the Israeli news magazine, *Jerusalem Report,* who also writes for *The New York Times* and the *New Republic,* appears to have a hit on his hands.

If such a varied representation of Jewish opinion as Mike Wallace, Rabbi Joseph Telushkin, Senator Daniel Patrick Moynihan and Abraham Foxman all consider a "must-read" verdict, then one supposes it is up to the reader

---

Jewish Power
Inside the American Jewish Establishment
J.J. Goldberg
Addison-Wesley, 1996   422 pages

---

to judge for himself. Certainly it is provocative. When Goldberg asserts that Jews are "losing interest in the institutions of organized Judaism," and that most American Jews "no longer pay any attention to organized Jewish community life," and that "... Judaism has become a private matter," the unpleasant element of truth is painful to read about.

It is also unpleasant to have to deal with a glittering generalization which overlooks the fact that a very strong "center" is not only holding, but apparently growing. In other words, those who are part of the "organized" institutional Jewish community are in it across the board, shoring up, not in desperation, but with persistence and initiative, the synagogues, JCCs, Jewish Family and Children's Services, long-term care facilities, day schools and all the other Jewish communal manifestations.

Goldberg's book does perform one great service: it successfully debunks the myth, believed by Jews as well as gentiles, that the Jewish political agenda begins and ends with Israel, and that Israel's support in Washington largely results from Jewish political power.

While it is not denied that the clout Jewish Americans exercise on the American political scene far exceeds our population, the active interest we take in public affairs, our willingness to work for causes in which we believe, our gift for organization and most of all our dedication to philanthropy, all support a new militancy. Goldberg is not at his strongest in the early chapters which survey, too quickly, the "ept" and inept machinations of early organizations such at the American Jewish Congress, the American Jewish Committee, B'nai B'rith, Hadassah and the Jewish Labor Committee. He is almost disdainful of these early efforts, but seems not to understand fully the difficult transition organizationally from the immigrant *landsmannschaftens* and burial societies to the new form of communal enterprise.

"The new militance of the American Jew," Goldberg argues, "was well suited to fighting for the disenfranchised and winning a place at the table. Painting the world in black and white energized American Jews, made them uncompromising in defense of their rights—and the rights of others. Once seated at the table, however, this newly energized Jew was ill-suited to coping with genuine conflict."

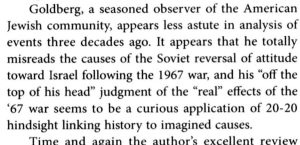

Goldberg, a seasoned observer of the American Jewish community, appears less astute in analysis of events three decades ago. It appears that he totally misreads the causes of the Soviet reversal of attitude toward Israel following the 1967 war, and his "off the top of his head" judgment of the "real" effects of the '67 war seems to be a curious application of 20-20 hindsight linking history to imagined causes.

Time and again the author's excellent review of the development of 20th century Jewish organizational infrastructure is diminished by sweeping generalizations and negative personal descriptions seldom based on personal knowledge. There is a persistent thread in these chapters of undercutting motives and actions.

Goldberg is perhaps at his best, on the other hand, in describing the development of the Council of Jewish Federations and, more particularly, Mark Talisman's role in initiating, drafting and nursing into law key legislation which in effect revised U.S. immigration regulations. It provided for the federal government to share in the resettlement costs of refugees from the Soviet Union in the 1970s and from the former Soviet Union in the 1990s. On this we agree completely: We owe a huge debt to CJF and Mark Talisman in this matter.

If *Jewish Power* exaggerates the effect of Kissinger's policies on Israeli security ("If there had been no October 22 [1973] cease-fire... Israel would still be at war with Egypt."), it cannot be faulted for charting the correlation between Jewish contributions to campaigns and the pro-Israel voting record of U.S. senators.

If his characterization of AIPAC (American Israel Political Affairs Committee) as having a "vast army" is a bit much, his discussion of the paradox surrounding Jewish media involvement is balanced and excellent. The complex issues stemming from the disproportionate representation of Jews in the media (as much as 25% of what is considered the "elite media"), measured against the often expressed Jewish belief that the American news media use a double standard, judging Israel more harshly than Arab countries, is brilliantly handled.

Goldberg demonstrates that "Jewish ownership in the mass media does not represent any significant concentration of Jewish power, however it may symbolize it in the popular imagination."

One concludes the following: The title is really wrong. But it certainly assures some extra sales. The book is about power, yes, but it is more about the development of communal process, not always a pretty picture. Even the chapter headings are mostly highly colored, setting a tone more to be deplored than praised. Goldberg has written an excellent book; it could have been a great book.

On balance, one supposes it is better to write an excellent book that thousands will read than a great book that dozens will cluck over.

December 1996

Personalities, history and politics and the quest for an Israeli-Syrian peace

ITAMAR RABINOVICH modestly supposes that he was chosen in 1992 by Yitzhak Rabin to head the Israeli delegation to the peace talks with Syria because of his academic specialization in Syria's history and politics. Your reviewer hasn't spoken with Ambassador Rabinovich in a number of years, but Rabinovitch remains the consummate teacher, aiming for even-handedness, yet admitting to bias. Your reviewer's own introduction to Israel, a quarter-century ago, included a two-day seminar at Tel Aviv University's Institute of Middle East Affairs (now the Dayan Center for Middle Eastern Studies), presided over by Rabinovich. He was then, as now, not a scintillating speaker or writer, but offered "a thorough and sober look at the positions and strategies" of the various parties involved. His appearance at the Tidewater Jewish Forum post-Camp David and pre-Intifada afforded us another glimpse of conditions in the Middle East from the perspective of what the author prefers to categorize himself—a diplomatic historian.

The Brink of Peace
The Israeli-Syrian Negotiations
Itamar Rabinovich
Princeton, 1998   264 pages

And so *The Brink of Peace* essays to convey the essential events of what must be considered to be a noble failure while placing them in the correct context and perspective. Rabinovich would insist that the question of whether the breakdown of the peace talks represented a missed opportunity is answerable only if we ascertain that there was really an opportunity in the first place. Rabinovich echoes and pretty much verifies Dan Kurzman's description of the macro events of this period. Rabin, perceived by the Israeli public as "Mr. Security," and Hafiz al-Asad, both with a background of half a century of impressive military and political success, dominated the negotiations. Both men knew, and had developed a grudging respect for, each other.

Rabinovich takes the reader through the numerous rounds of negotiation, in Rome, in Washington, aboard aircraft, in formal State Department settings, in hotel rooms. Regardless, the meetings took place in the context of other events. "All" that Syria wanted was "total Israeli withdrawal from the Syrian Golan occupied in 1967" and "dismantling of all Israeli settlements" in return for "termination of all claims or states of belligerency between the two sides." But what would be the effect of the Intifada and what of the demands of the Palestinians' "right of return"?

Without a doubt, the American presidential election of 1992 was bound to have a major impact on the negotiations. President Asad had developed a dialogue with George Bush and Jim Baker, personally, rather than as President and Secretary of State. Bill Clinton and Warren Christopher were an unknown quantity, as were the other members of their team.

We are led through the Jordanian-Syrian, Syrian-Lebanese, and other collateral aspects of the negotiations, to learn that Asad had basically achieved most of his demands, that a satisfactory resolution of U.N. Resolution 242 issues had been achieved. And here it was that Asad made what may be his greatest error. He hesitated. Netanyahu came to power. Nothing had been signed. All bets were off. As the new Israeli Prime Minister took on the mantle of security overall, Damascus probably finally desiring an accord, failed to come to terms with two Israeli governments.

The serious reader will enjoy Rabinovich's unraveling of the "myriad threads that run across the invisible line which separates..." past history and contemporary politics. He is empathetic to players on both sides, yet realistic about the change in perspective when the intimate relationship President Clinton enjoyed with Prime Minister Rabin was replaced by an at-best-awkward one with Netanyahu, and a shift in urgency to the Israeli Prime Minister's position of "Lebanon first," and the American concentration on the Israeli-Palestinian front.

March 1998

From a leading journalistic analyst

AHMED RASHID, whose *Taliban* deservedly reached #1 on the *New York Times* best-seller list, now offers all we may wish to know about the changing nature of Islam in Central Asia—and more.

The general reader may find *Jihad* fairly tough going, as Rashid takes us through the political, economic and religious history of a terribly complex region, made all the more so by the intrigues of imperial dictators and players in the "great game." The latter term refers to the decades-long chivvying between the imperial powers, particularly Britain and Russia, for influence in the buffer zone between Europe and Asia, for direct exploitation of the vast natural resources in the region, and for marketing manufactured goods. The "great game" continues today, both in the highly contested effort to dominate one of the last vast untapped oil and natural gas reserves, and for the hearts and minds of the millions of Central Asians of widely varying ethnic backgrounds.

Jihad
The Rise of Militant Islam in Central Asia
Ahmed Rashid
Yale University Press, 2002   281 pages

Rashid navigates the maze of tribal and linguistic diversity with notable dexterity; the names themselves, unfamiliar as they are to Western ears, echo dimly in our recollections—as the armies of Alexander the Great, Genghis Khan, and Tamerlane and the Mongol hordes swept back and forth through history. This reader found himself wishing for additional maps and some tribal/sect diagrams to help in keeping track.

But more recently, we read of Stalin's brutal repressions, and his arbitrary division of the area into five republics: Kazakhstan, Tajikistan, Kyrgyzstan, Uzbekistan and Turkmenistan, gerrymandered so that ethnic lines were crossed and recrossed, thus ensuring ethnic unrest and the inability of the tribes ever to unite. To this day, the demographic makeup remains an impediment to the creation of democratic government, setting aside if one can, the push for fundamentalist theocracies. Uzbekistan, the largest and most powerful of the Central Asian Republics, is made up of 69 percent Uzbeks, but Uzbeks make up anywhere from 13 to 23 percent of the other republics and live in considerable numbers in China's Xinjiang Province.

From 1939 right through to the breakup of the Soviet empire, Islam flourished underground, defying drought, civil war and the cruelest repression.

Post-September 11, the "Great Game" continues, but much changed. We now find China, Russia and the United States as major rivals in the area yet at the same time, somewhat united in the fight against terrorism and Islamic extremism. Finally, while the crisis in Afghanistan is arguably the most important external factor in the growing instability in Central Asia, Pakistan continues to educate Islam's militants; Iran has been the major supplier (prior to the U.S. involvement) of arms and ammunition to the anti-Taliban alliance; Turkey, despite its own economic and political crises, still entertains hopes of forging a pan-Turkic alliance; and Saudi Arabia has consistently backed the most extremist Islamic groups in the region.

The failure of Soviet colonizers to create viable infrastructure, the lack of economic opportunity and the repressiveness of regime after regime has created a swelling extremist Islamic tide. Organized crime, particularly in the manufacture and transport of heroin, continues to corrupt Central Asian society, and the machinations of Western oil companies has created an effete elite, which only increases the tensions in the area. Rashid finds hope, however in the aftermath of the war in Afghanistan, provided a stable government is created and provided the developed countries continue to display interest and lend strong economic support to the area. Rashid's latest work reaffirms his stature as the leading journalistic analyst and interpreter of the changing nature of Islam and politics in Central Asia. *Jihad* is an insightful work which will reward the careful reader.

May 2002

Why Morocco?

NOWADAYS it is fashionable to say that 70 is like 50; thus 60 is like 40, which goes in part to explain why a 62-year-old *bubbe*, Gloria Marchick, journeyed to Morocco on a Fulbright Foreign Grant. She chose Morocco because it is an Islamic country whose King Mohammed V refused to turn the Moroccan Jews over to Hitler during World War II, defiantly replying, "I have no Jews. I have only Moroccan citizens." So that explains "why Morocco?"

Shalom in My Heart, Salaam on My Lips
A Jewish Woman in Modern Morocco
Gloria Marchick
Micah Publications, 2003   170 pages

But what explains the *chutzpah* of this woman, albeit a highly experienced ESL teacher, who ventured to an Arabic-speaking country with a significant French- and Spanish-speaking educated class, herself gloriously monolingual, having no Arabic, practically no French, and only the Spanish learned in high school 45 years earlier?

Marchick's adjustment to life in Morocco is as hilarious as she appears to be particularly maladroit, getting talked into the wrong apartment, stepping into it literally, be it donkey dung, or mud, and figuratively, applying lipstick in public, being unable to order a decent meal, or refusing to enter her kitchen, having seen mouse-sized roaches. Her inability to communicate with servants, taxi drivers and the like often led to unintended consequences.

But the lady hung in there—even when it stopped being fun. And it stopped being fun when, shortly after her arrival, the second Intifada began, and the Arab-media inflamed Moroccans were outspoken in their hatred of Jews. Her eventual triumph after many false starts, her humane treatment of students, servants and language teachers (according to the author herself, this was one ESL teacher who demonstrated remarkably little linguistic aptitude) led to friendships, but friendships Marchick believed could not survive the knowledge that she was a Jew. So she hid that small fact, responding to all questioners that "no, I am not a Jew. *Je suis croyante*." (I am a believer.) We should not be quick to criticize, unless the experience of watching the tortured and mutilated corpses of the two Israeli reserve soldiers being thrown out the window took place in a room with deliriously happy and cheering Moroccans was shared by us.

The author, despite her vacillation between love of the land and the people, frustration over customs she could not deal with, and cold fear being a Jew in a Muslim land in a dangerous time, fulfilled her mission with sensitivity and cheerfulness, until her vision became affected by what turned out to be cataracts, and she was forced to return to America before her year was up.

One is reminded of Geraldine Brooks' *The Nine Parts of Desire,* and of course of the just-reviewed *Wedding Song* by Farideh Goldin, which both illuminate what for us is the dark mystery of Islam.

October 2003

Necessary reading

GABRIEL SCHOENFELD is senior editor of *Commentary* magazine and has written on world affairs for *The New York Times, The New Republic, The Washington Post,* the *Atlantic Monthly,* and *The Wall Street Journal.* Just published, *The Return of Anti-Semitism* couldn't be more timely, its arrival coinciding as it does with our Federation's creation of a Task Force on anti-Semitism.

Those who have read Daniel Pipes' controversial and disturbing *Militant Islam Reaches America* will recognize that Schoenfeld covers some of the same ground in his early chapters. His conclusions, moreover, are right up front: The most vicious ideas about Jews are not voiced primarily by the downtrodden and disenfranchised element of Islamic society, but by its most successful and best educated members. Thus anti-Semitism today is not cultured in the petri dish of the European beer garden, but on the college campus. And the anti-Semitism of the political right, expressed in its extremity by Nazism, a Nazism we mistakenly thought to be discredited, is now nurtured on the political left, surging on the current wave of Islamic anti-Semitism. Thus author Schoenfeld dubs his work *The Return,* as the extreme right consists of Holocaust deniers and those who criticize Adolf Hitler for failing "to finish the job," while the political left's hatred of the Jews is reminiscent of that of the 18th century, the so-called "Enlightenment."

The Return of Anti-Semitism
Gabriel Schoenfeld
Encounter Books, 2006   240 pages

It is understandable that Israel's success and freedom is a standing rebuke to all Arab regimes, regimes which are mired in a nexus of poverty, characterized by poor or unavailable health care, degraded habitat, dysfunctional educational systems and rising illiteracy (over 65 million Arabs cannot read or write). But how to explain the virulent anti-Semitism in Southeast Asia where there is no conflict with Jews and no Jewish presence? From the splenetic pronouncement of Malaysian Prime Minister Mahathir to 98%-Muslim Pakistan where there is no longer a Jew in sight, we find a society rife with fear and hatred of Jews.

It is one thing to understand that the "return" of anti-Semitism to France is strongly abetted by its huge and growing Muslim population, however in France, chants of "death to the Jews" are heard not only from the Muslim Students of France and the Committee of Moroccan Workers, but from officials of trade unions and members of the Communist League, the Communist Party, the Greens and the Human Rights League.

In Central and Eastern Europe, burgeoning religious and nationalism movements reveal anti-Semitism, particularly at the grassroots level, entrenched and lethal.

The crossover effect of anti-Semitism espoused by extreme right wing groups such as Islamist groups in America to extreme right wing non-Islamic groups and thence further to left wing groups, is a disturbing phenomenon that is apparently manifesting itself in ever-increasing fashion. Universities have been prime propagators of anti-Semitism in the U.S., from San Francisco State to the University of California; from Rutgers University to the University of Colorado; from Stanford University to Wellesley College.

And in the media we now see Democratic Presidential nominee candidate, Al Sharpton, treated with respect. Both Cynthia McKinney and Earl Hilliard, black congressional delegates were subsequently defeated, yet despite their outrageous anti-Semitic remarks, both were solidly supported by the Congressional Black Caucus and over two dozen congressmen contributed to their campaigns.

Even liberal columnists such as Maureen Dowd fell prey to connecting the perceived errors of the Bush administration in leading us to war with Iraq with mid-level Jews in the government such as Douglas Feith, Paul Wolfowitz, Richard Perle, Eric Edelman and Elliot Abrams who are accused of "running the Government." Echoes of 1918, when it was said "the Jews were responsible for pushing our country into WWI." So we are not surprised when a white congressman in Northern Virginia advised his constituents that Jewish power was leading our country into armed conflict.

What is worse, perhaps, is the role of self-hating and "renegade Jews" such as Noam Chomsky, the MIT linguist, who for years has been a fanatical denunciator of Israel and who with others, such as his acolytes Norman Finkelstein and Fred Kovel of Bard College, have been in league with Holocaust deniers and have exerted immense influence abroad. And of course those intellectuals in Israel itself, whose opposition to the existence of the Jewish state transcends simple party politics, but provides ample grist for the mills of Jew-haters the world over.

Finally, the phenomenon of what may be termed "Anti-Semitism Denial" is exposed. For the likes of Chirac, Farrakhan and Buchanan the very act of denying their anti-Semitism serves only to provide a platform for further Jew bashing. If we define anti-Semitism narrowly enough we must conclude with theologian Emil Fackenheim that "unless somebody wants to kill Jews he does not qualify as an anti-Semite."

One can only hope that each member of our Federation's Task Force on anti-Semitism will be given a copy of Schoenfeld's book which succeeds in being comprehensive, yet brief and eminently readable. Natan Sharansky believes this book is necessary reading to "anyone seeking to understand the causes of our troubled world predicament today." We agree!

February 2004

A grim overview

AUTHOR SABINA CITRON is an exceeingly sympathetic figure. An Auschwitz survivor now living in Jerusalem, she has devoted much of her life to outing and bringing to justice Nazi war criminals. Approaching 80 years of age and implored by her grandchildren to tell the story of her experiences during the Holocaust, she has chosen instead to gather up all the bits and pieces of her writing career, the essays and columns, the documents and the news clippings into an angry jeremiad, a "modern day *J'Accuse.*"

The Indictment
The Arab-Israeli Conflict
in Historical Perspective
Sabina Citron
Geffen, 2006   384 pages

Citron opens with a brief, perhaps too brief, recollection of the terrors of her and her family's suffering during the Holocaust, almost as though she felt the need to establish a kind of *bona fides*, as though those horrible experiences license the sometimes over-the-top presentation of her analyses.

She first attempts to show the roots of anti-Semitism, tracing the cause and relationship of events from the Council of Nicaea (325 CE) to Auschwitz. The litany of perfidious actions taken against the Jewish people by every Western country at one time or another is summarized in chronological fashion, from the expulsion of the Jews from the Frankish kingdom in 628; the slaughter of the Jews of the Rhineland in 1096; the anti-Jewish riots in York, England in 1190; all the subsequent expulsions and re-expulsions, burnings, massacres, forced conversions and ghettoizations in Spain, France, Italy, Germany, Austro-Hungary, Poland, Lithuania, Rumania and Russia extending right up to the advent of Fascism in Italy in 1922.

The negative aspects of every conflict since the creation of the State of Israel, of every peace effort, of every diplomatic initiative are emphasized, but Citron marshals her sharpest barbs for the British and her deepest anger for the merciless depravity of the Arab-Muslims.

Much of *The Indictment* is a kind of *Myths and Facts* with an attitude. The enemies of Israel and the Jews are no damn good, and there have been and are no friends, no friends at all. The United States, which stood by and let the Holocaust happen, was no damn good then, and because Bush and Rice are clueless about what needs to be done, is no damn good now. Somehow she fails to mention the billions of dollars in U.S. foreign aid and further tax-deductible billions allowed to be given by American Jews, nor the critical war materials sent by Nixon during the Yom Kippur War.

When all is said and done, hers is a grim overview of our history and the way it forms the context for the present Arab-Israeli conflict. There are a few interesting appendices, such as the U.N. resolution 242 which we hear mentioned so often, but may not know its contents or importance. Author Citron brings considerable passion and heated language to her subject, but lacks balance. Not that there need be "equal time" given to the side of the Nazis or the PLO. But some of her conclusions are simplistic and her research is sufficiently shallow so that *The Indictment* has a journalistic tone more akin to a greatly expanded op-ed column.

February 2007

Successes in Israel

DAN SENOR is adjunct senior fellow for Middle East studies at the Council for Foreign Relations. He has been awarded the Pentagon's highest civilian award for his many years of service in Iraq, as a Pentagon adviser to our Central Command in Qatar, and as a foreign policy and communications advisor to the U.S. Senate. Saul Singer, now living in Jerusalem, continues to write for *The Wall Street Journal, Commentary, Moment,* and *The Washington Post.* He has been an advisor to the U.S. Congress and is best known for his important book, *Confronting Jihad: Israel's Struggle and the World after 9/11.*

Start-Up Nation
The Story of Israel's Economic Miracle
Dan Senor and Saul Singer
12 Publishing, 2009   304 pages

Start-up Nation is an easy reading puff piece that clearly explains the underlying basis of Israel's extraordinary success and preeminence in creating and sustaining start-up companies, principally high-tech, and in creating lasting and highly profitable partnerships with international mega-companies such as Intel and Google.

Jewish News readers will not be shocked to read of Israeli chutzpah (Standard English now—no need to italicize) bred of desperation during the period leading up to independence in 1948. The need to raise money, to purchase and cadge arms, to manufacture arms and armament, was a matter of survival and Israel did what it had to do in order to achieve success against overwhelming odds. That spirit and that continuing need to assure survival led an improbable medley of cultures and political ideologues to create a society at once disciplined enough to offer up its youth to universal military service amidst a democracy free enough to encourage innovation.

What may be news is the role of Shimon Peres, that most conservative old-guard leader, in encouraging the creation of a major military-industrial complex capable of producing first-line battle tanks (Merkava) and high capacity jet fighters (Kfir). Peres remains, at 85, an indefatigable promoter of Israeli technology and start-up growth in particular.

Senor and Singer offer several theories, each of which in part explain the cultural background which nourishes the phenomenon of Israeli start-up success. First, of course was the need, mentioned above, to become partially self sufficient in arms manufacture.

Second was the need to create a large standing army and an effective reserve. Men and women who train together, serve together and then do their reserve time together create fraternal bonding that interacts throughout their careers. Each Israeli pre-inductee is tested to determine where they will fit in the IDF. Some will be selected for commando training; some few for the Navy; some fewer to train as pilots; and a group of elites among the elites for the special TALPIOT program which provides such specialized educational opportunities as to create a group indoctrinated to be innovative.

The IDF is the great democratizer of Israel. The son of a garbage collector can be a lieutenant commanding millionaires. One analyst has gone so far as to say that "the Israeli tank commander who has fought in one of the Syrian wars is the best engineering executive in the world. The tank commanders are operationally the best..."

Years ahead of its U.S. competition, the Israeli creation of an electrified grid to service electric automobiles built in partnership with Renault is virtually a one-man show led by Shai Agassi, a start-up company billionaire. An American executive from Google notes that while Google may outsource service work to other countries, Israel is the only foreign country where work on which they "bet the company" is entrusted. "The best kept secret is that we all live and die by the work of our Israeli teams."

The results are impressive: Cell phone penetration in Israel is 125%. As recently as the 1970s, telephones were so scarce there was over a one-year waiting period to get one. There are more Israeli companies on the NASDAQ than Japan, Finland, U.K., Singapore, China and the UAE combined. Israel boasts more venture capital dollars per capita than any country in the world, and a greater percentage of GDP is devoted to civilian R & D than in any country in the world.

Israel's success is understood to be ascribable to more than the talent of individuals. The authors offer comparison with two other countries that have universal military service, a highly developed technological industrial base, and a nominally democratic governmental structure: South Korea and Singapore. Singapore scores poorly in the creation of a culture of innovation due to the clamped down nature of its society, the rigid control exerted by its virtually dictatorial president. South Korea, more democratically free than Singapore, suffers from an Asian over-concern with "face." It is just too embarrassing to fail, and start-ups are notorious for a high failure rate. Israeli start-up executives, upon failing, just seem to pick themselves up, dust themselves off and try again.

The mixture of anecdotal evidence with hard data works well in *Start-up Nation*, but the book gets thin and somewhat repetitive near the end. One would have appreciated a bit more meat throughout.

March 2011

Author is part of *Israel Today* Forum

ONCE AGAIN, the complex matrix of organizations and interests that make up the Arab lobby is dedicated to the delegitimization of Israel. Once again Israel finds herself increasingly isolated, and at a dangerous point in time when rising generations of Jews, mainly out of ignorance, question the relevance of Israel in their lives and indeed fall victim to the anti-Israel agitprop. In an effort to counteract this, the Community Relations Council of the United Jewish Federation of Tidewater is planning an ambitious program, *The Israel Forum*. This program will bring author Mitchell Bard, among other speakers, to the Simon JCC. The Israel Forum will be geared to youth and adult participants and will provide a much needed outreach for Israel.

The Arab Lobby
The Invisible Alliance That Undermines America's Interests in the Middle East
Mitchell Bard
Harper Collins, 2010   412 pages

Which gets us to Bard's book. Those of us familiar with his epic *Myths and Facts* will not be dismayed by the fact-laden *The Arab Lobby*. In his acknowledgment he thanks several people who "slogged" through early drafts. Well, in some respects the book is a slog; loaded with fact upon fact, acronym upon acronym, it covers over a century of arabist activity—governmental, corporate, foreign and domestic. The interested reader will need to look elsewhere for a definitive study of the "original" arabist fascination with the language, art, and sexual culture of these modern-day tent dwellers. Suffice it to say that the "Lawrence of Arabia" brand of arabism swiftly gave way to a more practical variety, citing America's best interests while concealing a basic anti-Semitism.

The seeds of the Arab lobby lay not in Mideast oil, predating what Bard calls our "addiction" to oil and the discovery of the region's huge oil reserves. Christian missionaries were flummoxed by the lack of desire of Jewish "Christ-killers" to be converted. The boldly anti-Semitic post-Wilsonian State Department resisted all efforts to forward the intent of the Balfour Declaration, which urged the creation of a Jewish Commonwealth in Palestine. State Department arabists tried to persuade President Truman not to support the creation of a Jewish state. Fortunately, Truman never really trusted what he called the "striped-pants boys." Nonetheless, Bard reminds us that the Arab lobby achieved success during the first 15 years of Israel's independence by preventing the United States from selling arms to the new state.

As the Cold War pitted the United States against Soviet interests, warnings from the Arab lobby—that support of Israel could turn the Arab world toward the Soviets—were shown to be partly true, but only served to strengthen U.S. ties to Israel. The United States confronted the Communist world on three fronts: Europe, Asia and the Middle East. By the early 1980s we had huge military forces stationed in Japan and Germany at a cost of roughly $66 billion annually. No U.S. troops were stationed in the Middle East, but for a little over $2 billion in foreign aid, Israel successfully contained Soviet influence in the area.

Two key chapters are devoted to the rise of what Bard terms "the petro-diplomatic complex" and its increasing ability to influence our policy in the Middle East. The Saudis' profligate spending and their increasing belief that they can buy anything, coupled with the scare tactics of other oil producers, continue to prevent the United States from basing its relations on values and interests, and leads too often to sacrificing our principles.

Former President Jimmy Carter's "conversion" to embarrassing anti-Zionist standard bearer is dealt with rather harshly but deservedly. *The Arab Lobby* carefully distinguishes between the powerful support of Israel by right-wing Christian groups and the particular strain of fundamentalist faith embraced by Carter. His consistent apologetics for radical Islam, his consistent acceptance of what Arab leaders tell him in private, and his consistent overlooking of Arab human rights abuses, is made even more understandable in the light of his acceptance of millions of dollars of Arab donations to his personal causes.

Finally, while acknowledging repeated failures to create a truly indigenous American Arab lobby, Bard discloses the tremendous effort on the part of the Saudis to fund the creation of mosques in America—and, more importantly, to furnish them with basically fundamentalist clergy prepared to deliver Saudi-furnished sermons filled with anti-Zionist and anti-Semitic venom. In Bard's own words, it is clear that "the Arab lobby is a many-headed hydra that is less easily defined and less visible than its counterpart. It has no central address comparable to AIPAC...." Bard makes short shrift of Israel's detractors, such as Walt and Mearsheimer whose work, *The Israel Lobby*, has been the subject of almost universal derision. Yet, a vigorous Arab lobby does exist and at times exerts tremendous influence. For these and other reasons, the forthcoming *Israel Forum* initiated by the Community Relations Council of the UJFT is particularly timely and warrants interested community participation.

October 2011

Few solutions

S T E V E A . Y E T I V , an award-winning University Professor of Political Science and International Studies at Old Dominion University, has held a post-doctoral position at the Harvard University Center for Middle Eastern Studies. He has written several books including *Crude Awakenings: Global Oil Security and American Foreign Policy* and *The Absence of Grand Strategy: U.S. Foreign Policy Toward the Persian Gulf (1972-2005)*. Yetiv has been a consultant to the U.S. Department of Defense, the U.S. Department of State, the U.S. General Accounting Office and CNN International.

The Petroleum Triangle

Steve A. Yetiv

Cornell University Press, 2011   241 pages

In *The Petroleum Triangle,* Yetiv demonstrates the degree to which the threat of transnational terrorism, both that which is real and that which is perceived, has been influenced and nurtured by Middle East oil and the accelerated globalization of the last three decades. At the risk of being repetitious, the author over and over again refers to the "distorted prism" and the "distorted lens" through which Islamist groups, including Al-Qaeda, view Western and particularly American society, its values and its foreign and military policies.

Bankrolled by oil revenues and Saudi oil revenues in particular, Al-Qaeda at its operational peak was estimated to spend in excess of $30 million yearly to fund its efforts. Paradoxically, the Saudi infusion of hundreds of millions of dollars to subsidize the building of mosques and the operation of Madrassas may have actually succeeded in promoting Wahhabism—at the risk of increasing opposition to the Saudi regime itself and its tolerance of infidel forces in the land of the holy sites of Mecca and Medina.

Yetiv goes beyond the more obvious influence of oil and perceived Western designs on Middle East oil in creating the matrix of regional and international politics. There are numerous indirect influences in shipping, construction and weapons manufacturing that are all substantiated in detail. Yet this rather scholarly work remains very readable, while providing a clear timeline of the development of Al-Qaeda following the U.S.-supported effort to overthrow the Soviet occupiers in Afghanistan.

A survey conducted in six Arab states in 2003 revealed that looking through the "distorted lens," more than 80 percent of respondents believed dominating oil was an important motivation for America's invasion of Iraq, while 70 percent thought that support of Israel was important. Virtually no respondents thought the United States was seeking to promote democracy. That some Americans as well see "as through a glass darkly" is demonstrated by a *Newsweek* poll in 2010 where 31 percent of those polled thought it true or probably true "that Barack Obama sympathizes with the goals of Islamic fundamentalists who want to impose Islamic law [*sharia*] around the world." Clearly, oil-related issues have fed the phenomenon of anti-Americanism throughout the world.

The contribution of globalization to economic growth is unquestioned; however, it has led to great increases in oil demand along with geometric increases in global travel and transportation usage. At the same time, abetted by the advent of wireless communication, the infrastructure of support for Al-Qaeda, in terms of recruitment and financial development, went global. Yetiv argues that the Afghan fighters could not have grown into a transnational virtual state in a less globalized world.

The Petroleum Triangle makes a good argument for the schizophrenic nature of global oil, at once a global menace and the fuel of the global economy. Proposed solutions—other than to reduce our dependence on oil—are few.

December 2011

THIS
and
THAT

To Be a Jewish Woman
provides needed tools

FEW TOPICS in contemporary Jewish study encompass greater potential for divisiveness than that of Judaism and women. Most feminist literature cites the biblical account of Creation as the underlying font of Judaic sexism.

Yet, in our own community we know young, well-educated women who, despite the apparent inconsistencies between traditional teaching and current feminist advances, choose to be Jewish women in the traditional sense. How can they do it? How can they accept what appears to be totally unacceptable?

Lisa Aiken, a doctor of clinical psychology, may not always convince (that is really not what she has attempted to do), but always forces one to read on, to try to understand from traditional sources just what the teaching is and how the modern woman can accommodate herself to the tradition rather than attempt to reshape the tradition to accommodate the woman.

To Be A Jewish Woman
Lisa Aiken
Jason Aronson, Inc., 1993   282 pages

In many ways this is just another example of the tortured reasoning and convoluted interpretation often used with little success, except for the admittedly small minority who just accept. One thing is clear, however. Just as our grandparents didn't need to consult a text or employ a *mashgiach* to supervise the observance of *kashrut*, neither did they have to refer to a "guide" to inform and advise them on matters of sexual intimacy, birth control, abortion and divorce. They knew all about it. It was basic to their upbringing and education.

To Be A Jewish Woman provides the tradition, the source, and the rationale in highly understandable form. Aiken's search, as a Hebrew Day School graduate from a non-traditional home, for an authentic expression of Judaism ended in the embrace of the observant Jewish life. But her 15-year investigation revealed little written by knowledgeable observant Jewish women about topics relevant to women. As Aiken points out, "precious little has been written about how a modern Jewish woman can find a place for herself in traditional Judaism, especially if she is not married or does not have children. Almost all the books that address women's issues in Judaism have been written by men or by non-observant women."

Here at last is a guide written by a knowledgeable observant woman; it is at once a "how to," and a "why," which lays out the rationale for those who are open to acceptance.

One may not be entirely won over by her explication, for example, of the morning prayer: "Blessed are you ... who did not make me a woman," but the examination of the particular noun form (*ishah*), and the implication of the qualities exemplified by the use of God's will (*kirtzond*), may give the open-minded reader reason to pause and, possibly, accept a different interpretation of both the content and the intent of the two blessings.

The modern woman, whether more or less observant, would do well to understand the basis from which to create or depart from a traditional Jewish life. *To Be A Jewish Woman* goes a long way in providing women with some of the tools needed for them to be intellectually and spiritually honest as they grapple with the challenge of being observant Jews.

December 1993

Jewish Wedding book tells 'everything you need to know'

A DEATH IN THE FAMILY, even when expected, is so traumatic, so ultimate, that the principal players in the funereal drama find themselves at the tender mercies of family, friends and the professionals who make the arrangements, and literally carry them through the hours and days. The closest survivors make a few basic decisions, depending upon the tradition followed in their family, and then begins a set-piece in which each member of the cast plays his or her part, and the "audience" likewise responds on cue. This is perfectly understandable, necessary and customary.

Your Jewish Wedding

Helen Latner
Doubleday, 1985   190 pages

But why are we introducing a book on Jewish weddings in such a grim fashion? Ironically, the wedding, Jewish or otherwise, although a planned event, so often traumatizes those most closely involved that the players in this life-cycle event all too often find themselves also carried along a dramatic path, scripted and directed for them by parents and professionals, leaving them to act out a role in which it is sometimes difficult to detect or salvage some shred of their original intent.

Helen Latner, author of *The Book of Modern Jewish Etiquette,* has furnished us with ample evidence that it need not be so. *Your Jewish Wedding* is a complete guide to arranging a wedding, large or small, in the unique Jewish tradition. For those who want a traditional wedding, but simply don't remember or never knew just what is traditional, it is all within easy reach, and this becomes increasingly important as more and more young Jewish couples from markedly non-traditional backgrounds opt for traditional ceremonies. For those whose families have disparate wedding traditions, forcing the couple to serve as referee, here is an authoritative guide from which a middle ground can be reached, whether on the subject of *Oyfruf* or the *Yihud, B'deken di Kalle* or the *Huppeh.*

It goes without saying that herein is contained the latest on choosing a date, sharing expenses, the guest list and invitations and announcements. Realistically, this modern guide addresses the special arrangements which must be made when parents are divorced, and yes, even how to call things off when an engagement is broken.

Because, as author Latner puts it, "getting married (is) often defined by the three P's: parties, plans, and panic," she has thoughtfully provided an appendix which instructs on the keeping of an expense record, a countdown calendar-punch-list, and even a note for the non-Jewish guest.

Marrying couples of the Jewish world, rejoice! *Your Jewish Wedding* will tell you everything you need to know to make your wedding, *your wedding*, while dealing sensitively with the feelings of parents and the often dictatorial whims of the caterer. And the best part of it is that you can pick and choose—use what you will—assured that your wedding will be correct if you wish it, but *yours*!

September 1985

Ethical wills transmit value during lifetime

ROOTED IN THE BIBLE and the Talmud is the tradition of bequeathing spiritual legacy, according to Rabbi Jack Riemer and Dean Nathaniel Stampfer, spiritual leader of Congregation Beth David of Miami, Fla., and Professor of Jewish Studies at Spertus College in Chicago, respectively. Just as we are able to transmit our worldly goods during our lifetime by means of a will, so too have we, as individuals, been able to transmit our values during our lifetime, by means of an ethical will.

This collection includes traditional testaments, wills emerging from the Holocaust and from Israel, wills by contemporary American Jews, and a selection from classics of modern Jewish literature. Many of these wills were, of course, meant to be read during the lifetime of the writer, and some, rabbinic in nature, were meant for a broader

> **So That Your Values Live On**
> **Ethical Wills & How To**
> **Prepare Them**
> Edited and annotated by Jack Riemer
> and Nathaniel Stampfer
> Jewish Lights Publishing, 1991   237 pages

audience than the immediate family. The editors, while making no attempt to distinguish among such didactic tracts, the true testamentary (*tzavaot*) and the ethical letter (*iggeret*), nevertheless, by including examples of all three, enable the reader to consider the distinction while enjoying this fascinating collection. Reading this slim anthology is somewhat like experiencing, for the first time, an anthology of poetry and turning to the section on folk ballads. There are the ballads from the oral tradition, authors anonymous, passed down with inevitable editorial changes by generations of minstrels. There are the literary folk ballads, drawn not from remembrance of real life, mythologized, but from the poets' creative springs. Thus we are grateful for the inclusion of examples from modern literature; we appreciate the juxtaposition of the chilling selection by I.L. Peretz, a revered Yiddish author, with that eloquently simple testament of Noam Grossman, written in 1948 during the heat of the Israeli War of Liberation. It mixes ethics with material directions: "To be opened only after I die."

> *This will of mine is written hurriedly without the opportunity for a farewell, even in a letter.*
> *1. Bury me in Nahlat Yitzhak, Tel Aviv.*
> *2. No need to write anything about me in the paper.*

3. With my salary and any insurance my family receives set up a fund for buying guns for the Irgun.
4. Return all my personal belongings to my family.
5. Do not eulogize me; I did my duty!

It is like comparing "Lord Randall My Son," an ancient ballad, with "The Revenge of Hamish," a literary folk ballad by Sidney Lanier.

For those who have spent some time studying ethical wills, this volume will appear too lean. The body of material from which it is drawn is vastly deeper and richer. For those who have never looked in on this treasury, it is perfect, an eclectic mix which will whet your appetite for more. More importantly, the included *Guide to Writing Your Own Ethical Will* will be very helpful, and in this era when we are into oral history, through audiotaped and videotaped interviews, the benefits of written transmission of values need support.

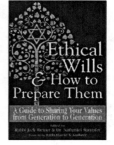

Just as a talking book is O.K. but not quite the same as a written book, these written views of the intimate values of the Jewish people are unique.

One final note, from literature. We have seen in Shakespeare all the richness and ills of history, such as the prevailing anti-Semitism of the time as evidenced by the values imputed to us in *The Merchant of Venice*. One also laughs, now, at the moralistic enjoinder of Polonius to Laertes as he begins his journey. We all remember: "To thine own self be true," and "neither a borrower nor a lender be," etc. It is now time to learn, with respect, of the admonitions of Benjamin M. Roth to his son, leaving for the United States in the mid-19th century:

> "Should you be forced, partly through circumstances ... to omit the ceremonial observances, you must nevertheless under no circumstances depart from the basis of religion: 'The Eternal, your God, is one, unique, single being.'
>
> "... never have any contact with missonaries. You do not have enough knowledge of the Holy Scriptures."
>
> "Avoid the company of drunkards and merrymakers."
>
> "Avoid Gambling."
>
> "Be Frugal and economy minded."
>
> "Give in to necessity, and patiently bear what fate has in store for you. That which is done cannot be changed; and what has been decided on high cannot be nullified or avoided."

Now I understand why I have always seen something Jewish in old Polonius of ancient Denmark.

We doubt if this exceptional work is readily available, thus we have given the address and 800 number. How else to get acquainted with a body of Judaica which will amuse and wrench your heart, as with these lines, written in chalk, and found next to the bodies of a Jewish couple after the Warsaw ghetto uprising:

"Fellow Jews, when you find us, bury my dear wife and me according to our Jewish faith. I request that you say Kaddish three times—for my little eight-year-old son, for my devoted wife, and for me. We lived, we loved each other, we fought, and believed in the God of Israel. – Berl Tomashelski."

November 1993

Stupid Ways worth the price of admission

VISIONS OF HELL abound in literature—vivid, terrifying and credible. Artists have had little difficulty portraying the horrors of Milton's *Paradise Lost*, Dante's *Inferno*, or Joyce's *Portrait of the Artist as a Young Man*. The problem seems to be an inability to depict, in literature or the graphic arts, a coherent vision of Heaven. The heat of the everlasting bonfire is easier to understand than the perceived-to-be insipid community of cherubs, angels and good souls.

So, too, in this halfway terrific little book. The "stupid" ways to think about God are amusing, funny, yummy, delicious,

Stupid Ways, Smart Ways To Think About GOD

James Shevack and Jack Bemporad
Triumph Books, 1993   117 pages

bright, and thoroughly debunk the silliest notions many adults have about God. And by God, the authors mean the God of all faiths... well, almost all. For whether they are debunking the God of the pre-Bar or Bat Mitzvah, "kind and loving, like Mommy," or "trustworthy, but firm, like Daddy," it is clear that we, as adults, gag on the ideas we were spoon-fed as children.

The authors—James Shevack, an advertising executive and award-winning copywriter and writer of numerous articles on religious subjects, and Jack Bemporad, a rabbi and leader in Christian-Jewish dialogue—by urging us to trade in outdated and ineffective images of God, trust that by so doing we will then, maybe, have an opportunity to understand and appreciate what the "real" God is about.

Ten stupid ways, then, include God the Cosmic Bellhop, God as Little Mary Sunshine and God the Godfather. The "God" in God the Cosmic Bellhop is the ultimate fixer, seeing to it that we have all the comfort items needed during our brief stay. Better to have been termed, in today's hotel parlance, the Concierge, the point is nevertheless clear. God furnishes TV, Porsche, mortgage payments, etc., attending on our snapped fingers of desire, whereas God, as Little Mary Sunshine, shines on us with pure love. But not real love, of course, for this God nourishes without disciplining, coddles without chiding, in other words, a love so simplistic it cannot be real. Don Godleone, Il Capo della Famiglia, is the God who fulfills all our worldly desires, providing, of course, that we are willing to pay the price. "We ask him for favors. And we live in fear of the favor he will one day ask in return."

From these witty discussions of the imminent God, we turn to the "smart" ways to think about God, God the transcendent one. Here the wit departs and we are treated to the same old soup about God the Beginning, God the Spirit, God the Creator—all the Aquinian rehash about prime movers and the like. Quite a letdown, one must conclude, but not sufficiently so as to justify avoiding this small work. The main course may be indigestible, but the hors d'oeuvres were delicious and worth the price of admission.

February 1994

Treasury of Jewish Folklore 'truly houses much valuable treasure'

IT HAS BEEN a fast-moving summer, and with *UJF Virginia News* off the air for a few weeks, this worthy collection of old legends of the *Agada* of the Talmud and the Midrash, cabalistic tales, humor, wisdom and songs has rested untouched well past its publication date in April.

Thus, with apologies to the editor and publishers, we hope to do justice to a "treasury" that truly houses much valuable treasure.

Those of us who attended the secular schools of the '30s were victims frequently of the trend toward realism in text selection. We learned to read books which told of real-life people—doctors, gas station attendants, farmers and so forth—and then in our university days made up for the loss of the classical mythology by taking survey courses. Those of the previous generation who were fortunate enough to go to school in the first place, learned to read using texts based on the great classical mythology. Similarly, as the editor points out, those children brought up in an orthodox Jewish environment were immersed in Jewish song and story as soon as they were aware of the world around them. It was in their blood. Once again, many of us lost out. This reader was frankly a bit awed by the size of the new anthology, but once the challenge was accepted, surprise surprise, what a readable, enjoyable treat was in store. This collection is very easy to dip in and out of, in small tastes or great bites. But this should be read, first, because of the unconventional but valuable manner in which it is organized, and second, because there are innumerable instances where the editor himself has created the story from oral tradition or foreign language sources.

> **Treasury of Jewish Folklore**
> Edited by Nathan Ausubel
> Crown Publishers, 1989   768 pages

As one reads, one chuckles:

> *"If I were Rothschild," said the* melamed *of Chelm, "I'd be richer than Rothschild." "How is it possible?" asked a fellow citizen. "Naturally," answered the* melamed, *"I'd do a little teaching on the side."*

One acknowledges wisdom:

> *Rabbi Wolf of Zbaraz had a stern sense of justice. One day his own wife raised an outcry that her maid had stolen an object of great value. The servant, an orphan, tearfully denied the accusation. "We will*

let the Rabbinical Court settle this!" said her mistress angrily. When Rabbi Wolf saw his wife preparing to go to the Court he forthwith began putting on his Sabbath robe. "Why do you do that?" she asked in surprise, "I can very well plead my own case." "I'm sure you can," answered the rabbi. "But who will plead the case of your maid, the poor orphan? I must see that full justice be done to her."

One partakes as well in the human comedy which we, as a people, have chronicled uniquely.

There is more, much more: songs, sacred and profane; demon tales; bibilical sidelights. This is a treasury which the family will enjoy.

May 1994

Two books, two viewpoints on planning and 'surviving' basic B'nai Mitzvot

WE HAVE PREVIOUSLY reported on a variety of "survival" guides for B'nai Mitzvot, for weddings, for holiday. None have purported to teach us how to make a profit through these events. None, that is, until Marvin Shapiro's *How to Survive and Profit from Your Son's Bar Mitzvah*. Shapiro, we are told, is the pseudonym of a nationally known trial attorney, writer and vice president of his congregation.

How to Survive and Profit from Your Son's Bar Mitzvah

Marvin Shapiro

Summit Publishers, 1995   95 pages

One is reminded of the canard about the family wishing to have a "theme" bar mitzvah which would outdo all previous "theme" events. They settled on an African Safari, wherein all the friends and relatives were flown to the Serengeti. Led by the headman, all the *tantes, bubbes* and *zaydes* were carried in covered litters; all the knishes, melting chopped liver platters, on the heads of the bearers, headed off into the jungle. After hours of hot trekking they came to a clearing and an abrupt halt. The father impatiently asked the head man the reason for the delay. The head man replied, "Sorry, bwana, two more bar mitzvahs up ahead."

If we poke fun at the lack of spiritual content frequently encountered in these life-cycle events, there is a darker side to the whole matter. But we dwell here on the outrageous tongue-in-cheek style which shows parents who face an average cost of $13,000 how to turn this potentially huge liability into a profit-making venture.... The imagination of Herschel Schmendrick Adams' family knows no boundaries when it comes to saving and even making money. Their *chutzpah* knows no equal.

Sharing flowers with a Christian family who is having a wedding on the same day is bad enough. Charging them retail for what you bought wholesale resulting in a profit of $100 is quite another.

It was definitely a stroke of genius that led to local real estate agents paying to have their message printed on the *kepot*, for a 25% profit.

No less ingenious was the sale of advertisements to local businessmen to appear in the program, which netted $3320.50. The creation of an internship for a student to do the videotaping and photography as "on-the-job-training" saved $500.

But the crowning devices had to be the use of local wine distributors to conduct a "wine tasting" which included hors d'oeuvres, thus saving many hundreds of dollars, and the placing of a cash register at the end of the buffet line, ostensibly to provide funds for their favorite charity, but which in reality netted a tidy sum.

On balance, most of the life-cycle events I have attended of late, however opulent, have shown a reasonable effort to be sensitive to the meaning of the event. It is possible to "do it well" while "doing it right." Shapiro's satire is aimed at those few who miss the point of the whole drill, but it does so in a rather hilarious way.

O N   T H E   S E R I O U S   S I D E of the street is this new publication from Jewish Lights, whose *Putting God on the Guest List: How to Find Spiritual Meaning in Your Child's Bar or Bat Mitzvah* by Rabbi Jeffrey K. Salkin was named the Best Religion Book of the Year (1993).

Bar/Bat Mitzvah Basics
A Practical Guide to Coming of Age Together

Edited by Cantor Helen Leneman

Jewish Lights Publishing, 1996   240 pages

Cantor Helen Leneman, who chairs the B'nai Mitzvah Network of CAJE (Coalition for the Advancement of Jewish Education), has organized an easy-to-read, practical guide that is relevant to Jews, regardless of their background. Rabbis, cantors and Jewish educators from the Reform, Conservative and Reconstructionist movements, parents, and teens speak from their own experiences.

Bar/Bat Mitzvah Basics is a tool to use in the preparation for the *simcha*, that the entire family may learn. It is a guide to the service and the ritual, whether traditional or creative; it provides an outline for planning and budgeting while maintaining the spiritual dimension we seek. But its distinction from earlier guides to *b'nai mitzvot* is its recognition of the particular needs of today's families, be they traditional, interfaith or divorced.

As much a challenge to families to preserve and enhance the inherent spirituality of the event, Cantor Leneman's book, with its introduction by Rabbi Julie Gordon and foreword by Rabbi Salkin, is a valuable "how to" resource.

May 1995

Open letter to Danny Siegel lauds *Unorthodox Book of Jewish Records*

DEAR DANNY SIEGEL, No offense intended toward your friend and co-author Alan Gould, whom I regret having never met, but I am mainly addressing my remarks to you whom I *have* met, with no regrets. It's been a long time since I have thought of you as a humorist. The way that it is in Tidewater, I review your mitzvah books and Rabbi Israel Zoberman reviews your poetry (noblesse oblige—purely), so we have spent the whole summer not reviewing your funny, funny *Unorthodox Book of Jewish Records and*

The Unorthodox Book of Jewish Records and Lists
Alan Gould and Danny Siegel
Samuel Wachtman & Sons, 1997   189 pages

Lists, arguing over whose territory it was in. This issue of literary pluralism tops my list of major concerns.

But if one is curious about the largest matzoh, or the largest matzoh ball or the largest challah in history, it's all in there, along with the famous "Phoenix Diet" by Rose Warson, who wore her fur when it was 118 degrees in Temple Beth Retired. The air conditioning failed and she refused to remove her stole, losing 17 pounds on one Shabbat morning.

To continue, Danny, thanks for sending *Heroes and Miracle Workers* to me. It would be easy to semi-dismiss it as a kind of update and rehash of other books we have received from you over the years. But just as the thirty-something generation learned from *Gym Shoes and Irises* 15 years ago, there is great need for the new thirty-somethings, and the twenty-somethings and even

Heroes and Miracle Workers
Danny Siegel
Town House Press, 1997   161 pages

the forty- and fifty-somethings to learn and re-learn what they may have forgotten or put aside in their hectic lives. Thus, your ability to reinvent yourself every now and then, to bring us a sequel to 1988s *Munbaz* or 1990s *Mitzvahs*, is remarkable and greatly appreciated.

I also think it is a pretty slick idea to include the "Annual Report of the Ziv Tzedakah Fund." I know there are many in Tidewater who are clueless about this magical effort (and it's hard to believe how it has grown). They can buy the book, or can write, call, fax or e-mail to Naomi Eisenberger to learn more about it: 384 Wyoming Ave., Millburn, NJ 07041; 201-763-9396; fax 201-275-0376; naomike@aol.com.

Well, keep it up, Danny, and keep in touch when you visit Tidewater again. I think it's time for you to meet with our young leadership and I'm hoping you are invited and that some of our not-so-young-anymore leadership shows up as well.

Kol Tov,
Hal Sacks

October 1997

Two books offer treasure trove of Jewish humor and cartoons

AT FIRST GLANCE, the twenty-buck pricetag for a slim paperback like the *Treasury of Yiddish-American Cartoon Humor* seemed excessively *chutzpahdik*. On second thought, one realizes that the emphasis belongs on the word "treasure." Dr. Albert Small's compilation is just that, a special treasure, since most of the Yiddish cartoons hark back to an earlier time, an earlier and perhaps less sophisticated era of humor, and particularly Jewish humor not necessarily meant to be shared outside the Jewish world. After all, the self deprecating or other group deprecating humor is frequently ethnically interchangeable. For example, the following from Hershel Shanks' *101 Best Jewish Jokes* (much less of a treasure but nonetheless not entirely without merit).

> **A Treasury of Yiddish-American Cartoon Humor**
>
> Edited by Albert H. Small, Ph.D.
> Companion Publications, 1999   93 pages

Consider the one about two retired Jews talking in Miami Beach:

"I just got myself a new car."

"Really? What kind did you get?"

"Blue."

End of joke. You didn't get it? Of course, it was a Caddy. The only question was one of color.

Now that dates it. In its day we might have substituted two members of a different minority. Same joke.

Today we might substitute BMW or Lexus, but regardless, the joke, as Molly would say, "t'ain't funny, McGee." We seem to have, happily, gotten away from the Jap, Polack, Newfie, Black jokes.

The trove of Yiddish humor, on the other band,

> **101 Best Jewish Jokes**
>
> Compiled and Introduced by Hershel Shanks
> Moment Publications   110 pages

retains its ability to charm us, largely one suspects due to the aura of nostalgia which surrounds it. This writer's generation grew up in the milieu, and the great success of Jewish comedians in the 1920s through the 1960s was largely due to the carry-over of the essence of Yiddish humor in their routines. Shanks freely acknowledges his debt to Joseph Telushkin, among others, a scholar who keeps his audience howling when he lectures on Yiddish humor.

An elderly Jewish couple, on their way to a vacation in Hawaii, get into an argument about the correct pronunciation of Hawaii: she is sure it is Havaii, but he maintains it is Hawaii.

When they get off the plane they hurry over to the first native they see and say, "Aloha! How do you pronounce the name of this island: Hawaii or Havaii?"

"Havaii," the man replies.

"Thank you," the wife says, triumphantly.

"You're velcome," the man replies.

Shanks' little collection is compared by him to a bag of potato chips: difficult to put down, you will want "just one more." Well, the analogy is correct in one respect: *101 Best Jewish Jokes* is more of a light snack than a meal, but a tasty one at that.

Albert Small's *Treasury*, on the other hand, has a unique format in that the cartoons, all chosen from the 1910–1930 era, are presented one to a page, with the Yiddish caption below. Beneath that caption is the Yiddish in transliteration, followed by the English translation. Highlighted at the bottom of the page are transliterations and translations of key Yiddish words used in that particular caption. The introduction, worth the price of admission, and the glossary of Yiddish, together make up half the book, which therefore serves as a text for the student of Yiddish as well as an anthropological guide to a particular time and a particular culture.

Of course, my use of the term "anthropological" is not intended to cloak Yiddish in the mantle of a dying language. Yiddish is spoken in religious communities, studied in schools and colleges, and Yiddish publications are again appearing. Nonetheless, the Americanization of the immigrant Jewish community in this country coupled with the destruction of European Jewry have left us with only a glimmer of hope that a real revival of Yiddish is possible.

In the meantime we can enjoy a 1923 cartoon which previews current views on sexual harassment in the office. Picture the shapely interviewee and the pot-bellied prospective employer.

Stenografistke: "Ir shaynt tsu zayn a guter altishker, ober eyder ikh farblayb bay aykh arbeyten, vil ikh ir zolt mit tsushtelen a reckomendatsie fun ayere frier-dige stenografistkes."

Stenographer: "You seem to be a nice old man, but before I take the job I would like you to provide me with references from your former stenographers."

Or in the same vein:

"Farvos iz dayn vayb azoy eyferzikhtig oyf dayn stenografistke?"

"Mayn vayb iz amol aleyn geven mayn stenografistke."

"Why is your wife so worried about your stenographer?"

"My wife used to be my stenographer."

And finally:

Er: "Hot ir epes geton a guten shidekh?"

Zi: "Oysgetseykhent! Mayn khosn fermegt tsvey million dolar, is 85 or alt, un hot a shvakh harts!"

He: "Have you made a good match?"

She: "Excellent! My husband is worth two million dollars, is 85 years old, and has a weak heart!"

Jewish humor, whether an uneasy reflection on the past, simple solutions to complex problems, or the much loved play on words, and Yiddish itself, has penetrated deeply into American English. We are accustomed to non-Jews using all the SH words: *schlep, schlemiel, shmoose, shmeer,* etc. It is not unusual to hear an African-American protest, "Don't make such a *tzimmis* over this!"

There can't be too many Jewish humor books, for, as author Small puts it, "Jewish humor is something special—even if once in a while there's a hint of desperation behind the smile."

As one Yiddish proverb goes: *Ikh zol handlen mit likht, volt di zun nit untergegangen:* "If I dealt in candles, the sun wouldn't set."

May 2000

Two audio novellas make good 'reading'

SO NOW WE KNOW that JCC doesn't only stand for Jewish Community Center. It could also relate to Jewish Contemporary Classics, (Inc.), publisher of "great Jewish books" on audiotape. We seldom review these, principally because we seldom spend enough time in our car these days to listen to a book, but we know some who do—and JCC is committed to producing audiotapes of high quality works, read by talented artists.

Envy, or Yiddish in America
and
The Pagan Rabbi
Cynthia Ozick
Jewish Contemporary Classics, 2000   4 hours

In this case, JCC offers two works of Cynthia Ozick, prolific and critically acclaimed author of *Quarrel and Quandary*, *The Shawl* and *The Puttermesser Papers*, among many other works of fiction and criticism. Ozick, herself preoccupied between the split in the human mind between the rational and the mystical, between the "restraint" of mainstream Judaism and the "unrestraint" of kaballah, between a world-view at once Hellenistic and Judaic, maintains the impossibility of the serious writer, living in a world of imagination, to be anything but a *vilde chaya*, a wild animal.

Thus we have these two marvelous novellas, rich in language, sometimes requiring a bit of extra attention to the Yiddish expressions (which are, however, usually translated in the text). *Envy, or Yiddish in America* is at once a requiem for the lost Yiddish language and the work of a large coterie of brilliant artists whose oeuvre, never to be translated, will never be known to the American public. Edelshtein, the poet, burns with envy over the success of Ostrover (Isaac Bashevis Singer?) whose "glory was exactly this: that he required translators. Though he wrote only in Yiddish, his fame was American, national, international. They considered him a 'modern.'"

Tony Award winner Ron Rifkin (*Cabaret*) reads *Envy* and Mitchell Greenberg (*Laughter on the 23rd Floor*) reads *The Pagan Rabbi*.

This is a very rich trove, for those who "read" audiobooks. Other JCC audiobooks include works by Malamud, Agnon, Singer and Bruce Jay Friedman. There is one cautionary note: When encountering works like those of the brilliant Ozick, they are not an "easy listen." Beautifully complex and multi-layered, they demand attention which is appropriately rewarded. The publishers recommend that these tapes be considered more as performance art, so on that basis we award "two thumbs up," and suggest you not listen to them while negotiating heavy traffic.

Jewish Contemporary Classics may be reached toll-free at 877-522-8273 or log on to wwwjccadiobooks.com.

June 2001

Books of Jewish content on audio cassettes

PROFESSOR RUTH WISSE of Harvard University believes that "with the exception of Theodore Herzl, the founder of political Zionism, no Jewish writer had more effect on Modern Jewry than I.L. Peretz." As the 19th century came to an end, Peretz was one of the leading advocates

The Stories of I.L. Peretz

Jewish Contemporary Classics, 2001   4 hours

for a Yiddish-speaking, secular Jewry in a Europe where Jews had no political independence or territorial sovereignty. Through his creative genius, an entire generation of Yiddish writers was encouraged to produce a literary treasure trove that was beloved by millions of Yiddish readers.

For audiobook enthusiasts therefore, this new release, unabridged and in English translation, will be a delight. Narrated by George Gudall, winner of the 1999 and 2000 Audie Awards, the audio industry's highest honor, and Susanne Toren, recipient of a "Narrator of the Year" award, the listener is rewarded with a bittersweet view of *fin de siecle* Jewish life.

Well known favorites such as *Bontshe Schweig, If Not Higher,* and *The Three Gifts,* are joined by a never-before-translated version of *All for a Pinch of Snuff,* and there is an afterword on the life and times of Peretz by Professor Wisse, author of *The Modern Jewish Canon.*

Also performed by George Gudall is Sholem Asch's gripping epic, *Kiddush Hashem* (literally *Sanctification of the Name*). Asch, one of the few Yiddish writers to become a popular success in America (some will remember *East River* and other best-selling novels of the '30s and '40s), weaves a magnificent tale of a Jewish family's fate in the Ukraine during the now-infamous Cossack pogroms in 1648.

WHERE I.L. PERETZ remained in Warsaw, surrounded by a coterie of aspiring Jewish writers, Sholem Asch, of the next generation, born to an orthodox Hasidic family in Kutno, Poland, immigrated to the United States shortly after the turn of the century.

Jewish Contemporary Classics has now issued a handsome catalog describing works by Nobel Prize winners S.Y. Agnon, Saul Bellow, Elie

Kiddush Hashem
An Epic of 1648 (unabridged)
Sholem Asch
Jewish Contemporary Classics, 2001   4 hours

Wiesel, and Isaac Bashevis Singer as well as works narrated by Theodore Bikel, Debra Winger, Ron Silver, and Elliott Gould. The reader/listener may call toll-free—1-877-JCC-TAPE (l-800-522-8273) or order directly from the web site at www.jccaudiobooks.com.

December 2001

Welcome additions

MANY WHO ARE UNFAMILIAR with Debbie Friedman by name are well acquainted with her music, as her "user-friendly" settings of such prayers as the *V'ahavta* and the *Mi Sheberach* have become standards within the Reform repertoire. She has been a welcome visitor to Tidewater on at least two occasions which come to mind, and her fans will welcome these two latest albums into their collections.

The Water in the Well
and
The Alef Bet
Debbie Friedman
Sounds Write Productions, 2002

The Alef Bet is basically a children's recording designed to help in the process of learning Hebrew, however, concealed within such tunes as *Bakitah, B'teiavon,* and *Im Ein Ani I,* is the usual welcome dose of Debbie values.

The Water in the Well contains 12 Hebrew and English numbers never previously recorded. For those hooked on Friedman, her rendition of *The Water in the Well, Devorah's Song, God my Shield, Hashkiveinu* and others will be irresistible. There are times when her modest, but adequate voice is overshadowed by the instrumental background, and there is some inconsistency of recording level from cut to cut, but overall the CD is a fine addition to her ever-expanding repertoire.

To order: 1-800-9-SOUND-9.

April 2002

Two Yiddish updates

WHY DOES ONE get teary-eyed when hearing "My Shaynele Belz," even if no one in the family or even a friend of the family came from there or has any memory of that place, that *shtetl*? We weep for a lost world that we really never knew, a world of piety and poverty, one of rock-ribbed theological certainty and total uncertainty about our place in it. When we reviewed in this column Michael Wex's translation of S.Y. Abramovitsh's 1865 literary landmark, *The Wishing Ring*, we felt unqualified to judge the translation itself. No such equivocation could be entertained at this time, for Wex, a novelist, university teacher, lecturer and stand-up performer, is recognized as a "Yiddish national treasure," bringing a welcome mix of wit and erudition to his subject.

> **Born to Kvetch**
> **Yiddish Language and**
> **Culture in All of its Moods**
> Michael Wex
> St. Martin's, 2005   303 pages

Born to Kvetch provides the etymological background for the development of Yiddish as we know it, through the population shifts and the vowel and consonant shifts of the Middle Ages and beyond. How much is Hebrew, how much German, Poylish, Litvak or Galitsiyaner? It all begins with the *kvetch*, which has its roots in the Bible, with the non-stop complaining of the Israelites, kvetching about everything under the sun, in Egypt, in the desert, about their problems and about the solutions. The next element is defined as the exile. Nothing can be quite right in exile and this was the Jewish lot for two millennia. And finally, the *mitsves*, developed from the Torah and the Talmud, these, in the context of eternal complaint, sentenced to wander the earth yet compelled to obey form the backdrop against which the ideas which led to the language developed over the period from the Exodus to about 1,000 C.E. Nothing is easy; nothing is just right.

Those of us who still dip into Leo Rosten's *The Joys of Yiddish* after reading Michael Wex are likely to agree with the author that it would be like watching Milton Berle today on television, which is not meant as a put-down of either Milton Berle or Leo Rosten, but mere recognition that things become dated and need to be made relevant to a contemporary audience. And relevant it is; the principal ingredients of all the old jokes are here as well as the philosophy which placed women in an inferior social status. Thus, when one chides another for failing to ask how things are, and the other asks, "So, *nu*, how are things?" the reply can only be, "Don't ask!" and a male is addressed as a *yid*, but the feminine of *yid, yidene,* is a pejorative expression, as in "you talk like a silly woman."

My mother-in-law came to America as a child from the Ukraine and her father-in-law, who lived with his son's family, came from Poland. She never let him forget that his Poylish Yiddish was of a much lower class than hers, and they had a lively time cursing each other in Yiddish. Wex describes such a curse (*klole*) as a kvetch with a mission, a descriptive activity that conveys disapproval. "My enemies should be as ugly as she is beautiful." "May an evil decree come upon you." "May only a tenth of what I wish you befall you."

The ultimately complex curse illuminates what the reader has in store in this treasure of a book which deals with business, life-cycle events, politics, child-raising, cuisine and our relationship with Gentiles (*goyim*).

> *"You should own a thousand houses*
> *with a thousand rooms in each house*
> *and a thousand beds in every room*
> *And you should sleep each night in a different bed*
> *in a different room*
> *and get up every morning*
> *and go down a different staircase*
> *and get into a different car*
> *driven by a different chauffeur,*
> *who should drive you to a different doctor—*
> *and he shouldn't know what's wrong with you either."*

Wex never loses sight of the grinding poverty which lay at the root of Yiddish life for hundreds of years. Even the reply to the greeting, "Hello, Moyshe. How's business?" *"lign in dr'erd un bakn beygl,"* (lying in the dirt and baking bagels)— not literally dead, but down and out and working at the miserably hot job of baking, has its reprise, with death, *"men est shoyn ire beygl"* (someone else is eating her bagels), and *"geyt shoyn in zayne shikh"* (someone else is already wearing his shoes). Not very nice—but direct.

WEX REFERS frequently to Uriel Weinreich's *Modern English-Yiddish Yiddish-English Dictionary.* And Sol Steinmetz, whose *Dictionary of Jewish Usage* was published last

Dictionary of Jewish Usage
A Guide to the Use of
Jewish Terms
Sol Steinmetz
Rowan & Littlefield, 2005   207 pages

year and is now in production as a paperback, credits the inspiration given by the late Professor Weinreich. Rabbi Steinmetz, a lexicographer, linguist and editor of numerous dictionaries, was driven to the creation of a dictionary of usage by his observance of the lack of standardization, discrepancies in the definitions of parallel terms, confusion in pronunciations and various etymological mistakes. Words used by English-speaking Jews, whether they be of Hebrew, Aramaic, Judezmo or Yiddish origin, are not foreign but by definition, *English*, and are designated *denizens* by the Oxford English Dictionary.

Such expressions as *aide-de-camp* and *table d'hote* are fully naturalized as to use, but not as to form, inflexion or pronunciation. Steinmetz' dictionary, then, is one of English *denizens* of Jewish origin, specifically as used by English-speaking Jews. But Steinmetz must first create a consistent system. Yiddish loanwords are spelled in English according to the Yiddish Romanization system and Hebrew loanwords according to standard Hebrew Romanization, yet he does not reject out of hand English spellings that do not conform to either system, yet have become commonly used. Thus generally accepted and recognized spellings are listed as main entries: *Hasid, kabbalah, yarhzeit;* common variant spellings are cited as separate main entries and cross-referenced: *Chasid, cabala, yortsayt.*

While the *Dictionary* necessarily carries the reader from *abba* (father, daddy) to *zugos* (religious scholars in the time of the Second Temple), when Steinmetz hits on a convenient grouping, he expands the entry such that under *music and dance terms* we find brief descriptions of *badchen, flash tanz, freylech, hora, kazatzke, niggun, and sher,* among others. Similar groupings are found under ritual terms, halachic terms and wedding terms, although some of the key terms so catalogued have individual listings of their own. From time to time the author treats the reader to a sidebar telling "The Story of a Name," such as Hadassah, or Maccabee, or a Word History, such as greenhorn, or leviathan. One can use this dictionary simply to look up a word, as we do with any dictionary, but the more time spent with this fascinating guide the greater the reward.

Don't throw away your Rosten or your Weinreich, but do update your reference shelf. These are two worth owning.

November 2005

A sentimental journey

OUR ESTEEMED EDITOR, possibly seeking to aid my convalescence with a marshmallow assignment, sent me off to Arizona with this recent CD by an artist who has spent his entire life in the theater, beginning in 1943. Classically trained (he played in *Streetcar* with Vivien Leigh—directed by Laurence Olivier, and *Love of Four Colonels* with Peter Ustinov). Bikel's folk records helped put our very young children to sleep in the late 1950s. He came to the musical theater fairly late, appearing as the original Captain Von Trapp in *The Sound of Music.* Many hits followed (and a couple of flops) including *Zorba, ThreePenny Opera, Jacques Brel is Alive and Well and Living in Paris* and *The Rothschilds.* But of course his signature work was as Tevye in *Fiddler,* which Bikel performed 2,094 times over 37 years.

In My Own Lifetime
12 Musical Theater Classics
Theodore Bikel
Jewish Music Group, 2006   LP/CD

Backed up by a 17-piece orchestral ensemble, Theodore Bikel, never a great voice but always an engaging singer, offers 12 standards from his musical stage repertoire and a 13th bonus track that reprises "If I Were a Rich Man" in Yiddish. *In My Own Lifetime* is a sentimental journey covering four decades of the kind of musicals no longer presented, except in revival.

January 2002

Alternate summer reading: luminous and insightful

Fed up with thrillers that don't thrill, mysteries that fail to mystify, novels that lack novelty? Why not try something different?

We've been reading and enjoying novels by E.L. Doctorow for about half a century. Many have been set to film; *Ragtime* and *Billy Bathgate* come to mind, although Doctorow, whose novels frequently make great movies, cannot be said to write for this purpose.

Every 10 years or so he collects some of his essays, book reviews, lectures and introductions, and *Creationists* is the latest. To some, this is merely the effort of declining writers to satisfy their publishers' demand for material. For this reviewer it is a great treat! Doctorow is the winner of the National Book Award, two PEN/Faulkner awards, three National Book Critics Circle awards, the Edith Wharton Citation for Fiction, the William Dean Howells Medal of the American Academy of Arts and Letters, and finally, the presidentially conferred National Humanities Medal.

Creationists
Selected Essays 1993–2006
E.L. Doctorow
Random House, 2006   176 pages

This particular gathering of essays is a modest celebration of the creative act, but the reader cannot overlook the author's title which, by its very appearance in common parlance connected to the thoroughly discredited antithesis of evolutionary science, serves as a roadmap to Doctorow's understanding of stories as revelatory structures of facts.

Beginning with a brilliant discourse on the *Book of Genesis,* wherein he concludes that it is God himself who is the most complex and riveting character, there are excellent and engaging essays on Poe, Harriet Beecher Stowe and Herman Melville, as well as reviews of biographies or new editions of works of such 20th century authors as Sinclair Lewis, John Dos Passos, F. Scott Fitzgerald and a brilliant bonus piece on Albert Einstein.

Selected essays 1977-1992 preceded *Creationists*, and informs the reader that fiction is Doctorow's métier, but when requested and commissioned to do so he will reward us with one of his beautifully written and brilliantly-thought-out essays on literature, politics and social philosophy. His essays on Jack London, Ernest Hemingway and Theodore Dreiser are brief, but belong right up there with the best of John Updike and Edmond Wilson, providing the "shock of recognition" that makes you feel you are auditing a master course in American Literature.

In this collection he takes aim at that "amiable dunce," Ronald Reagan, the "spiritually dysfunctional" Richard Nixon, that "stolid mangler of language," Gerald Ford, and that "well-meaning but terribly vacillating permanent-pressed piety," Jimmy Carter. Carter is dismissed as having run as a liberal and governed as a conservative. George H.W. Bush is roughed up pretty badly as Doctorow trashes the right for subverting antitrust statutes, withholding Social Security payments from the disabled, cutting off school lunches for needy children and allowing the rich to become filthy rich while the middle class was turned poor.

**Selected Essays
1977–1992**

E.L. Doctorow

Random House, 1993   203 pages

One of the centerpieces of this volume is Doctorow's take on the American Constitutional Convention, a coming-together of 55 men of America's upper class. Having written in observance of the bicentennial celebration of its creation, Doctorow summarizes some of the important commentary by succeeding generations and adds his own pithy analysis of what he considers to be the sacred text of secular humanism.

TO ROUND OUT the trio, *Reporting the Universe* is a collection of 14 short essays under the rubric of the William E. Massey, Sr. lectures in the history of American civilization. The avid Doctorow fan will appreciate the autobiographical material that highlights his boyhood and early success as a writer. Doctorow begins with Emerson and concludes with Whitman, but this collection is rich with philosophical commentary, historical comparisons, literary judgments and personal asides.

**Reporting the Universe
2003**

E.L. Doctorow

Harvard University, 2003   125 pages

Finally, Doctorow wonders (in 2003), as we find ourselves with a president elected under questionable circumstances, with all sorts of implications of sleazy business interests and a federal judiciary thick with right-wing justices, if what he calls a "rage" to deconstruct the Constitution and the Bill of Rights is connected with the increased presence of God in our political discourse.

What writer worth his salt, Doctorow asks, will fail to take on the universe? The three slim volumes discussed here reveal the novelist as a luminous lecturer and insightful commentator. They are all available at your public library and promise to take up little room in your suitcase or beach bag.

July 2007

Principles worth pursuing

RABBI SHMULEY BOTEACH, known almost universally by his first name, is the best-selling author of *Kosher Sex* and has been dubbed "Dr. Ruth with a *yarmulke*." A fixture of celebrity culture, rejected by the Crown Heights leadership with which he had been involved as a young adult, Shmuley shocked the Orthodox community with his gleeful discussions of intercourse and pornography. (His Tidewater Jewish Forum appearance some years ago met with a mixed, but mostly favorable, reception). Yet, despite Shmuley's iconoclastic reputation, *Kosher Sex* is a deeply traditional book.

Based on his show on The Learning Channel, where Rabbi Shmuley acts as a kind of *Nanny 911*, this anecdotal reprise of his

---
Shalom in the Home
Smart Advice for a Peaceful Life
Rabbi Shmuley Boteach
Meredith Books, 2007   288 pages

---

time spent with 10 dysfunctional families, interspersed with succinct lessons and "Shmuleyisms," delves into problems of adultery, teenage sex, self-esteem, toxic relationships, sexual intimacy, divorce, cultural pressures and the effects all these issues have on the family.

His own parents' divorce when he was a boy of eight, and which necessitated his spending a considerable amount of time on airplanes traveling from one parent to the other, led him to wonder what was the secret that kept a couple living happily together for their entire lives.

Shmuleyism #1: *Shalom in the home, domestic tranquility, is the ultimate blessing.*

If we recall the recent visit of Rabbi Irwin Kula whose book, *Yearnings*, was reviewed here, we can see remarkable similarities in their perspectives. "We are not meant to feel guilty for having enough, or even more than enough, money, a beautiful house, great sex, lovely clothes and delicious food, Kula asserted. His frequently anecdotal musings grapple with everyday issues as we search for truth by digging a bit deeper into our feelings and understanding our needs and how the satisfaction of them is prelude to our giving. Digging into feelings, understanding needs and helping families deal with them is Rabbi Boteach's *modus operandi*.

Shmuleyism #2: *Even if you can't live together as husband and wife, you can still parent together as mother and father.*

When charged with appealing perhaps too much to non-Jews, Shmuley's signature defense has been that broadening the visibility of Judaism to the general public would attract Jews. "To get Jews interested in the Jewish world," he said, "you have to get the non-Jews interested. The Jews will follow what the non-Jews are doing."

Other Shmuleyisms: *Adultery destroys families, not just marriages.*

Don't allow sexual intimacy and time together as a couple to be a casualty of a growing family.

Rules are an essential part of parenting. Children do not benefit from a life without boundaries.

Teenage sexual activity doesn't just expose children to pregnancy or sexually transmitted disease. It robs them of their precious childhood.

Although Rabbi Shmuley consistently applies Torah (cf. Rabbi Kula on "applied Torah"), with one exception it is unclear whether or not there exists any religious observance in any of the families studied, Jewish or otherwise. Shmuley does not claim to have worked miracles with these 10 families. In fact, he comes perilously close to abject failure in some of the cases, and shows little progress in others. One can only wonder if a pattern of observance, or at least a passing acquaintance with a religious or ethical system, was operative.

I know several families who might benefit from the information in this book, not because it comes as any kind of news flash. Any educated person might easily recognize the principles espoused. Recognizing that they apply to *them* is another matter entirely.

June 2007

Cursing, Yiddish-style

WHEN OUR SON was about four years old, he came running breathlessly into the house, demanding of his mother that she tell him if "get" was a dirty word. "Why do you want to know?" she asked. "Well," he replied, "Mr. Miller [a neighbor] always yells at me — 'GET off of my property!'" Does a word become "dirty" just in the mind of the listener (or reader)?

Talk Dirty Yiddish hardly competes with *Born to Kvetch,* Michael Wex's erudite and witty work of 1985, which in addition to updating Leo Rosten's timeworn *Joys of Yiddish,* provides the etymological background for the development of Yiddish as we know it. Whereas Wex gives wonderful examples of Yiddish curses,

---

Talk Dirty Yiddish
Ilene Schneider
Adams Media, 2008   176 pages

---

he completely avoids Yiddish curse words. You won't find them in his glossary. The whole point of *Talk Dirty Yiddish* is that a *curse* is not the same as a *curse word.* Author Ilene Schneider has a more finite objective.

A curse is a hex: *Zolz tsebrekhn ale dayne bainer az oft mol vi brekhts di aseres hadibres!* You should break your all bones as often as you break the Ten Commandments!

A curse word is an expletive: Lenny Bruce, a stand-up comedian who faced severe censorship in the early 1960s, is thought to have brought Yiddish expletives into mainstream English usage. Thus, words like *drek, shtup, putz, shmuck* were "allowed," while he would have been kicked off the stage had he used their English equivalents. Now, non-Jews routinely use these words in speech and print, frequently only vaguely knowing their literal translation. We regularly see words like *maven* in the *New York Times,* so it is not surprising that dozens of Yiddish words, from *bupkes* to *chutzpah,* from *shlep* to *shlock,* and from *shmooze* to *shtick* are common parlance, and they are all dutifully included by Schneider. One can only wonder if the creators of the popular *Shrek* movies were familiar with the Yiddish *shreck* meaning fear, terror, or a fright. I'll be convinced that these Yiddish words are truly cognates in the English language when my spellcheck includes them. Not yet.

I never heard my grandmother, grandfather, mother or father utter a curse word in English. However, my grandmother could turn the air blue in Yiddish. And my mother-in-law, when riled, could go at anyone in litanies of less-than-polite Yiddish that went over our heads completely. (Actually, we didn't want to know what they meant!) They didn't need to use curse words; they had creative Yiddish curses instead.

Zolst fahrlirn ale dayne tsain akhuts ainer, un in dem zolst hobn a shreklikher tsainvaitik!

You should lose all your teeth but one, and you should have a terrible toothache in it!

But, yes—the author does provide sufficient examples of dirty Yiddish. There are two pages of excretory words, sections on euphemisms for male and female genitalia, sex and a chapter on other bodily functions. But this is not all there is. Skimming through the chapter on *How to Insult Somebody* I found that I was familiar with most of the hundred or so insults listed. Does that mean we spend a lot of time insulting each other? Possibly. However, our people are better known for self-deprecation and many of the insults are applied to the speaker him- or herself.

Ilene Schneider has given us a wonderful primer of the words not taught in Yiddish classes. "With plenty of slang, curses and idiomatic expressions, this book gives our Yiddish vocabulary a real kick in the *tuches....*"

September 2010

Briefly noted

THIS NEW DOCUMENTARY, narrated by Dustin Hoffman, features a rare Sandy Koufax interview (he didn't give interviews) with recollections from Ron Howard, Larry King, Bob Feller, Bud Selig, Marvin Miller, Al Rosen and Hank Greenberg.

Of course, even younger baseball fans are already familiar with Hank Greenberg, Sandy Koufax, Shawn Green and Kevin Youkilis. However, they will enjoy learn-

Jews and Baseball
An American Love Story
Directed by Peter Miller
Docurama Films, 2011   91 minutes

ing about less well-known Jewish stars such as Buddy Myer, Andy Cohen, Sid Gordon, Harry Danning and Phil Weintraub.

Baseball is quintessentially American, and Jewish immigrants around the turn of the 20th century wanted nothing so much as to be American. They were drawn to baseball then, and Jewish Americans to this day are passionate devotees to America's pastime—in the stands, on the field and in the top levels of management and ownership.

This well-put-together DVD provides a welcome appendix to Ken Burns' seminal television series and will be greatly enjoyed by Jewish baseball fans, from little leaguers to dads and granddads.

MICHAEL KRASNY is credited with hosting the nation's most listened-to locally produced public radio talk show. Krasny, an agnostic since he reached adulthood, has written a deeply personal reflection on a lifetime of seeking, but not finding answers. And what a search!

Spiritual Envy
An Agnostic's Quest
Michael Krasny
New World Library, 2010   264 pages

Krasny, a professor of literature, invokes the entire bibliography of occidental, oriental and Asian holy texts, literature, philosophy and music. The songs of Jim Croce, John Lennon and Paul Simon as well as the poetry of T.S. Eliot, Dylan Thomas and Robert Frost provide grist for his mill. Surprisingly, his encyclopedic recall of several thousand years of man's attempt to describe, seek, obey and yes, fear God in the myriad manifestations ascribed to God, is not mere name-dropping. This is not your typical summer read. Krasny challenges the reader with his erudition and engages the reader more with his questions than with his answers.

But he does an excellent job of defending his position, while at the same time wishing he could change his position. *Spiritual Envy* explains why agnosticism is a valid and defensible position despite its reputation as being indecisive, wishy-washy—a kind of atheism-lite.

When asked if he believed in free will, Isaac Bashevis Singer was said to have replied, "I have no choice." Krasny opines that while we have the freedom to act we can also choose to do nothing. Thus, it is necessary to establish one's own code of behavior. He wishes he could know God; however the creator appears to be ultimately beyond human reason or imagination. As one philosopher put it, "Agnosticism is a learned ignorance based on self-knowledge and philosophical reflection." From Democritus who said, "Nothing means more than nothing," to the "Our nada who art in nada" of Hemingway; from Shakespeare to Faulkner; from Sartre to Beckett, the "dreadful freedom" gained by existential belief is somewhat alluring, yet there is a yearning for something more.

Despite his belief that religion was an instrument of intolerance and violence, Krasny kept on creating his moral code which includes respecting the beliefs of others regardless of how odd they might be, as long as they were not harmful. Certainly, he believes, religion may be toxic and thus provides good fodder for satire. He concludes, however, that belief can sow good, and deserves respect. Pithily, he observes that a lack of belief in the hereafter or in any kind of physical or spiritual reincarnation begs the question, "What is worth giving up one's life for...if not for belief...."

Krasny criticizes the atheists of the present atheist zeitgeist, such as Richard Dawkins and Christopher Hitchens, who offer certainty that belief in God and faith is scornworthy. He favors agnosticism as the means of signifying nonacceptance of all forms of dogmatic certainty. Agnostic doubt may preclude any certainty of discovering a way to satiate spiritual hunger. Nonetheless, Krasny still seeks to find, and still hopes to find, answers to what appears to be unknowable.

Krasny is learned but never dry, and the serious reader of whatever religious persuasion will be well rewarded by this challenging work.

June 2011

AFTERWORD

WHEN ASKED if book reviewing is a public service or an art, two well regarded contemporary editors agreed that it is basically a service. While there may be a modicum of art or craft involved, the point of the review is not the reviewer, it's the book. And yet, what the reviewer brings to the book—the reviewer's tastes, the reviewer's background, the reviewer's sense of obligation to the reader—matters. I agree with the editor who said that "when it comes to book reviews, critics should remember that the best thing they can do for readers is to be straightforward, unselfish, and to remember to get out of the way."

HS
Scottsdale, March 2015

APPENDIX

101 Best Jewish Jokes ed. Hershel Shanks...221
A Cuban Journey Hal Sacks..30
A Hole in the Heart of the World: Being Jewish in Eastern Europe
    Jonathan Kaufman 124
A Jew in America: My Life and a People's Struggle for Identity
    Arthur Hertzberg 157
A Living Lens: Photographs of Jewish Life from the Pages of The Forward
    ed. Alana Newhouse 135
A Pigeon and a Boy Meir Shalev...66
A Tale of Love and Darkness Amos Oz 161
A Thumbnail History of the Jews of Tidewater Hal Sacks.................36
A Treasury of Yiddish-American Cartoon Humor
    ed. Albert H. Small, Ph.D...221
And the Sea is Never Full: Memoirs, 1969 Elie Wiesel......................154
Ariel Sharon: An Intimate Portrait Uri Dan 18
Arthur Schwartz's New York City Food: An Opinionated History and
    More Than 100 Legendary Recipes Arthur Schwartz.....................87
Autobiography of a Delicatessen – Katz's
    Jake Dell and photog. Baldomero Fernandez.................................96
Bar/Bat Mitzvah Basics: A Practical Guide to Coming of Age Together
    ed. Cantor Helen Leneman 218
Beyond the Whiteness of Whiteness Jane Lazarre.............................122
Born to Kvetch: Yiddish Language and Culture in All its Moods
    Michael Wex...229
Broken Covenant: American Policy and the Crisis Between
    the U.S. and Israel Moshe Arens 108
Caspian Rain Gina B. Nahai...64
Chaim Potok: Confronting Modernity Through the Lens of Tradition
    ed. Daniel Walden 23
Chicken Soup with Chopsticks Jack Botwinik...................................163
Chinese Kosher Cooking Betty S. Goldberg 73
Chocolate Chip Challah and Other Twists on the Jewish Holiday Table
    Lisa Rauchwerger 84
Chutzpah Alan M. Dershowitz 12
Classic Yiddish Stories of S.Y. Abramovitsh, Sholom Aleichem and
    I.L. Peretz ed. Ken Frieden 56
Creationists: Selected Essays 1993-2006 E. L. Doctorow 233
Cuban-Jewish Journeys: Searching for Identity, Home, and
    History in Miami Caroline Bettinger-Lopez 132

243

Dictionary of Jewish Usage: A Guide to the Use of Jewish Terms
Sol Steinmetz..230

Dry Tears Nechama Tec 142

Ellis Island to Ebbets Field: Sport and the American Jewish Experience
Peter Levine...126

Enlitened Kosher Cooking Nechama Cohen 91

Envy, or Yiddish in America Cynthia Ozick 224

Escape to Shanghai: A Jewish Community in China James R. Ross.................104

Everyman Philip Roth..60

Fast and Festive Meals for the Jewish Holidays Marlene Sorosky.................77

For the Relief of Unbearable Urges Nathan Englander.................46

Founder: A Portrait of the First Rothschild and His Time Amos Elon.................120

From the Holocaust to Hogan's Heroes: The Autobiography
of Robert Clary Robert Clary 171

Gideon's Spies: The Secret History of the Mossad Gordon Thomas.................139

Growing Up Jewish in America: An Oral History
Myrna Katz Frommer, Harvey Frommer.................................112

Harriet Roth's Deliciously Healthy Jewish Cooking Harriet Roth.................74

Heroes and Miracle Workers Danny Siegel 219

How to Survive and Profit from Your Son's Bar Mitzvah Marvin Shapiro.................217

In Hitler's Shadow Yaron Svoray, Nick Taylor 183

In My Own Lifetime: 12 Musical Theater Classics Theodore Bikel 232

In Search of Anti-Semitism William F. Buckley........................176

In The Lion's Den: The Life of Oswald Rufeisen Nechama Tec 144

Intrepid Sailor Samuel Sobel..137

Israel To Go: Look and Cook Book ed. Lara Doel.....................96

Jerusalem, a Cookbook Yotam Ottolenghi, Sami Tamimi.................95

Jewish Community Club Comes of Age Hal Sacks.....................28

Jewish Cooking for All Seasons: Fresh, Flavorful Kosher Recipes for
Holidays and Every Day Laura Frankel.................................90

Jewish Cooking Secrets From Here and Far Lorraine Gerstl 75

Jewish Power: Inside the American Jewish Establishment J.J. Goldberg.................185

Jews and Baseball: An American Love Story dir. Peter Miller.................239

Jews of the Amazon: Self-Exile in Paradise Ariel Segal.................128

Jihad: The Rise of Militant Islam in Central Asia Ahmed Rashid 190

Kiddush Hashem: An Epic of 1648 (unabridged) Sholem Asch.................227

Kosher Kettle: International Adventures in Jewish Cooking
ed. Sybil Ruth Kaplan...77

Kosher Light Zillah Bahar 80

Kosher Southern Style Cookbook Mildred L. Covert, Sylvia P. Gerson 70

Little Cookbook Full of Secrets: Mark Stark's Amazing Jewish Cookbook
Mark Stark..81

Louis D. Brandeis   Melvin I. Urofsky 20
Lower East Side Memories: A Jewish Place in America   Hasia R. Diner.............130
Madeleine Albright: A Twentieth-Century Odyssey   Michael Dobbs....................14
Memoirs of 1984   Yuri Tarnopolsky..180
Minyan: Ten Jewish Men in a World That is Heartbroken   Eliezer Sobel............54
Miriam's Kitchen: A Memoir   Elizabeth Ehrlich..78
My Prison, My Home   Haleh Esfandiari..173
Nathan and His Wives   Miron C. Isakson 53
Our First Century and a Quarter, 1844-1969 and *Our Sesquicentennial:*
    The Past Twenty-Five Years, 1969-1994   Elise Levy Margolius...................110
Ravelstein   Saul Bellow..48
Remember the Catskills: Tales of a Recovering Hotel Keeper
    Esterita "Cissie" Blumberg 116
Reporting the Universe 2003   E. L. Doctorow..234
Russ and Daughters: Reflections and Recipes from the House
    That Herring Built   Mark Russ Federman 97
Selected Essays 1977-1992   E. L. Doctorow 234
Shakespeare and the Jews   James Shapiro..119
Shalom in my Heart, Salaam on My Lips: A Jewish Woman
    in Modern Morocco   Gloria Marchick..192
Shalom in the Home: Smart Advice for a Peaceful Life
    Rabbi Shmuley Boteach...235
Shanghai Remembered   Berl Falbaum..167
Sharon: Israel's Warrior-Politician
    Anita Miller, Jordan Miller, Sigalit Zetouni 16
Ships Cabin Restaurant   Hal Sacks...26
So that Your Values Live On: Ethical Wills & How to Prepare Them
    ed. Jack Riemer, Nathaniel Stampfer...210
Spiritual Envy: An Agnostic's Quest   Michael Krasny 239
Start-Up Nation: The Story of Israel's Economic Miracle
    Dan Senor, Saul Singer 198
Stupid Ways, Smart Ways to Think about God
    James Shevack, Jack Bemporad 213
Talk Dirty Yiddish   Ilene Schneider...237
The Alef Bet   Debbie Friedman 228
The Arab Lobby: The Invisible Alliance That Undermines America's
    Interests in the Middle East   Mitchell Bard 200
The Brink of Peace: The Israeli-Syrian Negotiations   Itamar Rabinovich...........188
The Catcher Was a Spy   Nicholas Dawidoff...106
The Children's Jewish Holiday Kitchen   Joan Nathan 76
The Color of Water   James McBride..121
The Conversion   Ahron Appelfeld...44

The Death Lobby: How the West Armed Iraq Kenneth R. Timmerman...........178

The Gefilte Variations Jayne Cohen...85

The Great Chefs of America Cook Kosher ed. Karen MacNeil.............................75

The Indictment: The Arab-Israeli Conflict in Historical Perspective
  Sabine Citron 196

The Jewish Gardening Cookbook: Growing Plants and Cooking for
  Holidays and Festivals Michael Brown...82

The Jews in America: Four Centuries of an Uneasy Encounter: A History
  Arthur Hertzberg 100

The Kidnapping of Edgardo Mortara David I. Kertzer 114

The Kirkpatrick Mission Allan Gerson...152

The Kugel Story: Not Just Noodle Pudding Nina Yellin...............................72

The Last Three Jewish Children in Alexandria, Egypt Hal Sacks.....................39

The Lonely Days Were Sundays: My Life and a People's Struggle for Identity
  Eli N. Evans...102

The Magician of Lublin Isaac Bashevis Singer...51

The Man in the Sharkskin Suit: My Family's Exodus from Old Cairo
  to the New World Lucette Lagnado 169

The March E.L. Doctorow..58

The Myth of Hitler's Pope: How Pope Pius XII Rescued Jews from
  the Nazis Rabbi David G. Dalin..148

The Pagan Rabbi Cynthia Ozick..224

The Petroleum Triangle Steve A. Yetiv...202

The Pigskin Rabbi Willard Manus..50

The Return of Anti-Semitism Gabriel Schoenfeld...................................194

The Stories of I.L. Peretz I.L. Peretz...226

The Tiger in the Attic: Memories of the Kindertransport and
  Growing Up English Edith Milton 165

The Transfer Agreement Edwin Black...146

The Unorthodox Book of Jewish Records and Lists
  Alan Gould, Danny Siegel...219

The Water in the Well Debbie Friedman...228

The Whole Foods Kosher Kitchen: Glorious Meals Pure and Simple
  Levana Kirschenbaum 93

The Wishing Ring S. Y. Abramovitsh...52

The Yiddish Policemen's Union Michael Chabon 62

To Be A Jewish Woman Lisa Aiken...206

Today I Am A Boy: The Bar Mitzvah Journey of a Grown Man
  David Hays..156

Treasury of Jewish Folklore ed. Nathan Ausubel....................................215

Visiting UJFT Project Sites in 2009 Hal Sacks, Judy Anderson 32

Wedding Song: Memoirs of an Iranian Jewish Woman Farideh Goldin 159

What's Cooking at Hadassah College?
    Recipes from the Culinary Arts College..91
When Light Pierced the Darkness   Nechama Tec 142
Your Jewish Wedding   Helen Latner 208

CPSIA information can be obtained at www.ICGtesting.com
Printed in the USA
BVOW05*1059300415

397375BV00003B/4/P